The Media Symplex

Also by Frank Zingrone

Works on McLuhan

Essential McLuhan
edited by Eric McLuhan and Frank Zingrone

Who Was Marshall McLuhan?
Co-edited by Barrington Nevitt with Maurice McLuhan

Poetry

Traces

Strange Attraction

The Media Symplex

At the Edge of Meaning
in the Age of Chaos

Frank Zingrone

Published in 2001 by Stoddart Publishing Co. Limited
895 Don Mills Road, 400-2 Park Centre, Toronto, Canada M3C 1W3
180 Varick Street, 9th Floor, New York, New York 10014

Distributed in Canada by:
General Distribution Services Ltd.
325 Humber College Blvd., Toronto, Ontario M9W 7C3
Tel. (416) 213-1919   Fax (416) 213-1917
Email cservice@genpub.com

Distributed in the United States by:
General Distribution Services Inc.
PMB 128, 4500 Witmer Industrial Estates, Niagara Falls, New York 14305-1386
Toll-free Tel.1-800-805-1083   Toll-free Fax 1-800-481-6207
Email gdsinc@genpub.com

05   04   03   02   01   1   2   3   4   5

Canadian Cataloguing in Publication Data

Zingrone, Frank
The media symplex: at the edge of meaning in the age of chaos

Includes bibliographical references and index.
ISBN 0-7737-3293-4

1. Television broadcasting — Social aspects.   2. Internet — Social aspects.
3. Mass media and culture.   I. Title.

P90.Z56 2001   302.23'4   C00-932846-7

U.S. Cataloguing in Publication Data
(Library of Congress Standards)

Zingrone, Frank.
The media symplex: at the edge of meaning in
the age of chaos / Frank Zingrone. — 1st ed.
[304] p. : cm.
Includes index.
ISBN 0-7737-3293-4
1. Mass media — Influence — Social aspects.   2. Technology — Social aspects.
3. Mass media criticism.   I. Title.
306.4/ 6   21   2001   CIP

Jacket design: Bill Douglas @ The Bang
Text design: Kinetics Design & Illustration

THE CANADA COUNCIL | LE CONSEIL DES ARTS
FOR THE ARTS | DU CANADA
SINCE 1957 | DEPUIS 1957

*We acknowledge for their financial support of our publishing program the Canada Council, the Ontario Arts Council,
and the Government of Canada through the Book Publishing Industry Development Program (BPIDP).*

Printed and bound in Canada

To the living spirit of Herbert Marshall McLuhan,
my teacher, mentor, colleague, and friend

To fight in another man's armour is something more
than to be influenced by his style of fighting.

— C.S. LEWIS, THE ALLEGORY OF LOVE

Contents

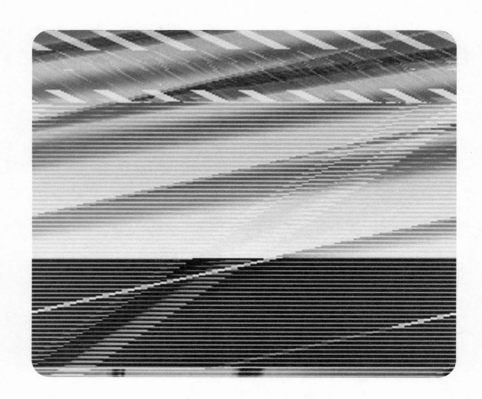

Preface

THIS BOOK IS THE RESULT of a persistent meditation on electric process and how it affects the human spirit. We like to believe that our values can resist technological change, but inevitably we realize that the opposite is true: our technologies, especially our media, create the spaces in which we live. Each technology makes new environmental demands on our lives. As we use technologies, they also use us. That, as Jacques Ellul (the French McLuhan) notes, makes us a technological society.

While advances in technology seem to represent progressive good, they also create social and economic chaos. Our willingness to replace life with information systems, along with the pseudo-evolutionary progress of virtual reality, adds complexities that have come to dominate our lives. We are now living in electric space and appear to be caught between two momentous states — the need to perpetuate civilized values while living under electric conditions.

All media translate experience into other modes of perception. Today, we are living stressfully between the virtual and the real, the simple and the complex. Simple truths now seem to us as complex as the archetypes that haunt our dreams. Electric media transform our rich, more natural lives by virtual simplicities — the programs of media, the video equivalent of life. We can only cartoon the truth with media that are at best the prostheses of amputated experience.

The structure of this book is not complicated. It is comprised of five main parts, each one simply a neglected fundamental dimension of communication. These pieces probe the dynamic interrelations of media and mind in preparation for understanding the deep structure of the complex and chaotic epoch that is dawning.

We are discovering new ways of rethinking the universe and human survival. The ecology of communication (communication considered as large process patterns) demands that we consider the complex grounds of all simple realities. A deep order, a breakthrough, is emerging from the breakdown of the old world view. This book is about these changes and the new values they imply.

Acknowledgements

This book owes its life to two rare men: Nelson Doucet and Paul William Roberts.

The book was faceted by Steven Beattie and polished by Ilana Weitzman. As well, I owe special thanks to Don Bastian and Jim Gifford at Stoddart; John Robert Colombo, Donald Theall, and Andrew Roberts; and for their pithy conversation, Bob Dean, Barrington Nevitt, Matthew Corrigan, Ian Alger, and the late Graham Crane. Thank you especially to my remarkable family: Delia, Francesca, Michael, Robert, Paul, and Joseph, for their love, support, and patience, and to Samantha, Rachel, Jack, Adam, and Dylan, who had more to do with this than they yet imagine.

Finally, my heartfelt gratitude to my many students in Canada and the United States who never complained of my practising on them.

The Bias of McLuhan

AT THE BEGINNING OF THE TELEVISION AGE and the rise of advertising, our ignorance of the effects of mass media persuaded Marshall McLuhan to take mass culture seriously and to introduce a necessary bias into the study of communication. This bias recognized the dominance of the technical means of communication over its contents, an idea that had also occurred to Harold Innis (*The Bias of Communication*),[1] H.J. Chaytor (*From Script to Print*),[2] and I.A. Richards (*The Meaning of Meaning*).[3] "The medium," McLuhan said, with some degree of hyperbole, "is the message."[4] He seemed to be saying that the medium is almost the whole message, that content counts for very little and doesn't have much to do with the reshaping of the senses effected by the technology of the medium.

This revolutionary insight denigrated contents to an unnecessary degree. My view of this was that if the medium is the message, then that message has to be expressed as content if it is to be understood, though it is a content of a deeper and more complex kind. The medium always re-enters content.

In the short run, as anyone who has watched a six-part TV serialization of a popular novel knows too well, media shape our perceptions of content. In the long run, however, media fade technologically. Like the phonograph, the telegraph, and silent film, older media pass the story on to other, more technically advanced media formats. The content is too often submerged beneath the novelty of the new medium's technology — as we saw with the "talkies," 3-D films, Cinerama, and IMAX. But it does appear that to each newly trained generation the content gathers livelier variance in new formats.

By 1964, the idea that "the medium is the message" had revolutionized our understanding of communication with the insight that media distort our perceptions by translating experience into simulations of the real. In fact, the structure of our social and psychological lives has become increasingly cinematic. Each medium adds its technical values to the experience it interprets. We have become so used to baseball as a televised event, for example, that most baseball stadiums have installed jumbotrons (giant video screens) so that both the fans *and the players* can see the game and its replays framed and up close. A virtual reality grows out of such a mergence of the real with the technical. This electrically driven, automated reality seems at times even somewhat robotic as we begin to understand that our technologies use us as much as we use them.

The original formulation of "the medium is the message" was meant to show media users not only how the structure of their perceptual awareness shifts from one medium to another, but that electric process accelerates the flow of information in all media while it shortens attention spans. McLuhan also described the instantaneous nature of electric process. He discovered that "[i]n a simultaneous world which structures information at the speed of light, effects are simultaneous with their causes, or, in a sense, 'precede their causes.'"[5] As technologies, media complexify; as processors of content they greatly simplify the kaleidoscopic flux of human experience. This aspect of electric media demands a new balance between the medium and the message.

McLuhan forced us to see how media alter reality by restructuring perception. He might have gone on to observe that electric media create a simultaneous union between the simple and the complex in their simplifying figures while *simultaneously* complexifying grounds. McLuhan always used the futurist implications of art and literature as the truest way to gain insight into how figure and ground relations work. He compared the disjointed figures of T.S. Eliot's *The Waste Land*[6] to the difficult figures in Pablo Picasso's work; Picasso insisted that he always began with a figure, even if his pictures often seemed all ground.

"The poem is rather like Picasso's cubism," McLuhan once offered.
"How like Picasso?" I inquired.

"Oh," he said coyly, "cubism is not hard to understand once you know what Braque and Picasso were up to. *They give you the ground — all four sides, top, bottom, inside, and out — in a complex set of interrelated planes which appear paradoxically as a figure on one surface.*" He went on to explain how a figure is meaningless without its deep ground to interpret it by. A book, as a figure, must be understood against the complex ground of print technology and the values of literacy.

This parable of information suggests that under electric conditions we all are trapped between simple figures and complex grounds, between the electronic poles of meaning. In this respect, I am reminded of Jung's *complexio oppositorum*, or the self that tries to realize itself through reconciling polarities: "[T]here can be no reality without polarity."[7] Literacy breeds cause and effect, either/or thinking. Electric process and the inheritance of uncertainty from physics requires more attention to both/and thinking.

After McLuhan, my own work has unavoidably led me to study the dynamic and simultaneous relations between simplicity and complexity that result from examining the medium and the message in the context of *virtuality*. This set of relations creates an infinitely vast interactive process pattern. (A process pattern reveals an underlying structure of meaning, as in Eliot's *The Waste Land*, where the surface seems chaotic and meaningless.) Deep structure is at the same time part content and part medium, that is, symplectic. The computer, operating by binary logic, exposes the lack of deep structure in post-modern communication: what is, simply is, and means only in terms of itself.

The view implied by the statement "the medium is the message," if taken to suggest that content is of no real importance at all, was less of an exaggeration in 1964 than it is now with virtuality massively affecting contents. The old view clearly

> The medium
> is never the
> whole message.

lacks balance. The hyperbolic bias of McLuhan's statement is meant to bring home an important point: *It is only through an understanding of the structure of a medium that one can gain real access to its message.* In the end, however, it is the message that we want and need.

Media tend to simplify complex human events for easy consumption. At the same time, they complexify events through exhaustive — even obsessive — coverage, but only at the level of low-cost entertainment. In television, redundancy serves as a replacement for complexity. Care must be taken to keep it simple and avoid alienating sponsors or consumers through real controversy, real introspection. The truth could put you out of business.

Contemporary skepticism regarding events reported by the mass media results in the tension of knowing, however vaguely, that we are trapped between the desire for simple views and the reality of their complex out-of-awareness grounds. This tension is a condition sufficiently stressful that it requires constant inhibition. Many of those thus inhibited — Trekkies, UFO mongers, celebrity trial devotees, or assassination buffs — exhibit an irrational addiction to imaginary grounds. Fantastic possibilities, electric circuses, clutter their lives in the form of television programs, while actual media news reinforces premonitions of immanent disasters.

Fantasy and reality are forced by media to fuse into virtual themes, like *Seinfeld*'s nothing or *The X-Files*' something, that only mime real life and real values. Morality under the press of media becomes surreal in its complex relativity, and so is effectively abandoned in practice. One person's morality is another's perversity. We are left in our cop shows to distinguish between the good pimp and the bad. Soap operas sub for Sunday school. Fellatio grips the global mind, is discussed at the breakfast tables of North America. Criminals seduce venal leaders everywhere, but we cry out to be spared such complex knowledge of our exploited and lobbied existence.

Willingly, to inhibit this debilitating stress, we numb ourselves down, narrowing our focus to exclude everything that is not self-referential. We call people so afflicted Yuppies or Yippies — Young Inhibited Professionals. Among many of these people, conversation, discussion, or debate takes on the drone and whine of talk show vacuity and megalomania.

Media operations on important events create an extreme disequilibrium, like speeded-up traffic flow hitting spatial gridlock or a riot flipping into a march, as with the assault on the Bastille in 1789. New kinds of order can break out of such chaos — unexpected, complex results of simple actions. Media constantly fuse content and context into ascending helical loops of virtualizing relations. Witness, for example, the furor over the *Survivor* program, one of the first "Real Television" shows, which has now spawned a bunch of clones. The fake voyeurism of this show is content that depends on the credibility of the context: people isolated on a desert island trying to win a million dollars, deviously conniving their own survival against that of the group to gain notoriety.

The Second World War continues to rise from a mountain of fact to achieve mythic status in public awareness. Each ensuing generation, more and more distant from the events of that war, has to be convinced of the awful events of the Holocaust through the continued use of black and white film — consider *Schindler's List* — though the actual film technology has developed very far from that early film form.

Access to awareness of message content is gained only through an understanding of the underlying structure of perception imparted by different media formats. The survival of simple human values depends on our developing a sense of the total complex effect of the media array. Consider the contribution of the media to our understanding of the values of love and family over the last few decades. Our present level of consumerism, for example — a direct result of television — doubles the need for family income, which in turn pulls even reluctant mothers out of the home and into the workforce.

Such economically liberated women tend either to delay maternal experience or to change mates and get involved with more than one family. The behaviour of the children of such increasingly tenuous familial situations is considerably altered from that of more traditionally fostered children. Championing moral behaviour in any media form has its actual effects in society. We may feel outrage at certain celebrated crimes, but if we watch them played out on TV and in the newspapers we stimulate their increase.

Like an enigma, the Net simplifies while simultaneously complexifying. Nobody can read more than a few screens' worth of text, so every subject gets paraphrased, in simple if not cogent form. The unimaginable complexity of our site-mapped cyberspace makes our use of it seem obsessively repetitious and depersonalized. But after you have visited a certain portion of this vast Net, you realize that each site is a node of relatively simple information. The complexity is in its configuration as an open system of knowledge, a complex mosaic of simple points in a complex design, not unlike a fractal. If the Net is a fractal in structure, the growth of the Net and its socio-economic ramifications become extremely complex.

Now that we can know so much about anyone, we are all becoming public people and feel ourselves to be "on" all the time. As we process more and more information faster and faster for longer and longer periods of time, we become like creatures trapped in a multimedia version of Zeno's paradox — the original strange attractor that can only define a "tendency to order" that is never arrived at.

Media are always much more complex than their messages, just as all grounds are more complex than the figures they support. The most complex messages imaginable can only approach equal complexity with the structural possibilities in the medium. No medium can be less complex than its message and still communicate. James Joyce's *Finnegans Wake*[8] is an example of a message approaching the same level of complexity as its medium; it is the most print will allow before all meaning disintegrates.

We seem to be getting closer and closer to the truth but never actually getting there because of the faulty bases of scientific knowledge in bringing us simple solutions. Now, having discovered these post-modern effects of electric process on communication, what is the next major step in surviving the onslaught? *Symplexity.* ˎ

The Symplex

The symplex is the most fundamental characteristic of electric media; it is the fusion of simple figures with complex grounds, created by virtual additions to an evolving technical reality. When nothing is seen as simple and everything appears complex, the survival of our sense of reality demands a turn-down in information processing. When technical complexity consistently devours simple realities, the result is symplectic awareness, which recognizes the impossible need to simplify life in the face of its evolving electronic complexification.

A symplex is a content that reflects its reliance on the medium being used. A simple and useful example is a film about the making of a film — such as Fellini's *8½* or Truffaut's *Day For Night* — or a show that is both a show and a show about the show melded together. This can be subtle, as in Francis Coppola's *One From the Heart*, or crude, as in *The*

Larry Sanders Show, which even mixes video and filmic effects to create an authentic "feel." This double vision results from the simple and the complex merging into a virtual relationship. The viewer apprehends this polarity all at once.

The entire sensorium, trained by media to adapt to media forms, has become symplectic. All perceptions are adulterated by the values implicit in media translations of reality. A trip abroad tends to become coincident with the photographic and Handycam validation of it. In fact, the trip can become nothing more than a photo-op for the folks back home, a non-trip, an image-making junket, a travelling media frenzy. Even driving a car into the countryside takes on cinematic characteristics. We have been trained by media to see the exurbs rolling by as in a pan shot.

In the Age of Virtual Reality, the medium and the message are swiftly merging. It is no longer useful to say that "the medium is the message" because the message is now gaining significance through its marriage to the medium's structure. Paradoxically, symplectic double vision is added to the way we actually see reality. Our view of nature and reality has become symplectic. Briefly, *symplexity is the effect of the process of virtualization on reality*.

It seems paradoxical that we get closer to our goals by degrees of technological extension. But NASA exists to confirm this technological obsession to reach the stars. In becoming increasingly technological in our understanding of reality, we create the ultimate complexity: an overloaded matrix of networked simplicities. But there is no experience of deep content in the Net as there is in the profound power of a great poem like Eliot's *Four Quartets*[9] or a novella like Tolstoy's *The Death of Ivan Ilyich*.[10] Most of what we know is derived from second-hand, indirect, or mediated information. This is a form of propaganda. Our knowledge of humanity, when it comes to us almost exclusively through simplifying media, is functionally diminished.

McLuhan's quest for the humanistic implications of technology was always moving forward into new provinces of the mind: advertising, media analysis, culture as business, cliché and archetypal relations, split-brain theory, tetradic analysis, discarnate electronic being. None of these were wholly original ideas. He took the "global village," for example, from Wyndham Lewis, and "the medium is the message" came from the title of a talk by Ashley Montagu, "The Medium and the Method." The tetrad is simply the scientific notion of "phase transition" (the idea that systems pushed to the limit of their capability reverse into their opposite) adapted to humanistic application. McLuhan's brilliant technique was the assimilation of the ideas of others into a new style of perception — a vision of electric reality — of which he was the undisputed author. He discovered integral grounds for disparate ideas, which he regarded as figures of thought, unowned, in an intellectual commonwealth.

His study of mass media was so thorough and prescient that McLuhan was on the edge of discovering virtual reality. Consider the following insight from a talk he gave in 1965 at the Buffalo Spring Festival of the Arts,[11] in which he intuits VR's principle of replacing experience with playful simulations. Talking about the new environments created by media, he observed, as if talking about cyberspace: "We have as a world gone through the looking glass. At the other side of the looking glass you are in a new kind of space, one in which the human observer creates his own space and his own time." This is the technologically induced condition, he says, of "[w]orld as artifact, world as art form, world as programmed experience." In other words, world as virtual reality — a virtuality that is the basis of symplexity.

Symplexity and the Virtual

Symplectic perception is one of the two most revolutionary effects of mass media; it is the complement of virtual reality. VR is a special case of symplexity in which nature and technology are seen as continually merging. Electric process is completely changing the structure of reality through a bias for virtual formats. Virtuality can be crude, as in a headset visor full of elementary simulations, or subtle, like a time-lapse film of an opening rose that reveals the ineffable motion of a flowering bloom. Having experienced the rose in this simulated way, we may never again be able to look at a rose, or any flower, innocent of the virtual vision granted by our technological aids. Similarly, our belief in germs is greatly aided by microscopic photography.

The dual aspect of virtual reality — the technical and the natural merged — gives rise to simplectic perception. These are moments of instant mythic awareness in which the thing is perceived in an implosive instant like an epiphany, a perceptual freeze frame. Now such effects are normally part of media-trained habits of perception. In a virtualizing world, we can no longer keep the simple and the complex ·

apart in our perceptions. Take, for instance, the symplectic image of the mushroom cloud from an atomic blast. The future-casting world of physics, while pursuing the angelic agenda of surpassing the speed of light, has left us to live with fears of a physics-inspired holocaust. This is the simple and complex married.

Through media views of nature, everything becomes reinterpreted until there really is no longer a nature independent of technological distortions. Our idea of nature is constantly being reworked and now imitates its own colourful, hyperactive Disney-like version in our virtualizing mind's eye. Electric process forces us to perceive paradoxically that everything is both itself and something else — both real and virtual — simultaneously. And despite the optimistic notion of information as negative entropy, it is now clear that there is too much information in the world.

An unhealthy overload of complex stresses is spiralling out of human control and into automated, robotic systems that use us and make us subservient to their socially blind, engineered interests — everything from anti–lock braking systems on cars for icy roads to anti-crib-death monitors. We are even systematically looped in media overkill, the obsessive over-coverage of news events. This excess of virtualized reality is no panacea for our ignorance and can be a danger to our humanity. Too much of anything makes us likely to care less about civil or humane outcomes.

Symplexity and the Media

As electric media simplify human experience with increasingly complex technologies, they suppress and inhibit the true complexity of reality. Media leave out the parts of experience that threaten the balance of established consciousness and normal perception. The disgusting banality of physical violence is often glossed over, trivialized, or romanticized in some way that masks the reality of actual violence — the gut-wrenching sounds of victims, the broken teeth, the flesh split to the bone, the unexciting pop of real bullets, and so on. Film and television's simple view of reality is one in which sensory stimulation is proscribed in important conventional ways. No time is wasted in cleaning up. Stars are never killed in car chases. The painstaking efforts of real achievement are evaded, spliced out.

Information overload forces us to suppress the growing complexity of life. But this constant action of suppressing complexity results in rising political, personal, and economic angst. This general anxiety is the pervasive tone of modern life.

> Virtuality simplifies perception but complexifies the real.

Symplectic relations driven by media dominate the ordinary experiences of daily existence. Take, for example, the case of the JFK assassination. The simple story that unfolded on television was in immediate conflict with more reflective media and private consensus. As time went on, public misgivings developed — which persist to this day — that the complexity of the event had been oversimplified. The simple TV narrative has been pitted against suspicions of a complex conspiracy theory. From now on, *neither the simple nor the complex views of these events can be extricated from each other*. They must live together, forever linked on the edge of meaning in a symplectic relationship that dominates all historical events with a deep, media-sustained, perceptual ambiguity. All mediated news now bears this permanent, dynamic, ambiguity, whether the content is focused on a president's sex life or the apparent theft of a trillion dollars from the American taxpayers by S&L managers.

Awareness of symplexity is beginning to dawn on us. We have discovered that the underlying structure of events, the out-of-awareness aspect of reality, is of more than equal importance with their superficial appearance. We learned from Fellini's *8½* that a movie about making a movie can be intellectually more engaging than most ordinary films. Increasingly, the making of every movie is a story in its own right, like *Hearts of Darkness: A Filmmaker's Apocalypse,* produced by Bahr and Hickenlooper, a fascinating look at the making of Coppola's epic, *Apocalypse Now*. Celebrity exploitation magazines take the reader behind the scenes.

The French Lieutenant's Woman is another example of a simple story read against a complex substructure in which our attention is drawn to both simultaneously. The roles of the male and female leads in "life" are reversed in the plot of the film. Each is seen as both dominant and passive-aggressive, depending on whether we're in the film-within-the-film or in the "real life" of the film's frame tale.

Media values increasingly dominate contents and become a new kind of deep content. The medium and the message are merging in new, interesting ratios. Every action thriller, with its arsenal of explosive production values, not only entertains but also trains the viewer in symplectic awareness. The apparently simple business of rigging a scene for exploding bullets is in actuality rigorously studied and computerized. Production values require complex skills for simple effects.

Life lived under electric conditions exhibits symplectic structure. A film, for example, is a relatively simple translation of a life situation that splices out the complexities of wider experience. The filmgoer only half knows this while the sensory training in cinematic values takes place. Films tend to be taken as parables of reality. Thus film or video that tries to deal more aggressively with real-life complexity and its dirty details loses its mythic edge and becomes incomprehensible as a whole.

> A symplex results when a virtual addition to an event intensifies awareness of the complexity of its deep content.

Documentaries are not reality on film; like all films, they have a deliberate and biased structure. But their simple themes are so accessible that the role of the medium itself in the message is obscured. In documentaries, one is less apt to think of lighting or sound problems, scripting difficulties, retakes, or the miles of film simply left out of final production for various reasons. Documentaries simply give the impression of "natural" filming, a camera running in the face of reality.

We should keep in mind the powerful evolutionary benefits of simplicity. Simplicity produces a serenity and clarity of vision, and a strong belief in achievable goals. We are naturally inclined to try to understand things; simplicity is our reward. The price of simplicity is eternal vigilance and inexhaustible adaptability. We have had priests and bankers, heroes and poets to handle the complex. Now, with our information coming at us through a multimedia network, we must play all these roles; complexity is revealed behind every event and produces a pervasive quasi paranoia. Why is it that in an information-overloaded reality we usually feel that we are not given enough information to act safely upon?

E-mail is often shared between people with Net identities only. These are personae so simplified that they are literally discarnate or cybersomatic — that is, needing no body to maintain their virtual identities. This stripped-down facelessness is a minimal perceivable personality, but increasingly it's all we need in a virtual world of symplectic tensions. What we do about retaining our spirituality is another matter.

All experience is now partly virtual, composed of synthetic percepts embedded in whole human experience (for instance, the way we recall last night's weather forecast to start the day). Any experience beyond normal vision, technically aided, is virtual — like looking at microbes or molecules through powerful microscopes, or "seeing" the sound of the Big Bang through a radio telescope. Our simple awareness of a complex world of microbes when cleaning house is rudimentary symplexity. The symplectic fear of errant emissions of electromagnetic radiation from a microwave oven or computer monitor, imagined or real, turns a simple meal or work session into a complex subliminal worry about cancer. Listening to economists give simplifying explanations on TV of unknowably complex financial events is an ongoing staple of investigative television, one which exposes instead the symplectic dread of viewers who strongly fear that they are being bamboozled or lied to.

Also symplectic is our conflicted perception of, and disdain for, governments of all kinds, which may be related to the media techniques that manage public consciousness finally becoming visible to us. The sleight of hand of the gatekeepers of power and finance is slowing down. We feel strongly, and may yet understand, these deep aversions to the subliminal fascism of our consumer culture and its corporate oligarchy. Our constant need to escape the understanding of complex issues makes us seem less fully human: less moral, less ethical, less caring, even less intelligent — in short, dumbed down.

Whether we notice it or not, it is the relationship between the simple and the complex that splits the world into those capable of pattern recognition, real perception, and real work, and those who are being left behind in the information revolution. The simple, linear, logical, and categorical minded are left groping for simple cause and effect connections between events.

Whatever the present positive benefits of symplectic awareness, it is likely that future generations will feel themselves trapped between the desire for a richer interior life and the inundation by shallow, secular trivia. They may find it very difficult to escape the me-first, anti-social

horrors of fiscal idolatry and the depersonalization that arises from
overuse of electronic media, especially the computer.

Our increasing disconnection from tradition will even further
diminish the reflective, introspective skills of humankind. In short, discarnate people, etherialized by information technology, will have
to learn to live not only without bodies, as McLuhan warned, but also
without souls. Many, we hope, will not accept such a fate. Besides, the
pendulum of change is always moving. Some of us want to believe that
our adaptation to the electric obsession of the world guarantees movement in the other direction.

A Parable of Symplexity

One Monday evening in the mid-seventies, I went down to the coach
house to see McLuhan in one of my rare visits to his Centre for Culture
and Technology. The special guest that evening was Geoffrey Payzant,
a friend and confidant of Glenn Gould, the internationally famous
Canadian pianist and frequent breakfast partner of McLuhan. Payzant
spoke eloquently and movingly about Gould, who had retired from the
concert stage in 1964 — the same year that *Understanding Media* was
published. In spite of Gould's legendary disdain for the concert hall
audience, some of us still wonder if McLuhan had a part to play in the
pianist's momentous decision. Did McLuhan's work convince the pianist
that the concert stage was no longer the right venue for music in an
electronic age? Gould finally retired to a basement studio to produce
music with full electronic control of its effects.

Payzant brought with him a three-minute piece of Mozart on tape,
which he played for the assembly. We listened expectantly, but simply
heard a fine piece of music masterfully rendered. When it was over,
Payzant asked if anyone had heard anything unusual. No one had, but
one fellow, probably guessing, said he may have heard a splice. Payzant
assured him that though he probably hadn't actually heard a splice, he
could have, since there were thirty-two separate splices in the tape.
None of us, including some well-trained musical listeners, had heard
them. We were astounded at the perfect melding of the pieces into a
unity. We were then informed that each of the thirty-two pieces of the
tape had been produced from *thirty-two separate playings of the piece*.
What I didn't realize at the time was that this remarkable display of a

mergence between technology and music changed my understanding and appreciation of music forever.

We spent the remainder of the session that evening discussing the role of the acoustic engineer in the production of the music. The virtual concert can be so perfectly engineered that, as Gould worried, the artist who enters the concert hall to present a real concert will constantly fail to live up to the impossibly high standard set in the studio. The relatively simple effect had been produced by a dauntingly complex means.

In another ridiculously extended case of symplexity in virtuality, an award-winning popular music group was exposed as having not played or sung a single note on an album entirely produced for them by relatively unknown studio personnel. The revelation of this real fraud destroyed the group in question. It would seem that symplectic perception is the antithesis of the wilful suspension of disbelief. Symplectic perception, in fact, liberates one from media controls on perception.

Axioms of Symplexity

Information overload requires excessive simplifications.

The death row case under appeal is 1,200 pages long. The governor just wants the three-line summary.

Media simplify complex reality.

"Where were you when the Gulf War started?" "Watching *The Price Is Right*."

Symplectic awareness makes us feel that we never have enough information to act on.

The environmental assessment of water and land contamination will have to go through endless studies before anything can be done on an authoritative, trustworthy, or politically sound basis.

Language is made simultaneously simpler and more complex by electric process, which tends to implode language into acronyms.

"I'll be POed if IBM and GM merge but TWI and AOL are not likely to scream unless the GOP leads the way with a push from NASDAQ."

The Media Symplex

AS BENJAMIN LEE WHORF, the patriarch of anthropological linguistics, has demonstrated, it is mainly by language that we structure reality by simplifying experience. This can be dangerous — an oil drum marked "empty" can still be full of explosive gases. More recently, we are faced with understanding reality in terms of how all media change the structure of our perceptual lives. By splitting experience into media forms that have become increasingly complex through their virtual effects, we create a revolutionary change in experience that makes our real world, in turn, increasingly more complex. Ilya Prigogine, a Nobel biophysicist, puts the conundrum clearly: "Biological or social evolution shows us the complex emerging from the simple. How is this possible? How can structure arise from disorder?"[1] This is the fundamental question for the emergent Age of Chaos. Under electric conditions, this is happening everywhere.

This is the essential paradox of all communication: the basic *divisiveness* of communications technologies in their operations on reality. *The Media Symplex* is a study of the failure of communication to unify thought and perception, and offers some suggestions for understanding and reconciliation between the simple and the complex. To begin with, it is necessary to understand the most important negative aspect of the richness of media diversity: the loss of stable meaning.

Globally, cultures are being surrounded by technology and are taking on its technical obsessions, its automated systems, and its fiscal fixations. Pushing worldwide "democracy" and humane social values seems too simple a response to the complex demands of an electronically systematized globe. On the contrary, the communications envelope that contains the planet is being pushed by inhumanity and criminality; venal celebrity is invested in trivial characters to the detriment of real human achievement.

Everywhere in the world, democracy seems critically ill, perhaps by virtue of its being sold globally as simple staging for the management of complex tribal despotisms. Freedom now equates with the freedom to consume; in fact, freedom may soon depend on one's ability to say no to the none-too-subtle and pervasive coercions of consumerism. Is electric process, with its information overload and its virtual culture, at odds with human liberty? Yes. Has modern life been seriously destabilized by the excess of every kind of information? Yes. Can the simple socio-political order we crave emerge from the chaotic complexity of this data deluge? I hope to show that it is possible. Powerful new forces are afoot which we have yet to recognize. Pessimism in such dynamic times may be somewhat naive, even if partly justified.

In order to survive in this electronic labyrinth without walls, our natural reaction has been to shut down and to simplify our sensitivity to the quantity and quality of life itself. Drugs, alcohol, inattention to social obligations, a general lack of commitment, depersonalization, overwork, media deflections from reality — we do whatever will erode the acuity of our sensitivity. This state of being partially numbed, this condition of sensory inhibition, pushes everyone's perceptual capacities toward extreme disequilibrium. This sounds bad, and often is, but is not necessarily so. What are we to make of schemes for dismantling meaning as an oppressive obsession? The Deconstructionist movement led by the French thinkers Derrida and Foucault has proposed that, as with matter itself, when you break meaning down further and further into smaller and smaller particles, both substance and meaning disappear. It is easy to see some merit in this approach to meaning, but is it this easy to dispose of the primary essential of sociality and institutional life?

The world's sanity is poised on a fulcrum of chat. Communication is meant to stabilize human interchange. If so, why does the attempt to communicate effectively so often fail? (McLuhan used to say that it was a miracle we were able to communicate anything.) Others take what we are saying, however minimally, in some way other than we intended. Why? Do we aim to produce simple, clear, sincere statements of meaning or are we really testing each other?

The answer is deeply rooted in the nature of complex systems. Nobelist Ilya Prigogine has enunciated a general principle: "The more complex a system is, the more numerous are the fluctuations that threaten its stability."[2] In fact, there is intense competition between "stabilization through communication" and "instability through fluctuations."[3] A fluctuation is a point of directional change like a vibration or oscillation. If you want simple (i.e., minimally fluctuating), dependable information, then you must be sure that the stability of that information is sufficient to support the gamble of your actions. Every businessperson bets one way or the other on the innuendoes from Mr. Greenspan of the Federal Reserve Bank. Financial talk is always thick with insider speculation.

Language as the basis of all other media is the prime example of the complex arising from the simple. The Gospel of John begins, "In the beginning was the Word . . . and the Word became flesh." Language contains all other media as subsystems or extensions of the word. Changes in any or all of these media result in fluctuations that alter the relations between all parts of the media array. This can produce a very large communications ripple — the media version of the butterfly effect — extremely small stimuli producing very large effects. Knowledge of events is always more complex when arrayed across a media spectrum. An idea presented through a mass medium as a mosaic of sound bites is not even half formed.

Advertising has trained us to perceive in metaphorical and paradoxical ways. All meaning in advertising is layered, multiplex. Puns abound, especially visual puns. Meanings are allusive, suggestive, indirect — anything but simple. McLuhan's career began with the publication of *The Mechanical Bride*,[4] an extremely astute analysis of the techniques of psychological manipulation employed by successful advertising. In *Advertising as Communication*,[5] Gillian Dyer has examined the rhetorical basis of advertising, exposing all the techniques of formal persuasion, including synecdoche (part for the whole), ellipsis

> For the first time, our very survival depends on our having *simultaneously* both simple and complex awareness.

(inference of the part), hyperbole (implausible exaggeration), and all the other five hundred figures of rhetoric that have always been the successful forms of psychological inducement in communication.

We live in an environment in which a simple act of consumption is underwritten by an extremely complex management scheme for public consciousness. The constant suspicion that everything has a deeper and subversive meaning liberates us, apparently, from having to commit to anything. If we are aware at all of how the media operate, our sense of the simple has been devoured by the complex.

In James Joyce's *Ulysses*,[6] the central figure, Leopold Bloom, earns his little living on the edge of the ad world. As we follow Bloom about Dublin on June 16, 1904, we become aware as readers that every page of this symplectic novel requires knowledge of the complex underlying structure of the book if any sense is to be made of it. On the surface, things could not be simpler: the almost plotless story takes place on one day, and simply involves two men meeting while a cuckolding takes place involving Bloom's wife, Molly. Bloom wanders about, attends a funeral, places an ad in a local newspaper, thinks about his dead son, and finally meets Stephen Dedalus, with whom he carouses in Dublin's Nighttown. Certainly, when I was studying Joyce in relation to my work with McLuhan, it quickly became clear that I had to become professionally familiar not only with Homer, but with all the references set loose in Joyce's artfully oblique work, which alludes to nearly the whole of Western literary tradition. Each line takes you not only forward, but requires that you branch out into the complex associations demanded by the novel's structure. This was the first symplectic novel in which explicit plot is minimal and the extremely complex structure of the novel is everything. Joyce, who jokingly said he had the mind of a grocery clerk, developed a writing style that perfectly blended and reconciled the simple and the complex, the mundane and the metaphysical, and the reader is aware of this reconciliation.

One of Joyce's close friends, Stuart Gilbert, tells the story of meeting Joyce in Paris at a favourite magazine kiosk. Gilbert asked how the writing was going and Joyce replied that he had been working on a single sentence all day. Gilbert smiled the smile of understanding: "I see, looking for the *mot juste*, eh?" Joyce seemed irritated and shot back, "No, I've had the words from the beginning. I've been looking for the correct order."[7] The simple, deft selection of exactly the right word, and setting it in precisely the right syntactical order, is a symplectic arrangement. As the old communications adage has it, it's not what you say that's important, but how you say it measured against all the other ways you might have said it. The unstated is always implied. As Hazlitt once observed, at the moment a statement is made the doubt of it is born.[8]

Without expert knowledge of the structure of any medium, you cannot gain access to its real contents. The cultural code shared by the bard and his audience in aural societies makes it possible for them to fully enter the content of an epic poem. In print culture, all the Homeric values shift to favour a book version of the epic. Print has a different idea of what the bard is singing about. All our media watching is done with coded perceptions. There is a tacit grammar to each medium that gives us a different way to put the pieces of experience together, in accordance with the perceptual bias of that medium. Print gives lengthy descriptions of scene; film pans; TV avoids everything but the close-up.

The comparatively simple richness of small-town community life is being replaced by complex media controls that seek to effectively manage human consciousness everywhere as if it were an advertising demographic. The gatekeepers of this control activity are very large transnational corporations.

Media ownership and control is oligarchic. As ownership is made simpler through the merger and concentration of capital, the problems of freedom of information are greatly complexified, while socio-political controls are greatly enhanced. Under the electric conditions of dissomatic (bodiless) computer isolation, the only revolution possible is the revolution of one person. A single individual with a brilliant idea and an attractive web site can start a billion-dollar business. That hope drives the new Net economy. Borrowing from Thomas Jefferson, one person with a network is a majority. That is why the attempts by governments to control the Net are unrelenting. The small fluctuations of one person's articulate dissent, added by media to a stressed political disequilibrium, can "become amplified into gigantic, structure-breaking waves."[9]

The national attempt to reconcile French- and English-speaking Canada through the Meech Lake Accord was frustrated and reversed by the dissent of a single, almost anonymous, Aboriginal backbench MP named Elijah Harper, who had the entire Canadian communications network disseminating his crucial dissent. The weak, disaffected, and disengaged citizen has never been potentially more powerful. The branching complexity of modern life is rooted in the technological evolution of human awareness.

The point of all communication is to extract the central meaning, the essence of events and experiences, in order to share them as coherent contents. In fact, our survival depends on how we simplify experience. We must remember that the content of a medium's content is the process of communication itself; *deep content* is symplectic because it is the interface of two or more media: the tacit media contained within the newer medium. For example, radio and film are tacit in the explicit medium of television. At such an interface, the time/space interactions are extremely complex. Physicists would call this a "many-body problem," producing an exponentially great number of possible relations between a system's parts; chaoticians might regard this as a "period three" event, where an orderly bifurcating system suddenly flips into complete, disorderly chaos.

Put more simply, the interrelations between three or more media must be suppressed in order for the dominant medium to control the impression it gives. Growth of awareness of the importance of film sound is a case in point. There is a very important tacit relationship between sight and sound in movies, but for a long time we were not supposed to think about sound values when viewing a film. Special lenses and booms, too, are part of the complexification of the film medium. The contentless action film is what we are left with — a long and varied advertisement for the playground of technology. Even film documentaries like to suppress awareness of the camera's presence as much as possible in order to negate the possibility that what is being recorded is in any way "performed."

> The most revolutionary fact of contemporary existence is the overwhelming amount of information we consume daily.

Considering the growing complexity of our information environment, it is increasingly difficult to find a basis, an objective principle, for our actions. In politics, religion, and education, we lack stable grounds for decisive action. Our problem is less a specific one, and more an overlaying malaise about the uncertainty and ambiguity that information overload introduces into our understanding. In medicine, for example, while we may worry about having too few nurses and too long waits in the ER, we are also aware of new realities regarding the whole conception of disease.

There is a new, symplectic reality destabilizing medical specialization. Our survival requires a shift in medical awareness. Our MRI, CAT, and PET scans are in fact media of medical communication, conduits of massive information flow. Medicine has become symplectic; the overload of information about any illness or therapy outstrips clear understanding. Consider that doctors themselves have become a major source of illness (Iatrogenics), to some extent through carelessness, incompetence, and overwork, but mainly by the excess of information in their fields of specialty.

Because of our ability, through media, to represent experience in a variety of ways, everything appears to be both itself and something else. The paradoxical conditions created by electric media subvert our good intentions. Individually, media simplify, but as a whole array, the structural interrelations between media paralyze the will in its desire to make meaning. It is difficult for electric media to support a sense of purpose to life beyond money and entertainment.

Religions, for example, work best in local environments where the competition from other religions is small or non-existent, and controls over worship are effective. Reading about other religions, seeing films about them, and watching television shows that reveal their admirable qualities tends to diminish the intensity of devotion to any one religion as the true way to God. In other words, media tend to foster the growth of ecumenical attitudes in religious awareness. Inadvertently, media expose the flaws in every human institution. The simple faith required to commit to any system of belief is pushed in the psyche to the breaking point, the point of reversal. An overload of information about religions can greatly diminish specific clerical controls over their masses. Local violence then follows, as we have been seeing, as electric media encourage global awareness and spread religious indifference throughout the world.

> A medium of communication is a technology for investigating new ways to perceive.

Perceptions become virtual by taking on the structure of the medium that informs them. I've always found it interesting that, for example, Emma Bovary, the protagonist of Gustave Flaubert's masterful novel,[10] is actually little more than a cartoon-like projection, a Rorschach ink blot in print, variously filled in by the reader. Flaubert does not describe her in great detail. When cast for film, however, our experience of her and our understanding of the story are greatly altered by the film's high visual definition and the specific personality of the portraying actress — a personality which may have little to do with Flaubert's intentions in drawing Emma. The casting director's view of her steals our own creative response to her sketchy appearance. More than one great director has pointed out that when the casting of a film is set, the film is eighty percent finished. And on television, Madame Bovary is reduced by the medium to the stature of a soap opera denizen, operating in close-up and medium close-up performance in accordance with the demands of that medium. The sophisticated scope of her personal drama is seriously diminished by TV's inability to survive rich language. Each medium produces its own Emma.

The role of all media is to simplify human experience by leaving out parts, by giving it form and structure and a reasonable interpretation that we can act on. The art of any medium is how it leaves out parts of perception. A video view of reality is too often cartoonishly oversimplified. If you don't understand the medium's structure, you can't judge how it adulterates our knowledge of the real. Still, the childish simplicity of TV seems quite all right as a surrogate reality for many of us.

> Normal ratios between the simple and complex have been greatly imbalanced by electric process.

There has always been a balance between the complexity of experience and its simplified record as memory. It's the difference between history and myth. Myth implodes aeons of ritual and science in simple but dense formats, while history expands on events, endlessly discovering neglected insights of fact. Overall, culture itself serves as permanent propaganda for the folkway against the complexities of the future. No culture publicly shows reality in its true complexity, but rather propagandizes its citizens to hold simple, enculturated views, a set of rules for conformity and simple order. Faith springs from mythic assumptions; belief is rooted in history.

Electrically driven, multimedia, simultaneous, overloaded complexity has become a serious threat to understanding events historically and is pushing all meaning to the edge of coherence. Now everything is both itself and something else, both myth and history simultaneously. Star Wars is the name of a movie and a trillion-dollar US strategic defence initiative — a clear case of history and myth merging. Both are true and not true at the same time. Every expert knew that the technology wouldn't do the job, but the threat to outspend the USSR by a trillion or more dollars did work. Paradox reigns everywhere in the electric world. Even when I park my car I'm never quite sure if I am buying time or renting space. The linear expectation of the historical-minded suggests that given enough time, all apparent complexities surrender to the simplifying techniques of category, thesis, and formula. This will no longer do. Under electric conditions, the simple and the complex are operating simultaneously; they drive the engine of critical meaning and, since much of what we take in is of the nature of entertainment, this makes it very difficult to find solid grounds on which to base action or insightful perception.

The action of media in simplifying experience produces an exponential growth in the amount of our rejected experience. Rejected experience appears to be stored in the preconscious mid-ground of the psyche, the region between consciousness and the intractable unconscious. The preconscious is always lurking just below consciousness and influences it. Thus we constantly suspect that simple human events are at the same time more complex — boding potentially disorderly conditions. Awareness expands, insight deepens, and truth becomes more elusive when it is perceived that everything in the stable conscious mind is rooted in the unstable preconscious. As W.B. Yeats suspected, everything is indeed rooted in its opposite.

> In electric culture, everything is both simple and complex at the same time. Only awareness varies.

We deeply fear feeling cut off from complex meanings, yet entertain ourselves by attempting to simplify everything for easy future recognition. Complex cultural artifacts are constantly being simplified: Romeo and Juliet becomes the Broadway show and then the video; the Gulf War becomes the ad agency yarn, the network animation masking death and destruction; the destruction of the environment is reduced to the minister's three-page summary for the House. We label our ensuing feelings as paranoia, a misnomer that refers to the preconscious role in mental stability.

As we simplify awareness with multiple media treatments, we simultaneously complexify the associations in broader patterns of meaning.

Our attempts to simplify characters through more intense focus on their true natures usually backfires on us. I recall the lesson I learned when I had to teach a course in the Bible as literature and I began to search for the true Job, the ancient and the modern Job. I gathered many editions of the *Book of Job* and carefully read about this enigmatic character, the apparent recipient of God's injustice. I particularly found Carl Jung's *Answer to Job*[11] useful for purposing a psychoanalytical dimension to the figure, and Archibald MacLeish's play *J.B.*[12] offered me playful variations on the character. As I learned more about the character of Job, he was at the same time becoming more complex. In fact, with several ways to view Job at hand, I had been driven close to the edge of meaning. Much post-modern speculation describes the dilemma of not having sufficient grounds for supporting statements of precise meaning. I had sufficient grounds for too many meanings, which results in no meaning at all.

You can also make more out of less information. There are many examples of this phenomenon, but few as powerfully subliminal as our current habit of submitting our idea of nature to cinematic treatment. It has been well documented that from the ecological perspective, the filmic view of nature falsifies the true operation of natural processes. A nature film shows things happening in flowing sequences that tell more about the rhythms of film editing than about the time frames and visual availability of creatures living in the wild.

> By simplifying awareness, media create mythic expectations.

Dramatic events are always occurring in the media's simplified cinematic wild. In sound bite nature, you don't need to have the patience required for complex observation and real understanding. Creatures simply appear.

The simple and the complex are constantly shifting. What was complex becomes simple, as with Ptolemy's attempt to explain the heavens through their earth-centred movement. What is simple becomes complex, just as that system became increasingly unable to account for perceived discrepancies in observations, which made way for the revolution of the Copernican heliocentric view. The simple earth-centred view is maintained by suppressing new perception; the complex view is always burgeoning with new links and associations.

Clear vision has an irresistible power. True wisdom — brilliantly simple solutions to ineffably complex problems — is still awe-inspiring. Increasing awareness destroys the simple view. The management of public consciousness is effected by complex arrangements of information, like demographics and propaganda, which enforce simplistic views, whether social, political, or religious. The simple and the complex are inescapably interdependent.

Small variations in any dynamic system when driven at computer speeds mount up to extremely large differences. See for yourself: set up a closed loop of a videocam shooting a monitor. Light a match between the camera lens and the monitor screen. The effect is magical.

> A fractal is the most complex mathematical figure possible and is created, amazingly, from the simplest formula of the type: $X^2 + C = X$, the formula for *iteration*, which is *repetition* with *feedback* driven by computer at electric speed.

Every random flicker of the match becomes part of the evolving structure of the iterating, orderly pattern. This technique produces a spectacularly beautiful image approaching infinite complexity.

The productive tension between complex systems (media) and simple contents (messages) is not novel; it characterizes all attempts to accumulate knowledge. Complexity, like chaos theory, is often associated with mathematics. However, because the idea is fundamentally *subjective* — Complex to whom? When? — can we find a way to talk about complexity that is scientifically useful and is also humanistically insightful?

As McLuhan once observed in this regard, "There is no technical alternative to humanism . . . Innovation is obsolete."[13] Technology is always in a state of speeded-up obsolescence. Where is our obsession to complexify everything leading us? Are we reading the feedback we're getting from the human condition in ways that are useful to promoting a general improvement in life conditions?

Recently, Neil Postman and others have been expressing doubts about the wisdom of our present obsession with the computerization of everything. A backlash against our electric panacea seems likely as its gains on the human level come into doubt. Presently, our monopolistic obsessions with money and guaranted bank profits deflects us from seeing that power is returning to the individual. Our social instability may be a sign of an impending leap into a higher order. The streets of North America could easily become gridlocked with social protest again.

As Ilya Prigogine has shown in his revolutionary study, *Order Out of*

Chaos, the increasing complexity of our reality is a competition between stabilization through communication and the instability created by fluctuations — the unpredictable motion of subsystems within larger and more orderly systems. It is this role of communication in setting up conditions for stability that interests this study. This relationship is a helical loop, in which the movement from the simple to the complex cannot be detected moment to moment, nor can the movement from the complex back to the simple. The simplicity/complexity relations are a communication problem.

Let's begin the investigation of these new dimensions of communication theory as simply as possible.

An easy way to demonstrate the relationship between redundancy and complex communication is by examining the structure of language. It is a well-known conundrum in linguistics that language is a finite system, infinitely extensible. That's a paradox worthy of meditation. Language is growing and expanding like the universe itself — one can't imagine its limitations. But we can know the underlying structure of its rules.

> *Complexity* is made possible through the simplifying action of *redundancy.*

Here is a little game I used to play with my students:

If there is potentially an infinite number of possible sentences, what are the chances that if I pick one of them you can find out what it is within a hundred guesses? Not a chance, they always bet, even though I wager that they can do it in less than one hundred guesses and I try to get odds. I have my sentence. We begin.

"What is the likeliest first letter in my sentence?" Almost always someone says "t."

"Yes it is. Now what letter is most probable after a 't'?"

An "h," of course.

Now they are catching on. Usually we have "the" in three guesses. The next letter is purposely rare. We waste some guesses on more probable next letters, but soon someone tries a less probable one. I wait until "q" comes up. It never takes twenty-six guesses. After "q," "u" must follow, and "a" comes soon after. With "qua" it takes no time to get "quality." With a few more guesses, "of" is discovered, and "mercy." Frequently, some Shakespeare student starts reciting, "The quality of

mercy is not strained, it droppeth as the gentle rain from heaven . . .".
And my point has been made — that the statistical structure of language
is partly redundant and partly news and that redundancy gives us
access to the greatest complexities of language.

These two aspects of language work together to create the great
complexity of linguistic communication. I have yet to use one hundred
guesses, and I never lose money on this demonstration of the profound
relationship between simplicity and complexity. A chart may be useful
here.

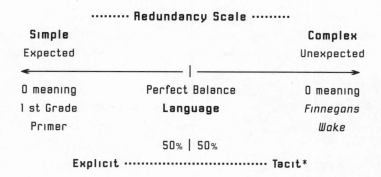

········· **Redundancy Scale** ·········

Simple		Complex
Expected		Unexpected
0 meaning	Perfect Balance	0 meaning
1 st Grade	**Language**	*Finnegans*
Primer		*Wake*
	50% | 50%	

Explicit ······························ **Tacit***

**If one measures redundancy in a lengthy text, the familiarity gained through
time and exposure actually increases the effect of redundancy considerably,
up to 85%.*

The term tacit *is used here in the sense defined by Michael Polanyi in*
Personal Knowledge[14] *as "latent, inarticulate knowledge."* Explicit *knowledge
refers, of course, to the "unambiguous knowledge" of precise, objective
knowledge, like that used in science.*

As Colin Cherry, commenting on redundancy and Zipf's Law, has shown,
it is an intriguing statistical property of the printed English language
that it is approximately fifty percent *expected* (redundant), and fifty percent *unexpected* (surprising).[15]

It is the essence of complex processes that they are full of unexpected, non-redundant data. Put another way, in media, complexity
shows up as news, since whatever is unexpected lacks redundancy and
requires simplification. The shock of a news bulletin carries very little
explicit meaning. The event must unfold into simple units of meaning.
Each of those units can be broken down further into an increasingly

complex array of possible other meanings. But it is the job of mass media to control the depth of inquiry and limit speculation of further complexity by simplifying the reports of events. Complex programming stifles the selling capabilities of mass media.

Extreme redundancy approaches zero meaning, as does extreme complexity, but in the other direction. Take, for example, a droning chat about the weather with a neighbour that is interrupted by a sudden announcement that you have been to Mars. The latter statement is pure news, too irrational and inexplicably provocative to bear much meaning. The weather chat is so lacking in significant data that it, too, approaches zero meaning, but at the other end of the spectrum.

We entered historical time not haphazardly but through the phonetic alphabet, which allowed us to make records of past events. The simple linear measurement of complex events as recorded historical facts removed once and for all the domination of events by heroic action and archetypal symbolism. The line, the uniform motion in a straight line that idealized movement in the Newtonian universe, wiped out the mythic vision of the European Middle Ages and created historical time and, soon after, the myth of progress that still operates as a contemporary ideal. Most importantly, the line brought in the heavy reliance of modern thought on reductionism.

Simplicity/complexity loops move up or down in helical spires.

The dynamic relations of simplicity/complexity are implicit in the movement of awareness down the reductionist helix into the true nature of matter.

5 Fundamental Dimensions of Perception

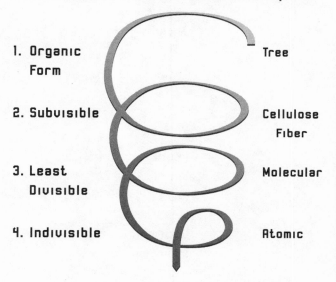

1. Organic
   Form

Tree

2. Subvisible

Cellulose
Fiber

3. Least
   Divisible

Molecular

4. Indivisible

Atomic

5. Subatomic Particles
No Substance
Pure Energy
Ethereal

*The simple view of a tree becomes complicated when it
is pointed out that the underlying structure of that tree
is cellulose fibre. Further complications arise when one
discovers that cellulose fibre has a molecular structure that
is even more essential to understanding the substance of the
tree. And finally we come to the smallest, indivisible element
of that molecule, the atom. Unfortunately, the archetypal
simplicity of the atom is flipped into abject complexity
through the splitting of the atom and the release of myriad
subatomic particles. At this level of material existence,
there is no longer any substance, or stuff, to matter;
it has become instead a series of pure energy transforms.*

5 Fundamental Dimensions to Meaning

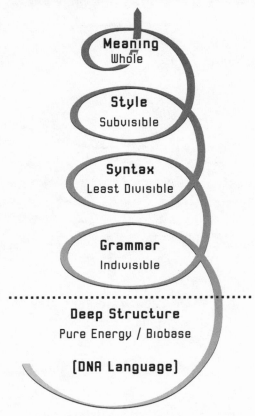

Meaning
Whole

Style
Subvisible

Syntax
Least Divisible

Grammar
Indivisible

....

Deep Structure
Pure Energy / Biobase

[DNA Language]

Just as computers have special languages rooted in arcane codes, so too is language itself rooted in a deep substructure: the biological material of DNA. Nobelist George Beadle[16] and others have been investigating the biological basis of language, where differences in communication result in different species of creature. Noam Chomsky sees man as a linguistic animal carrying the capability of learning language inherently. So, we are born to learn grammars and, having done that, can fashion the subtleties of a specific language, its syntax, style, and meaning.

There are more than a thousand books on the Second World War; it is now the most complex war in history. The more we try to clarify and simplify the military events from 1939 to 1945, the more the historical connections proliferate and interact. All simple views of the war now seem naive except to those who re-fight their wars in a fog of nationalist propaganda. Complexity in systems is the joint creation of the system and its interaction with other systems. In other words, when you probe any complex system, it always becomes more complex. Simplicity does not need to be itself transcendent; it is true and satisfying when most like a formula for scientific or philosophical use. "All humans are love-seeking creatures" is a statement of simple tendency toward absolute truth, but it is not absolute, and psychoanalysis gives it the lie, at least partially. It's as close as simplicity can come to escaping complex grounds.

> In all communication, the amount of complexity created always outstrips the simplicity gained. The demand for increasing simplicity must always be rising.

In conversation, people want to agree and disagree simultaneously. To be in conversation is to agree to talk. But maintaining an element of difference in order to establish one's own position is crucial. To share information is to suggest that some common ground of understanding can come of it. No one wants to be absolutely unique in their views. Overlap of attitude and position of some degree is usual in most chat. Ten people in mutual conversation produce ten variations on a theme. One should have a different view of a conversation between two people, as there are really six people present: (1 and 2) each person as seen by the other, (3 and 4) each person as she sees herself, and (5 and 6) each person in reality. Add media to this mix and the symplexity of ordinary interrelations is made exponentially dense.

> Communication is basically divisive and bifurcating; the inevitable result is complexification.

Our motivation in all communication is always bifurcating, splitting into lines of agreement and disagreement, understanding and misapprehension. When our conversation is finished, a line of disagreement can often be traced through a filigree of tenuous agreement that the respondents have tacitly agreed not to recognize, but which remains a serious obstacle to true understanding. This I call "teleramic communication" (see below), which traces the branching or splitting of points of information into cruxes of divergent meaning. This wilfulness in avoiding complete agreement is the essence of the act of communication.

Communication grows complex like a nervous system or a tree, branching out to reach ever farther up toward the light. Trees and nervous systems are not symmetrical but are self-similar in their growth patterns. Each maple tree is unique but looks unavoidably like a maple tree. Balance in earth for straight growth and the quest for sunlight are the hidden attractors of apparently random tree growth.

Communication seeks a similar balance, as language itself always does, but can appear extremely desultory moment to moment. At a certain point in any smoothly bifurcating system, the system goes off balance and chaos ensues. This happens when a system starts to divide in an unsymmetrical way, as when a conversation becomes overwhelmingly one-sided.

An examination of any conversation shows strong unconscious recognition of these elements, which bring disequilibrium and divisiveness to the communications act. But the simple fact of having to communicate quickly and efficiently for practical purposes often demands that we suppress such awareness of complex interrelations. Differentials in power are also suppressed in the interests of maintaining a semblance of democracy. We should not see the lobbyists and special interest groups at the government's elbow. Civilized society and its institutions are based on this suppression of awareness. Electric culture, unfortunately, eliminates this civilized advantage in the interests of entertainment.

The communications gestalt, or deep pattern, is always more complex than its surface. Beneath every apparently idle conversation pulse the deep psychological biases that define personal interests in even the most trivial things and events. True agreement in any conversation is impossible because it is impossibly complex. A simple pattern of coincident, overlapping, and temporary willingness to operate as one voice is the best we can manage, and often even this is too much for our fundamentally dissenting natures. We can agree on basic consumption patterns but reserve the right to differ in brand preferences. This is the difference of no difference but serves the purpose of creating illusory individuation for our sameness.

Part of the problem in attaining precise agreement in communication is the role played by non-verbal communication in all attempts to coincide in opinion. The kinesic component alone, gestural and facial, muddies the communication waters immeasurably. Add to that the paralinguistic elements — the non-verbal, meaningful array of sound produced by people often unaware of voice set, pitch, stress, and juncture in undermining the clarity of their message — and you have a very dense set of interrelations. Like the many-body problem in physics, which makes it impossible to pin down for more than three particles precisely how all the parts are positioned for meaningful relationships, these non-verbal aspects make exact communication difficult.

The conceptualizing, theorizing, specializing, ordering — that is, the simplifying — mentality exhibited by all human beings always has two basic effects. First, it makes it possible to have a basis for action, scientific or artistic. Second, by leaving out parts of experience, and thereby simplifying it, we create a huge number of simple units for the generation of even more complex, or mosaic, patterns of knowledge in the future. Thus simple systems create complex realities.

The difference here is between linear systems ("Consider a feather falling in a vacuum"), which are easy, and dynamic systems ("Explain the migration of birds"), which are much more difficult. The complexities of dynamic systems have always confuted science and presented serious obstacles to study. Complexity is definitively dynamic, just as simple explanations are basically linear. It is the difference between life and law. Culture is a varying technique that selects and simplifies reality; it also suppresses holistic, more complex experience. Unfortunately, the linear and the dynamic almost always clash. Symplexity is dual, a complementarity of mutually exclusive modes of awareness.

> Simplicity is integral, systematic, and linear; complexity is turbulent, dynamic, and patterned. Reality is both.

The symplectic vision of reality tends to be holographic, each point of insight being both simple and complex and tending toward wholeness. On the other hand, each node of insight is part of a greater complexity. This is the basic structure of systems theory. A greater complexity can be itself a node in a yet larger complexity. But what happens when all these concentric systems are interacting all at once?

The world of such events becomes a giant *strange attractor* (an invisible point that dominates the behaviour of a dynamic system, like the point that pulls a pendulum back to zero) in which some invisible future reality is pulling chaotic events into the peculiar unity of a grand tendency to order, an order which is never achieved but is predictable. The implicit dynamic turbulence of such an environment can be understood only with a new vision of the behaviour of the material world as it begins to link itself spiritually with a new science that understands the normal aspects of chaos. In heart rhythms or brain wave studies, certain chaotic rhythms are thought to be normal. The simple objective of maintaining good health sets loose the very complex conflicts of nutritional claims.

Now that electricity drives all information sources, the features of dynamic systems take over from the simple linear modelling of experience.

Parables of Electric Process

Dr. Victor Frankenstein does not record the exact method by which he infuses life into his mosaic man, the Frankenstein monster. Though his studies have taken him through chemistry and anatomy, it is clear that the doctor has been caught up in the excitement generated by Galvani's paradigmatic breakthrough in physiology. In his famous experiments in bioelectric magnetism, Galvani was apparently able to "animate" severed frog's legs by touching the cut nerve ends with magnetic plates. The legs jumped and twitched as though still attached to their host. Scientific imagination was profoundly stirred by this discovery.

Frankenstein, having assembled the exhumed and purloined body parts into a whole, had to breath life into this clay. What power did he use? It appears to be electricity.

> It was a dreary night of November that I beheld the accomplishment
> of my toils. With an anxiety that almost amounted to agony,
> I collected the instruments of life around me, that I might infuse
> a spark of being into the lifeless thing that lay at my feet.[17]

This "spark of being," which had become a widespread scientific and philosophical curiosity, is probably a reference to the work of Galvani as proof of the *élan vitale* or "vital spark" of Bergson. There ensued a hot controversy about the significance of Galvanism, or the idea that electricity flows in animals.

Less dramatic but more inspirational, Alessandro Volta later showed how Galvani's effects were achieved — dissimilar metals, zinc and iron, were used in his probes. They were both right about one very important thing: neuroelectricity and electricity are compatible forces. The body is electric and electric bodies often seem somewhat human. This discovery produced an almost instant electric craze.

> Volta made the first portable source of electricity, the "pile" or battery. Electricity was feverishly and imaginatively applied to broadly promote profits by exploiting health worries.

In the annals that catalogue the early swoon of science into the electric embrace, very little can match the strange activities of James Graham of London. Graham exemplifies how far-reaching this desperate quest for electric therapy had come.

> One of the most bizarre results of this craze for the new force [electricity] was the establishment in London, by James Graham, of the Temple of Health. The principal attraction was a great "celestial or magnetico-electrico" bed, in which childless couples might indulge in reproductive activity under the influence of the therapeutic electric field.[18]

This activity took place in the round, before spectators. There seems to have been more conjugal activity in the celestial bed than that aimed merely at reproduction, nor were all the Temple members simply voyeurs or low-lifes. It is recorded that "one of the ladies who acted as 'goddess of Health and Hymen' on these occasions was no less a personage than Emma Lyon, later to become famous as Lady Hamilton, Nelson's controversial mistress."[19]

The frivolous rush to exploit electricity produced a panacea of products, all promising improved health: electric chairs, beds, and girdles, along with general devices for universal relief of pain. The tradition of embracing electricity had already been established in America and Europe when Franklin's experiments demonstrated the link between electricity and lightning. The fashion world quickly followed with a popular ladies hat topped with a lightning rod and trailing a ground wire onto the walkway. With such strong interest exhibited by charlatans and amateurs in playing with the new force, it is not surprising that the serious scientist was exceptionally careful to avoid association with

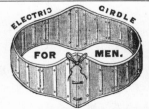

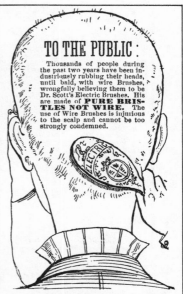

any of it. Bioelectriomagnetism has been a relatively neglected field of medicine ever since.

The context of all modern communications results from the fundamental characteristics of electric process. The underlying structural effects of electrification permeate all media today, even print, where docutext machines take computer disks and turn them into books at great speed.

In the 1960s, when McLuhan was establishing the fundamental characteristics of electric process, he determined that the process had three categories: (1) decentralization, (2) integration, and (3) acceleration. Some years later, working closely with Barrington Nevitt, a communications engineer, a possible fourth category was added: resonance, which was to account for the special way in which a broadcast field required a receptive resonant vibration in the antennae of receivers. Not a lot of work was done at the time, or since then, to develop our understanding of these crucial terms.

I have tried to add to and extend these very important insights because they condition all other thinking about electric forms. Their critical functions fall into place when it becomes clear that the fundamental characteristics of electric process are symplectic in form; that is, they are dual and divided in one sense and form a complementarity in another very important sense.

The fifth fundamental characteristic of all technological processes, and especially all electrical systems, is the tendency to group into syncretic forms: radio and silent films come together inevitably to produce talkies; radio and talkies syncretize to produce television; telephone and photocopying technologies produce the fax. The same is true of the earliest forms of technology, where a man's arm/fist combination by logical extension becomes the stone/shaft, producing a rudimentary extension of great value to early humankind.[20]

1. Decentralizes Information/Centralizes Power:

Think of a network as a simple set of intersecting horizontal and vertical lines. At every point of intersection, a datum of information entering the network is instantly available to everyone with access to that net. At the speed of light, the information is everywhere. The decentralizing effect is to create a universe in which spatial separations matter less and less. Everywhere is anywhere; anywhere is everywhere. Even the most

······· Symplectic Characteristics of Electric Process ·······

1. Decentralizing/Centralizing =
    Simple — media awareness everywhere
    Complex — power/monopolies/mergers

    ·····························

2. Accelerating/Instantaneous =
    Simple — time and space relations obsolescing/race of progress
    Complex — time and space relations from speed-up ⟶ speed of light

    ·····························

3. Inhibitive/Projective =
    Simple — reduced awareness through reduction in sensitivity
    Complex — information overload

    ·····························

4. Integral/Holisitic =
    Simple — pattern recognition/control of meaning/movie screen/CRT
    Complex — preconscious bias/subliminal/parts as wholes/parts in
    parts = wholes = extreme complexity/biotechnology/gene swapping

    ·····························

5. Bifurcating /Syncretic =
    Simple — conversation tree/media/Net
    Complex — pulling disparate parts together into resonant wholes
    — paradox and ambiguity re-established/global divisiveness and
        violence as planetary business

    ·····························

Events are both simple and dynamically complicated at the same time
because the rational mind is formed by the tension in resolving these
mutually exclusive extremes.

remote areas participate in the urban culture of the great media centres. In some crucial respects, small-town America disappears.

Besides making everywhere a receiving centre, the decentralization of information condenses power in the hands of the owners and managers of the public airways, which are not public at all. It is also important to know that a single gatekeeper has allowed that datum of information into the net. That person or executive group has great power over the agenda of news coverage, essentially deciding what will and what will not be broadcast. The very few who control the decentralization agenda to reach the widest markets have the greatest power imaginable. In spite of the appearance of there being many channels, owners become fewer in number as they consume each other through mergers and buy-outs. These commercial interests now have set their sights on controlling the one area of democratic communication left — the Internet.

2. Acceleration/Instantaneity:

While Einstein was introducing the Theory of Relativity into science, the mass media were becoming the instrumentality of relativism in everyday life by introducing a variety of views of events. Each medium's mode of perception becomes a special case of observer orientation. The "truth" becomes much more difficult to ascertain.

Electric media create the virtual collapse of time and space. A phone call to San Francisco is near instantaneous; the transcontinental distance is absorbed into the spacelessness of all telecommunications. Having eliminated time and space as factors in common awareness, and having created a relativistic sort of time-space, we notice that all communication is speeding up to a very high pitch. Some lines multiplex messages, which hurtle at the speed of light down channels that carry billions of bits of information per second to a great number of receivers.

When technology speeds up, life follows, becoming hectic and nerve jangling. The stress of keeping up with faster and faster information processing becomes a serious health hazard for many. Machines that can process billions of operations per second are breathtakingly demanding on human beings who are being used by this technology. Is there any limit to the acceleration of our lives? Just how adaptable are we? The rise of inhibition is a clear indicator that we have crossed a fine line of tolerance for the schizoid overload of information we face every day.

3. Inhibitive/Projective:

When we experience too much information for the senses to process, as with some music shows and workplaces, and the urban scene in general, we must inhibit the assault. The pain can be evaded by turning down our sensitivity, by inhibiting the continuous openness to the deluge. The nervous system begins this process automatically. When any sensory provocation is too complex to process, we lose feeling and begin to approach sensory closure, numbness. In fact, too much stimulation can induce temporary blindness or deafness.

Broadcast is projective, the opposite of turning inward. It fills the stratosphere with information, like an envelope containing the globe in the embrace of a dense network of programming. Now work becomes a project, because increasingly work means the processing of information, which involves sending it out to many centres.

As we know, this process inevitably tends to produce far too much information. Information overload drives communication systems to critical disequilibrium, a precarious state that threatens system breakdown. Patterns of coherent, enhanced meaning can emerge from what may appear at first as chaotic disarrays. As information mounts beyond the capacity of consciousness to attend to it, beyond the level of energy required to stay with the program, it can reach critical mass and flip into a mythic condensation of a higher order.

Overload conditions are always tending to extreme disequilibrium. Yet new order is achieved by managing disequilibrium. This is the true meaning of the tetrad that McLuhan was trying to work out. A tetrad asks, "What do technologies (1) enhance, (2) obsolesce, (3) retrieve, and (4) reverse into?" These are the questions — each an attempt at pattern recognition — that McLuhan was playing with without emphasizing their progressive complexity. The first three steps are *progressively more complex* projections until, like any system pressed to the limits of its capability, the tetrad reverses and flips into its opposite.

In my view, the tetrad is a symplectic device, taking huge amounts of complexifying information and imploding it into simple transformations.

4. Integral/Holistic:

The simplifying, imploding capability of the mind condenses vast amounts of disparate information into single nodes of powerful perception — so-called epiphanies or ontological illuminations, in which the deep meaning of a thing or event is made evident in a unitary way, in a flash of insight. The "exact whatness" of the thing is revealed. This simplifying aspect of cognition suggests that the entire point of consciousness is its role in establishing equilibrium between the simple and the complex.

In spite of all the careful, redundant training we receive in responding to simple linear models of reality, that is, the literate processing of reality, we still have a natural tendency to guide ourselves through our use of pattern recognition. Patterns are dynamic, organic, alive; linear models are theoretical, limiting, and often irrelevant to wide and lively purposes. Make precise plans for the week and see what happens.

A pattern has integrity and contains all the parts of a whole observation. A gestalt is an elaborate pattern in which the whole is even greater than the parts. The unifying effect of electric process pulls together information from many different fields into a patterned representation of reality that goes beyond the artificial boundaries of category or specialist discipline. Wholeness in our calculations makes it possible for us to solve complex environmental problems that could not be touched by knowledge from any one special discipline.

5. Bifurcating/Syncretic:

Meaning is constantly branching, splitting, and bifurcating, as well as pulling together. Any point of agreement in meaning will not remain one thing for long; as it is passed from one person to another or as a conversation between two people progresses, it is persistently becoming something other than original designation. No message is transmitted intact. Some part of it is always lost or changed as something not intended is added. After several transmissions, an original message evolves into a decidedly altered form.

Because of this splitting action of transferred messages, the counter-intuitive reality dawns: *communication is fundamentally divisive*, always bifurcating. Something of the original intent gets through, but, as the original message threads its way through a series of branching changes, it is simultaneously divisive. Consider the following exchange as an example of positive and negative interests trying to find enough common ground for action:

First person: "Hello, I'm collecting signatures to petition for the protection of the local green belt."

Second person: (*Looks like a professional tree hugger to me.*) "Well, yes, I'm in favour of saving our parkland too."

First person: "You see, we want to keep it in its natural wild state, not develop it into parkland."

Second person: (*Anti-development, I knew it.*) "But it's preservation for local citizens' use?"

First person: "Yes, preservation, and Dan Johnson is all for it."

Second person: "Do you think the city council will spend that kind of money on this project?"

First person: "The reform wing is committed to it."

Second person: (*Why should I make those pinkos look good*?) "It will probably take a majority of council to swing it."

First person: "Probably so. Are you in favour of this initiative, then?"

Second person: "Absolutely, for my children and my grandchildren."

First person: "Good, will you sign here then?"

Second person: "I don't want to sign just yet, but you can count me in as favouring the objective."

First person: "Okay, then let me leave you our brochure."

Bifurcation points produce increased complexity, with *emergent* or unfolding phenomena. In this ramification, the complexity level shifts as we move through conversational space. The splitting action, rather like cell splitting (meiosis) but at very high speeds, creates both a *syncretic* agreement pathway as well as a *divisive* differential that remains unstated.

Paradoxically, *agreement* (syncretism) masks a fundamental *disagreement* (divisiveness) built into the communication process itself. Any country's constitution is a good example of this suppressed divisiveness of communication. Lawyers can argue on any constitutional point, at odds with each other over the very document that binds us. Two people in conversation tend to split each point made by the other. Part goes toward agreement for practical, social, or psychological reasons, but another part is always reserved in order to separate individual communication from that of the other. This latter insight is often the only information we really want to have. As soon as you know that the person you're talking to is possessed of a powerful religious or political bias, all the rest of this communication is bifurcated along these lines of awareness and reservation.

This deep, unconscious commitment to divisiveness and to the bias of one's own reality, along with the necessity to cohere in the intention to communicate, is symplectic; the simple attempt at agreement is undercut by intimations of a larger and deeper commitment to the out-of-awareness aspects of the communication. The act of communication is teleramic, branching away from direct coincidence of opinion. We literally weave our way through myriad obstacles to clear, concise communication.

I am reminded of an incident concerning a big-city politician who was trying to sell the idea of progress to a country audience. After delivering a powerful and eloquent statement to the rural audience, the orator was glad-handing the crowd when an old farmer approached and said, "You know, what you said was true; it just ain't my kind of truth." It may be that the agreement to disagree falls into this category as well.

Pattern Recognition

Machines seem to get simpler by resolving the design deficiencies of old technologies. To do this, they must also become smaller and electronic. The obverse of mechanical simplicity is electronic complexity.

Consciousness reflecting on consciousness is always incomplete. A mind cannot know consciously everything that's in it. In its true nature, consciousness is an evolving system of expanding awareness driven by technological extensions of human characteristics, physical and mental. These technological extensions add virtuality to an evolving reality. It's hard to imagine a world without guns and bombs. This extending activity is an implicate system of unfolding, limitless awareness that is the deep structure of our present globalism. Our ability to survive in an increasingly populous and socially complex world depends on how we simplify the global reality created by communications. People used to say that knowledge is freedom; now we are beginning to wonder if knowledge does not also enslave. Life without simplicity is hardly worth living.

It is certain that we have to acquire greater facility in symplectic pattern recognition in order to keep up with the escalating speeds and complexity of electric culture. Some historical examples of how pattern recognition works may be helpful here.

Exemplary Patterns

Print technology simplified the recording and distribution of ideas, but greatly complexified social, religious, and political realities. The linearization of thought, with its left/right bias, its categories and fragments, its boundaries and borders, and its subjects and disciplines, follows from learning to assimilate knowledge from the printed page. This epochal linear project immeasurably complexified and institutionalized the human condition while making physical survival and material prosperity simpler.

Pressed to the limit, print becomes an overload phenomenon precisely at a time when the competition from other media is greatest. With too many books, the reading audience becomes fragmented. No dialogue of common literate interests can survive the onslaught, the excess. Without dialogue and critical understanding, the best go begging for a central place in the culture while popular non-books hold centre stage.

The changes forced on print by the electric media greatly complexify its new role for an audience that increasingly avoids serious reading while consuming many bestsellers. Ironically, following James Joyce, our best books have never been more challenging to read — Gaddis' *The Recognitions*, Pynchon's *Mason & Dixon*, DeLillo's *Underworld*, Salman Rushdie's *The Satanic Verses*, Calvino's *Invisible Cities*. It may be that we now sell so many books because we no longer know how to read.

$E=MC^2$ greatly simplifies our understanding of the operations of the universe by setting up new relations between mass, energy, and the speed of light. But, at the same time, Einstein's Theory of Relativity was the first step into a conundrum of complexity regarding the nature of matter itself, which is now regarded, however counter-intuitively, as nothing but transforms of pure energy. And relativity as a general concept has greatly increased cultural problems by illuminating the general futility of all absolute systems. Relativism has led to our uncritical acceptance of variant attitudes in all areas of social, political, and moral thought. As for the philosophical effects of relativity, we have failed to see that the real challenge is in finding out what is not relative. As the pattern of the speed of light and the behaviour of mass is constant and absolute (so far!), what are the moral equivalents? All this simultaneous simplicity and complexity is symplectic.

Parable of the slime mould. The powerful and neglected relations between simplicity and complexity in nature can be wonderfully illustrated by the now almost infamous slime mould. These simple, single-celled creatures produce complex, communal survival tactics that are a marvel of instantaneous, though temporary, complexification. When the environment of the one-celled myxomycete goes critical, these elementary organisms are capable of assembling into what one scientist calls "an erect penile shaft." Once the entire community is incorporated into this body (it is now big enough to be seen by the naked eye), it falls over and instantly develops a functional "head," middle, and tail. This slug-like thing, which is really a very complex act of social survival by the whole community, wiggles away to find a new and more propitious environment. When a new home is found, the slug erects itself, then dissolves quickly into a widespread community of one-celled individuals, with each unit going about its simple business of ingesting and eliminating food. This is symplexity at the heart of nature.

MRI, PET, and CAT scans, precise and unobtrusive ways to monitor the workings of the brain, are the result of extremely complex technologies that create relatively simple and useful images of internal brain functions. Because of its bloodless intrusion, this technology greatly simplifies diagnostic work in medicine, helping to discover complex brain mal-functions and many extremely complicated disorders.

At the same time, there is an interesting turnaround in medicine that sees complex wonder drugs being replaced therapeutically by herbal remedies and other simple, alternative medical sources.

Miniaturization. What are the limits to smallness as a desirable pattern for technology? For one thing, the smaller machines get, the less energy they require. The complex theoretical research into the piezoelectric effect, in which electric fields appear in certain materials when they are minimally stressed, has produced wonderfully simplified technologies for transducers of all kinds (devices that convert one form of energy into another), including quartz watches, which are a symplectic marvel.

All media are headed toward some omega point of complete synthesis in the never-never land of digital processing. When McLuhan pointed out that the content of any medium was always another medium, he was making an astute observation. Today, the contents of media are multiplexed with all other media: a novel is a film is a video is WebTV is HDTV is a DVD.

> The reverse action of bifurcation is the implosion of information, or syncretism.

Media are recombinant forms. Like cellular matter, they tend to agglomerate into more complex organisms by wedding their energies and increasing the power of their organic effects. Any technology is an extension of a combination of human functions; a fork is the extended hand and tooth; the wheel is infinite walking, with many little feet on spoke legs joined at the hub of an infinite hip; an automated factory is a city of slaves, and so on.

When language entered the visual grid of 3-space, print was inevitable. The handwritten gossip of Nathaniel Butter combined with print to give us the modern newspaper. When Reuters heard about sending impulses through wires over great distances, he sold his carrier pigeons and began a worldwide telegraph news service. The television, typewriter, printing press, and telephone syncretically meld into computers. Attached to networks, computers succeed in syncretizing all media into one, multiplexed form.

As media change, they change their audience. In order to assimilate the effects of a new medium, one must be able to suppress the habitual perceptions from the use of other media. That is why truly literate people can't stand watching television and why a generation raised on television values has great difficulty becoming truly literate. Using one medium predominantly risks losing, or never gaining, the perceptual virtuosity required to understand our world. Television uniquely usurps our allegiances to other media.

TV is hotting up. Originally a black-and-white medium of high sensory involvement in a low-definition picture, television has evolved technologically towards higher definition. The perceptual changes related directly to the changed technology tend to primitivize viewer responses, to get viewers more involved with the rich colour and the in-line precision of the harder-edged image. (Now, with the complete digitalization of the TV image, some say that TV is dead and that we are dealing with a new high-definition medium.) Beyond that argument, TV is a physiological experience, not an intellectual one. That's why a reasonably intelligent person can sit and watch utterly puerile drivel for hours on end without coming to the awareness of the complete waste of life that this activity involves. Nothing is more ephemeral on television than the infamous "talking heads" format — one of the few instances when intellectual debate or critical analysis is attempted in television programming. No one remembers what anyone says on television, only how it felt to perceive the figures on the screen. The high levels of general anxiety in the body are quelled by the pacifying medium.

The more that media come together in new combinative forms to create even newer media, the more it seems clear that all media are moving toward one overwhelmingly imploded medium, of truly epical structure, with everything in one. The computer is not so much a separate medium as a hyper-medium (of the cathode ray tube, CRT type) in which the expected benefits of several media come together in a synergistic set of possibilities. The computer is capable, under certain operations, of producing exponential effects. Nothing is a clearer example of this than the DVD version of a film or a fractal on your VDT, an ultimate process pattern. And considering the action of digitalization itself, we can see that it is exquisitely imploded. In the memory realm of multiple gigabytes, the vastness of cyberspace is encountered. It is possible to put entire libraries, several movies, and more on one small disk.

Presently, bookstores don't seem to know what to do with CD-ROMs or DVDs, which appear as a general threat to books. However, because radiant light of any kind is very hard to read by, most likely these new formats, rather than replacing books, will find their literary place as research sources and documentary backgrounds for the great figures of art.

The Internet is the syncretic result of the pairing of the computer and the telephone. It trains us to perceive the ultimate simplicity of the telephone, joined to the complex coded abstractions of the computer. The result of this pairing is to make every individual a communication centre. The power this confers on the individual can best be seen in the dot-com businesses that start up out of nothing but an idea and rapidly become billion-dollar enterprises.

> The Internet is prime training for symplectic awareness.

The Internet is also the ultimate symplex. In promoting e-mail, the Internet has seriously altered the way people, even close friends, communicate. The simple joy of a handwritten letter is becoming a rarity, a disappearing vestige of the past.

The Net simplifies all communication point to point by putting information into an electric vise that truncates, paraphrases, and generally implodes texts. In most cases, the user becomes someone addicted to short-form representations of larger, more complex, texts. And the almost infinite exfoliation of simple sites in cyberspace suggests a vast, evolving, and complex structure. The Internet will not produce scholars, but it is a scholarly tool and will certainly increase the number of dilettantes among us.

The complexity in Internet use comes from the vast increase in the scope of awareness, perhaps our finest evolutionary advantage. The "dumbing down" surface sampling of the Net user eliminates all the nice structural detail that enfranchises the expert view of any subject. Net users are aware that they can never be experts on anything because of the simplified nature of most Net contents. Still there is some advantage in developing expertise for configuring general awareness. Our ability to pattern widely and to access information quickly has greatly increased our general knowledge, but does little to aid our critical thinking or interpretive skills.

The Myth of Electric

ALFRED NORTH WHITEHEAD HAS PROVOKED traditional historians by observing that "[t]he real history does not get written, because it is not in people's brains but in their nerves and vitals . . . The trouble with history is that there is too much of it."[1] History, he seems to be saying, is a matter of "embodiment." Each individual is a walking, talking, variant node of historically random memory. That is, there is no history other than the aggregate of all of these nodes, which together represent the myth of history. As an art, not a science, history is a random array of exemplary moments. The understanding of historical events exists in each mind, like a mosaic of juxtaposed and interilluminating fragments of a picture too complex to be seen whole. The many voices of the official records are always at odds on the important points. Listen to generals, like Grant and Lee, or Montgomery, Patton, and Rommel, discuss a war. To use Joyce's insight: "History is a nightmare from which we are trying to awaken." Equally despairing of a real history, G.M. Trevelyan complains that "[w]e never know enough about the infinitely complex circumstances of any past event to prophesy the future by analogy."[2]

In media, the link between history and myth is technological. Because of mass media, our lives are full of paradoxical and ambiguous events that gravitate toward simple interpretation. In fact, much of our historical awareness is actually based on cinematic perceptions. Film splices out, cuts in, dissolves and fades, zooms in and out, and twists and distorts facts in the interests of creating simple feelings. Film is essentially metaphoric, dealing in perceptual analogy. The rhetorical declaration, "That man is a wolf," is a metaphoric comparison between the rapacity of wolves and human behaviour. In film, the case becomes a mythic virtuality, with actual wolf transformations — as in a film like *An American Werewolf in London*. Vampire and UFO movies, or television's *The X-Files*, establish the same kind of metaphoric relations with the contemporary psyche. Straight-up history yields to science fiction, which better predicts possibilities for real future events. The US Star Wars SDI (Strategic Defence Initiative) takes its name from a fantastic movie, yet played a key role in bringing down the Soviet Union.

> Electric power transforms all culture. We are liberated by electric process from the nightmare of historical time, but are forced to re-enter the mythic world of preliterate values.

When I was hired to teach at MIT in 1966, my division threw a party for new faculty. I was expecting a typical academic affair, with sherry imbibed in a tweedy environment. This faculty get-together was staged near the revamped commercial wharf in Boston's north end, in the lofty pad of the division's administrative assistant. Large balconies at both ends overlooked slips full of parked yachts and sailboats. No dusty, musty faculty club for MIT. The band almost blew the room apart, an early rock band putting out over 20,000 decibels of acoustic abuse. The dancing was spastic, anarchic; Dionysian gyration between flashes of stroboscopic pulse. I did my best. But I noticed about a couple of hours into this intense assault on my body that my vision was fading and my ears were hardly registering sound at all. Clearly, my senses were approaching physiological closure. I soon would be temporarily blind and deaf. I went outside into the sea air and relative quiet and experienced the overwhelming relief of negative inhibition: with the overstimulation suddenly removed, I became extremely aware of its effects on my senses. But before I cut it off, I was directly experiencing a feeling of hallucinatory, wild, primitive release, a special sense of freedom generated by this bacchantic hyper-media event. Harvard was still tippling sherry, but MIT was something else!

Under electric conditions, the psychic faculties that were suppressed by the ethos of the industrial era begin to make their return. New media forms regenerate the mythic sensibility: literacy is eroded and the loud, stereophonic throb of tribal music prevails over more structured and civilized ideas of reality.

Narcissism, as a natural consequence of the crudity of electric media and their depersonalizing effects, threatens traditional social relations and institutions. Old cultures retribalize, protecting obsolete local mores in the hope of retrieving the identity eliminated by global electric values. Reality gives way to the more commercial realm of virtuality. Being true in *effect* but not in *fact*, virtuality is the agency of electric mythology.

The word myth has come to mean a "lie," a "fabrication," or an unimportant aberration of fantasy. The opposite is true, of course. Genuine myths are the most dependable truths we have. We are so biased, so imbalanced by our historical indoctrination into linear time patterns and cause and effect reasoning, that we become impermeable to the thrust of electric media, which reinstate certain preliterate forms along tribal lines.

Myth is the story of a universal truth. Consider the ritual relationship between fathers and mothers and sons and daughters; it never changes, though it may have slightly different cultural styles. The hidden ground to these relations is the timeless incest taboo. Picking up on the primitive myth, Sophocles created a magnificent drama that pulls the pieces together in a perfect order of tragic relations. Inadvertently, Oedipus kills his father and marries his mother — the fundamental fear, or perhaps desire, that underlies family life.

We see in this process a literary mechanism of myth-making that implodes and thus refines the mountains of material amassed over time, finally flipping the material into a formal myth, a form that is sitting on top of a deep and complex resonant ground. History ignores this mode of understanding. Most students are required to study some history; they almost never study myth, but they live it, in depth, through media transformations on reality.

Myth has been our time-honoured technique for virtualizing experience. Life rarely takes on the shape of formal tragedy, but the effect of horrendous events can be dramatized without the actual facts of death and disaster. In fact, it is the virtual form that makes such events fully meaningful. This relationship between the virtual and the real still exists, except that the techniques of aural culture have now given way to the technologies of mass media.

The imploded patterns of electric process are mythic structures, especially in the way they collapse the values of time and space. Just as the telephone eliminates the distance between callers, film technology leaps symbolically from one point of association to another in its myth-making structure. The viewer is transported by film and television through a novel time and space to potentially embrace the entire imagination and fancy of humankind. The structure of our awareness is only partly literate and historical; it is also primarily mythic, as we are beginning to understand. A symplex is reality and myth married with full awareness, as in the case of drugs and sport — we know that winners have a chemical edge. Consider, too, our "democracy" and its ruling class; the rich and the educated, the social and economic elite who run the CIA, the great foundations, the National Security Council and much more are the tail that wags the governmental dog. Congress hardly matters anymore in terms of real power.

> When myth and reality merge, the result is uncertainty.

All philosophical systems are at base autobiographical. Personality adulterates even the most universal questions. From the arguing heroes of relativity and particle physics — Einstein, Heisenberg, Bohr, Schrödinger, Fermi, and others — we inherit the ineluctable truth at the heart of all science: *uncertainty*. The world is powerfully changed by this fact.

The deepest cultural truths we can apprehend are revealed in the new kinds of metaphors we create to replace the old. Every age creates a new set of analogies, which function as a breeding ground for new technical forms. The content of technology, then, is insistent fantasy, mythic scenarios becoming real, like the dream of flight or the conquest of space. In short, reality and myth are always connected technologically. A new system of metaphor is the principal device for expressing a continual re-evaluation of our position in the evolution of awareness.

We trust media to show us aspects of things and events that we might miss with unaided senses. But a new medium is a metaphor, a way to plumb elusive dimensions of our present, ever-changing reality. Aristotle believed that "[t]he greatest thing by far is to be a master of metaphor. It is the one thing that cannot be learned from others. It is the mark of genius."[3] Others hold the view that extended metaphor can be used "as a tool for scientific discovery." Today, Aristotle might have been in favour of mastering media.[4]

Metaphors are never wholly what they appear to be. They are both themselves and something else, a little system of crossed analogies. "My love is a red, red rose" is a sentiment that relates love, heat, blood, red, and a woman to the unfolding flower. A metaphor takes you across to the other side of its meaning and back again, making a connection that flips the comparison up into a higher order of understanding and expands insight. Ilya Prigogine thinks that such systems of order, the action of metaphors and the action of organic systems, are linked. At least, if language structures the reality we live, then metaphor, as the bedrock of linguistic meaning, structures all our scientific perceptions and statements.

Once humankind lived mythically and deeply, desperately trying to synthesize some sort of order out of the whirling flux and make sense of the hidden processes of an overabundant nature. Humankind built meaning by collapsing great amounts of orally transmitted information and behaviour into a mythic code for the simple retrieval and transmission of the important aspects of life. The *Gilgamesh* epic, Homer's *Odyssey*, the *Tao Te Ching* — all these strategies for survival against schizophrenic chaos were successful attempts to synthesize history and myth.

Life in this prehistoric era was dominated by primary-process, mythic thinking, which was pictographic and aural judging from the palaeolithic caves at places like Lascaux, Altamira, Levanzo, and Les Trois Frères. The word was regarded as sacred, with any utterance having the power to mentally invoke the thing to which it referred. Everything that matters, that is "real" in such a world, participates in the power of the exemplary models or archetypes of mind; all else is not sacred, merely profane — that is, of no actual importance.

Pan-spirituality, like a ground fog, purled about humankind at its dawning and lingered until the invention of method. Religion trained perception by juxtaposing the natural and the supernatural in a reality construct that was spiritually dynamic and dangerous. In some ways, this world was a mirror opposite of ours: aurally biased, mythically based, perceptually holistic.

Lévi-Strauss, writing in *Réalités*, expresses his belief that "primitive man is clearly capable of logical thought . . . but it is his myth-creating capacity which plays the vital part in his life . . . I believe that these two ways of thinking have always existed in man, and they go on existing, but the importance they are giving is not the same here as there."[5] Interestingly, the title of this article is "Man Has Never Been So Savage As He Is Today."

After print's civilizing effects, electronic media make us more barbaric. Our penchant for violence is mythic. Our loss of identity, resulting from global technologies and media, exacerbates the violence. We have relegated the mythic process to media formats. Now immersed in the effects of electric process, and with society disintegrating around us, we are coming to recognize the integrating, synthesizing, mythic properties of that technology.

H.J. Chaytor says that the auditory world was "drowned in printer's ink."[6] We became rational, and the main work of defeating nature went on until we were almost completely divorced from nature and its processes. Logical, analytical, literate strategies seemed to be doing so much for us. The world, demystified, became irrational in a more profoundly threatening way. By making reality appear relative, media changed the nature of communication profoundly.

Cultures change at a much slower rate than technological innovation. The global, or collective, values of technology appear to eliminate local cultural values and to bring everything in the world close to an intolerable sameness, a situation that will not support life. So much for information as life-enhancing negative entropy! Simplicity as sameness is lethal to cultural health. Only when in interplay with complexity is simplicity dynamic and alive. We thrive on the novel, the news, the unexpected — even chaos and its new deep order of surface disorder.

So culture tends to fight technology. People turn away from the positivistic panaceas offered, too long now, by science and technology as a replacement for a more holistic vision. Ecology is at war with economy. Biotechnology may become the central site of this war to conquer nature once and for all. Our fate hangs on whether the globe will become a technopoly (Postman's term for totalitarian technocracy) or a place where technology is surrounded by a new, viable, global culture. Ecological problems will inevitably draw us all into the global network of honest, mutual concern needed to cure the madness of a present world order based on the corporate obsession with global markets and exponential profits.

Ironically, technology is the most essential enemy we have. We are not a preliterate people trapped in the cultural limbo of perpetual dawn. There are too many of us to go back in time. We can't disinvent technology, but we can — and must — surround it with human values, with culture. Without electric machines, many of us would not be alive and complaining. Culturally, we must go on to "make it new," as Ezra Pound insisted. Micronizing technologies makes this a reasonable goal, since each of us is now empowered as a hyper-individual with a communications centre of our own that can reach anywhere in the globe.

In technological culture, we are always the lab rats of change, even while appearing to be the beneficiaries. Our conscious intentions have a very small role in determining the future. It is more important to know how media shape our perceptions and to understand the changes to inner states that this shaping breeds. Technology, while bringing us certain material benefits, makes an environmental mess; new technology chases out the old and escalates

Our future is imagination technologized.

the complex environmental chaos it created. The benefits mount into a heap of unnecessary and disquieting "conveniences," all associated, ironically, with the better life technology offers us. The strange fact is that the faster our computers become, the higher our levels of frustration and anxiety that they are not faster still. Next year, surely, they will be. Or won't they? This inner turmoil is at least a boon to psychiatry.

A deeply conditioned perceptual sameness results from our attempts to reconcile our inner and outer states of being with electric process. This global tension creates local adamancy against the erosion of regional cultures, which, at the same time, fails to thwart awareness of the consumer values of electric communications, leaving us only virtualizing global images with which to govern the soul.

Electric Process and Acoustic Space

Anyone brought up on pre-television radio, with its dramatic appeals to the inner eye of the listener, has an implicit understanding of acoustic space. The inner sensory response to certain music also reminds us of the profound significance of acoustic space. Acoustic space individuates our responses as we build an acoustic memory against the music video–style

> Through electric process, we re-enter acoustic space. A movie needs a soundtrack richer than its images. Telephones can't let you "see" your respondent. Radio is rich in voices. The digitized image is losing its credibility.

approach to sight and sound relations. The deep resonance of acoustic space forces the absorption of unpredictable patterns of imaginative interplay at the speed of light. Electric process makes this happen everywhere.

The interconnectedness of resonant frequencies is not a visual, but rather an acoustic relationship. Broadcast is an electromagnetic emanation, and there is an important analogy between these connections and the general auditory sensibility that is so well developed through telegram/fax, telephone, radio, and e-mail. Electronically transformed aspects of the human voice, projected through space in a net of resonant frequencies, are more affective than simple image tracks. In film, God can have a voice but never an image, if credibility is to be retained.

Electric process trivializes visual values by presenting them in multi-sensory contexts, thereby introducing ambiguity into the meaning of images. At the same time, electric process enhances acoustic values by using auditory effects at a high premium. In any film, the auditory values far outweigh the visual. Increasingly in modern life, we are being brought back to preliterate responses to auditory power in psychoanalysis, radio astronomy, rock music, and, of course, television viewing, which, as McLuhan first pointed out, is audile/tactile (*audile* meaning "referring to the sense of hearing").

All the affective power of television is in its sound effects. Sound enhances the tactile dimension of TV's main sensory effects. There is a grotesque banality to most of the rest of it. When a "good" program is presented, it is almost always "good" because of the superior effectiveness of the sound component. *Twin Peaks*, for example, was mainly a sound event, as is *The X-Files*. It is the sound that determines how much one wants to touch the figure on the screen with the hand in the eye.

If one needed stronger indicators of the return to acoustic values, consider twentieth-century art — everything from extreme Rothko to feverish Pollock — which has been a clear record of the downgrading and, in cases, complete obliteration of visual values. Ours is now an interior art, having little to do with the rendering of external objects, but rather with an attempt to directly present inner processes. In acoustic space, the processing of language, especially by computer, requires that we hear acoustic images again, the inner speech essential for true literacy.

What if it were true that we are what we hear coming out of our mouths? Most people read aloud badly. One is left to wonder how their inner speech sounds to them. Take the situation confronting the VDT operator who is processing little more than visual tokens, which lack any inner voice connections. The processor has not heard this material and is somewhat alien to its meaning. If the material is verbal, it will not flow without a voice being added.

> Computers transform print into visual symbols, without our really hearing them. Words become visual images detached from inner speech, mere mute verbal tokens.

The operator presented with an intensely lit iconic picture of a page on a VDT will first experience the desire to let the eye rove over the whole in a jerky action. An overcompensation is required to keep the eye moving on its saccadic way, line by iconic line. This work is hard on the eyes and on the nerves. Even the most adept operator must allow for frequent re-scanning over the entire cortex. The flow from left to right and back again in the brain is deeply disorienting, and makes the disparity between the job and the technology produce maximum stress. In addition, the low-definition icons on many screens require the operator to abandon the visual economy of seeing mainly the top half of every line. On a VDT, all of the line information must be taken in, and this wearying and frustrating slow-down of perceptual habit greatly increases operator stress.

The desire to inhibit the incessant intake of information mounts. The stress of prolonged VDT operation, sometimes rising to intolerable levels, increases to the point where serious illness can result. Fatefully, the attempt to improve the quality of onscreen print cannot alter the fact that the radiant light background of the VDT can never duplicate the effect of a paper page — a crucial distinction, as we shall see.

Though it is clearly a visual stimulus, television has an effect like the linking of the auditory and tactile senses. McLuhan spoke of the hand in the eye ceaselessly limning the TV image, and drew attention to the crucial role of sound in completing

> High visual stress eliminates the auditory resonances of mythic perception.

and interpreting the image. McLuhan was describing a medium that sets up sensory conditions that foster in-depth mythic awareness. Myth, not reality, is the subject of our entertainment media.

Bimodal Consciousness

> Recently, a little girl who was dying of cerebral convulsions had one-half of her brain removed. She is now doing fine, leading an almost normal life.

Perhaps no metaphor so epitomizes this movement back to aurality and myth as the current fascination with split-brain theory. This is the view of the brain as bicameral, producing a bimodal consciousness, which suggests that each personality is a complementarity of two obverse halves. Hemispheric specialization, a well-established view of how the mind works, illustrates the futility of talking about facts when we know so little about the structure of human consciousness — one which is probably holographic, so that every cell is both specialist and generalist.

The structure of the mind seems to reflect a deep mythic desire for wholeness in human actions. The quest for more holistic perception would seem to involve reversing the technique of reductionism and returning to the integrity of mythic awareness. Once the splitting-up of things into smaller and smaller parts for analysis comes finally to the limit of subdivision, the system under investigation flips into its opposite — a whole new vision of matter and the incredible powers it can release.

The enormous propensity of human thought toward dualisms of every kind, the binary notation of the computer not being the least among

> A sophisticated era of dualistic thinking came upon us when the surgical split-brain experiments of Nobelist Roger Sperry revealed the strange powers of a bifurcated brain.

them, and the hemispheric specialization of the brain suggest that the structure of the brain may be at the root of the mind's dualism.

Joseph E. Bogen, quoting a nineteenth-century observer on the effect that the cerebrum is double, like the organs that exercise it, has chosen the terms "propositional" and "appositional" to describe the fundamental differences between the left- and right-front brain.

One of the most obvious and fundamental features of the cerebrum is that it is double. Various kinds of evidence, especially from hemispherectomy, have made it clear that one hemisphere is sufficient to sustain a personality or mind. We may then conclude that the individual with two intact hemispheres has the capacity for two distinct minds. . . . In the human, where propositional thought is typically lateralized to one hemisphere, the other hemisphere evidently specializes in a different mode of thought, which may be called appositional.[7]

The appositional, or comparing faculty, does its job more or less out of our awareness and without disturbing the dominant functions of the left brain. It is curious how almost every investigator of this split-brain phenomenon building on the work of others, attempts to establish new terms of difference for the split. The overall characteristics of the left and right brain have been designated temporal/spatial, analytic/synthetic, sequential/simultaneous, expressive/perceptive, realist/mythic, and so on to great length. The new myth of the emergent mind is remodelled with an essentially binary structure.[8] It is a protean subject, defying definition. But it is interesting to see how split-brain research is a case of the theory proving the method of inquiry.

This is a dangerous theory. As soon as the list of terms for left and right functions is compiled, the matter is reduced to cartoon dimensions: this on the left/that on the right — a wonderfully clear visual model. Unfortunately, this approach falsifies the infinitely complex phenomena it attempts to describe. Action in the brain is going on at nearly the speed of light, which means everywhere at once, with more or less emphasis here in this area and there in others. All of the brain is involved in all its activities all the time.

The two brains do not exist isolated from, or independent of, each other. The corpus callosum appears to function as an organ of flow between the two sides. This body of millions of neural links sets up something like a dialectical process, which joins the activities arising from either side into a synthesis or resolution of essentially conflicting impulses. Wholeness requires a reconciliation of both modalities.

The evidence also suggests that there is drift of lateralized functions to the other side. There is some verbal facility on the right side, but only a childish command of language. Male and female stroke patients show a difference in verbal recovery, with women much more capable of retrieving lost speech than men. This finding tends to support the suspicion that women are more global in their brain activities than men. But left-handed men, like McLuhan and Postman, seem to function more like women in this respect because, it is thought, of the feminine thickness of the rear portion of the corpus callosum in left-handed people.

> A profound complementarity of two incompatible modes of thought is at the base of all educational systems.

Although they go by other names, the two modes, simplicity and complexity, co-exist at every moment of thought. The rules of the culture tell us explicitly what to extract from perception and what to ignore. The metaphoric wholeness of right-brained thought gives way to the selective "leaving out" characteristic of the more focused and analytical left hemisphere.

In the first year at school, children's artwork shifts from a free-flowing expression of whole feelings to a highly linearized grappling with the simple mystery of perspective illusion. The immemorial kindergarten house on a horizon, with two windows, a door, a chimney with pencil-line smoke rising, and a v-form path and a tree in the yard, can be seen as a sad day for the child, who is thus starting the elaborate training to move exclusively left in the brain. The emphasis is on the visual representation of the simple logic of a space. External reality may appear to be ordered, but every child quickly learns that feelings are always more complex than simple thoughts.

Arthur F. Deikman has divided bimodal consciousness into its "active" and "receptive" functions.[9] The active mode manipulates the environment and is associated with a high beta-wave dominance of the brain-wave mix. Along with a high level of boundary perception, this mode emphasizes formal characteristics over the sensory, shapes and meanings over colour and texture, and is generally perceived to be a state of outward striving for objective logical goals.

Television reverses the hemispheric dominance of the brain. The receptive mode takes in the environment and produces only low-intensity alpha-wave activity. Low-level boundary perception, diffuse attention, and a general domination of the formal by the sensory characterize this mode. These receptive conditions are maximal in the infant state and in viewers of television.

Deikman believes that the action mode gains a natural priority over the receptive mode in order to maximally ensure biological survival. As human organization becomes more complex, the receptive mode exists as an interlude between increasingly longer periods of domination by the action mode.

Civilized society tends to regard right-brained functions as pathogenic and regressive, and resists intrusions from the right into its world of rational order. The entire balance of the left/right ratio is thrown off by new experience. The divisive tensions that polarize every society are usually between the left-biased *line-integrators* and right-biased *point-integrators*. These are mutually exclusive visions of reality; to contain them peacefully, every society must be, in itself, a complementarity or a despotism.

The chief social device for controlling right-brained activity is the institution of the arts. Compartmentalizing the irrational and the imaginative by giving it an acceptable role has left the way clear for the linear agendas of technically advanced cultures. Now, modern media blur the distinction between art and reality, encouraging the irrational to re-enter ordinary life. The result can be seen in the hordes of fantasy-oriented children queuing up to have life dispensed to them by professionals — actors, video game designers, athletes. They are attempting to inhibit real life altogether with their preference for fantastic shows.

Regarding the wholeness of one's vision of reality, Georg von Békésy has observed that "thought is always interested more in one part of its object than another."[10] The specific blindness necessary for specialist selectivity helps us learn more and more about less and less, producing a narrow but intense knowledge in a context of general ignorance. But the roots of whole thought seem to be in the depths of the right brain. Once, when asked to explain his thought processes, Albert Einstein replied:

> Dim apprehension
> is the
> mother of invention.

The words or the language, as they are written or spoken, do not seem to play any role in my mechanism of thought. The psychical entities which seem to serve as elements in thought are certain signs and more or less clear images which can be "voluntarily" reproduced and combined.

There is, of course, a certain connection between those elements
and relevant logical concepts . . . This combinatory play seems to
be the essential feature in productive thought — before there is any
connection with logical construction in words or other kinds of signs
which can be communicated. The above-mentioned elements are, in
my case, of visual and some of muscular type. Conventional words
or other signs have to be sought for laboriously only in a secondary
stage, when the mentioned associative play is sufficiently established
and can be reproduced at will.[11]

It appears that Einstein's ideas developed in the right brain and moved
left. He was inhibiting the established patterns of verbal, logical, and
numerical habit from interfering with the birth of new ideas. This may
be about as close as we may ever get to understanding how thought
emerges from the dark side of the mind into the daylight of rational
scrutiny.

Alfred North Whitehead also recognized the one-sidedness of
rational thought and believed that imaginative invention originated on
the non-linear side of mind.

Human life is driven forward by its dim apprehensions of notions
too general for its existing language. Such ideas cannot be grasped
simply, one by one in isolation. They require that mankind advance
in its apprehension of the general nature of things, so as to conceive
systems of ideas elucidating each other. But the growth of the
generality of apprehension is the slowest of all evolutionary
changes.[12]

These "dim apprehensions" are probably pre-verbal, right-sided, primary-process wholes that are taken over for shaping and limitation by
the process of analysis. This process takes the products of a generally
integrated sensorium and submits those products to processing by
visual methods. But all that is changing now that electric culture has
begun to reinstate the dominance of acoustic space in the form of the
resonant frequencies of electronic media.

Some information acts to reduce sensitivity to other forms of information. The balance of the relations between the senses can easily
throw the operations of the sensorium off. The visual sense is notori-

ously isolating, cold, distancing. Tactility appears to embrace all of the senses indirectly. Our eyes are highly dominant; our skin covers us all. Some information is more useful to life processes. Though it may seem utopian to say it, perhaps we should always judge the value of communications by their ability to foster good health.

Electronic media — television, and film in particular — present simulated perceptual wholes, biased in their multi-sensory impact on right-brained stimulation. This media effect trains perception to be fundamentally biased toward the mythic view of reality and results in a hyper-complex pattern of life that transcends everything the left-brained bias has built as civilization.

Are life values enhanced by this transformation that brings the darker side of the brain back into play? Does the mythic dimension of the mind have an important role in our survival today? Is it good that the pressures from electric process turn us from literate and logical perspectives of reality toward patterns of a technically induced mythic awareness?

Above all, myth is in-depth training in understanding the uses of paradox and symbolic relations. Myth is anti-line, anti-model, anti-absolute; it is pro-pattern, pro-synthesis, pro-auditory, pro-cinematic. It is easy to see that this mindset is fundamentally healthy.

Electronic media alter the relationship between the values of time and space, enormously confusing the ability of people to deal with the highs and lows of real life. In media, the lows are spliced out, and the resultant sequence of highs is a serious falsification of the process of actual human existence. Nature ceases to exist; it is replaced by Disney's virtual nature, which has something dynamic and exciting happening every minute on a film that took the film team months to gradually accumulate. It includes pans, aerial shots, extreme close-ups, and, above all, stupendous colour. The disjunction introduced into our lives, the split between life and its representation, can only spawn severe anxieties for those who do not understand the tricks that are being played on their perceptions by media, film and television in particular. To live mythically and in depth is to sense chaos in one's soul.

"Men's progress was the work not of the mind but of the hand."[13] By the work of the hand, Democritus means science, measurement, and system.

I have already published an account

of the last day I spent with Marshall McLuhan in August 1979, wandering the Bloor Street area near the University of Toronto. At one point in our meandering, I took him into the Bob Miller Book Room and induced him to buy a copy of Giorgio de Santillana's *Hamlet's Mill* by insisting that it is the most important book in Western civilization after the Bible. That touch of hyperbole exhilarated him, and he bought the book with alacrity. (I had had the good fortune to be a junior colleague of de Santillana's at MIT, where he was furiously working to finish the book before he died. He just barely managed to do that; it was a heroic battle won with the energetic help of his collaborator, Hertha von Dechend.) A few nights later, I received an eleven o'clock phone call from McLuhan in which he thanked me for the tout and gave the book his vigorous praise. "Full of insights, full of insights," he said, which was saying a lot for him, his highest compliment.

Hamlet's Mill is concerned with the role of myth in human culture. De Santillana's discovery was truly profound, but it is not easy to understand immediately just how profound the central insight of the book is. De Santillana had once been reading *L'Origine de tous les cultes* by Charles Dupuis in the basement recesses of Harvard's Widener Library, one of the great libraries of the world. According to de Santillana, no one had looked at this eighteenth century book since its being placed in the Widener stacks. In this tome, the great Galileo scholar found the sentence that became the breakthrough concerning mythology and science that is *Hamlet's Mill*.[14]

> "Le mythe est né de la science, la science seule l'expliquera."[15]

"Myth is born of science, science alone can explain it." What this means is that myths are coded secrets of scientific content. The first science of man that is referred to here is astronomy, and *Hamlet's Mill* is a magnificent beginning at decoding some of the fundamental myths of the northern peoples using the figure of Hamlet or Amlodhi, who configures the Nordic sky. With von Dechend's help, the exposition of the Hamlet myth finally becomes universal — myths unfold the deepest scientific knowledge of ancient man. Learning how to crack these special myths is a way to disclose the inner workings of the ancient mind and the crucial knowledge it produced.

This insight then shed light on issues that we are still grappling with.

The ancients, for example, were extremely astute in reading the heavens, including precise observations that accommodated their beliefs. De Santillana presents a very convincing case for locating the Star of Bethlehem, "a thrice-repeated Great Conjunction of Saturn and Jupiter in Pisces in the year 6 B.C. or BCE."[16] De Santillana reminds us that precession, or the slipping back of the signs of the zodiac, moved the constellations "standing" on the vernal and autumnal equinoxes so that when it is said that Christ was "born of the Virgin," what is meant is that Virgo is the constellation standing on the autumnal equinox at this time. And it was extremely important to know what signs stood on these dates, because it was believed that they were the principal gates through which the souls of the dead could get out of earth's sway and enter heaven.

Myth is the art of mixing scientific evidence with the most fundamental cultural values. This produces a code that, when broken, reveals a great deal of information about people's beliefs and values; most importantly, such codes reveal the impressive rudiments of early empirical science, beginning with astronomy, the king of all sciences.

Electric Mythology and Chaos

Light uncollected, through the chaos urged
Its instant way, nor order yet had drawn
His lovely train from out the dubious gloom.[17]

About seven or eight years ago, I recall being astonished by a magician's extremely accomplished sleight of hand. The finale of his act involved an apparent psychokinetic event. By grimacing and straining his facial muscles and uttering the word "now" appropriately, he succeeded in turning a beaker of solution from clear, to red, to blue, to yellow, and back to clear again. I was astonished, since he had almost no chance to interpose anything physical with the system before him, though he did pass his hand with a typical flourish over the beaker to begin with. A little later, in my ongoing study of chaos theory, I discovered how he did it. He simply had activated a chemical clock, which was undoubtedly the simplest trick he ever performed.

Prigogine and Stengers, in *Order Out of Chaos*, discuss the chemical clock, a truly remarkable phenomenon of far-from-equilibrium conditions. A chemical clock is a mixture of molecules that behave with absolute regularity after crossing a threshold from utter chaos of behaviour. This is a self-organizing system that, they emphasize, is an extremely unexpected occurrence because of how we think about these matters.

> Suppose we have two kinds of molecules, "red" and "blue." Because of the chaotic motion of the molecules, we would expect that at a given moment we would have more red molecules, say, in the left part of the vessel. Then a bit later more blue molecules would appear, and so on. The vessel would appear to us as "violet." . . . However, this is not what happens with a chemical clock; here the system is all blue, then it abruptly changes its color to red, then again to blue.[18]

The authors point out that because this constant colour change has atomic precision, "we have a coherent process" that can be used as a very precise clock. So that we do not mistakenly think that what is happening is merely "chemical," Prigogine and Stengers continue with an extremely important general observation about such events.

> Such a degree of order stemming from the activity of billions of molecules seems incredible, and indeed, if chemical clocks had not been observed, no one would believe that such a process is possible. To change color all at once, molecules must have a way to "communicate." The system has to act as a whole.[19]

This parable of communication is an entirely new way to think about information transfer. Such a pattern of communication links our understanding to chaos. In the sense of unmanageable, random disorder, chaos has been, as the Bible indicates, the nemesis of reason from the beginning of time; chaos is the antithesis of heavenly order. The first large-scale scientific achievement was the reduction of the chaotic array of the heavens to a few relatively simple, fundamental rules of astronomical movement. We have been refining such movements ever since, with no end in sight. The more finely we measure the heavens with our simple physical laws, the more visually coherent the universe becomes and the more infinitely complex and boundless in extent.

Human cultures are stressed to the limit of survival by the sheer overabundance of information. The global values of electric technology subject us to an increasing disorder born of the unmanageable, burgeoning complexity of information overload. Surely it is obvious even to the most casual observer that the globe is transforming itself into a dynamic, computerized information system of chaotic speed and complexity. This chaos is actually a new form of order, revealed only by moving information at electric speeds to produce mythic cultural patterning.

Recently, because of the exciting developments in non-linear dynamics and related work, like the Theory of Dissipative Structures of Ilya Prigogine, the cosmological idea of chaos, of finding new orders in chaos, has taken on an immense significance. Chaos theory creates a way to find a more holistic, higher, and more useful order out of what appears to be erratic, incalculable disorder. It deals with natural, dynamic, non-linear systems on their own structural and behavioural terms, not merely by linear approximations and models. This new mode of scientific inquiry produces completely unexpected patterns of material behaviour. It's just what we need in an environmental era.

> According to Prigogine, all living things and many non-living things
> are dissipative structures. That is, they maintain their structure by
> the continual flow of energy through their system. That flow of
> energy keeps the system in a constant state of flux.[20]

In certain situations, these fluctuations increase to a point where a fast-forward effect is generated that agitates the system by violent fluctuations into a higher state of order.

> The fluctuations feed off themselves, and the amplification can
> easily overwhelm the entire system. When that happens, the system
> either collapses or reorganizes itself. If it is able to reorganize itself,
> the new dissipative structure will always exhibit a higher order of
> complexity, integration, and a greater energy flow through than its
> predecessor.[21]

As such self-organizing systems transform themselves into ever higher states of order, this "increased complexity creates the condition for evolutionary development." This is an astounding and ground-breaking linkage: chaos with evolution, and then with information.

> Like Prigogine, many scientists are coming to view evolution as
> the tendency of all living systems to advance toward "increased
> complexity of organization." Organizational complexity, in turn, "is
> equivalent to the accumulation of information" . . . *In other words,*
> *evolution is seen as improvement in information processing.*[22]
> (Emphasis added)

Improvement in information processing is certainly not a given under overload conditions. In fact, quite the opposite is true if the overwhelmed individual has adopted an inhibited approach to the environment, which results in an unconscious dulling of the senses. It follows that such a reverse strategy can also be seen as an anti-evolutionary development. Electric process may be counter-evolutionary in some important ways.

At the heart of the chaotic myth of electric process is the engine of iteration — the repetition at the speed of light and with almost instant feedback that only electric process can produce. In fact, without electric process, none of this could be observed at all. At the speed of light, the smallest mistake or variation in any system becomes an enormous chaotic aberration. But chaos is not only man-made, it lies at the heart of nature:

> Some populations multiply rapidly, others quickly die out; some rise
> and fall with a regular periodicity according to the laws of . . . chaos.
> History is replete with examples of populations out of control: the
> release of a small rabbit colony in Australia whose progeny exploded
> across the entire continent; the conquest of the north-eastern United
> States by the gypsy moth caterpillar that escaped from a Boston
> laboratory; the migrating tide of killer bees; the waves of influenza
> which appear to lie dormant for years and then travel across the
> globe as pandemics, only to die down again before the onset of the
> next cycle.[23]

The eruption of dormant nodes of chaos can, in some instances, like gypsy moth multiplication, be tracked mathematically. More often, the chaos is unexpected: a preference that is not properly marked or a defective transistor can bring the world to a halt. A tiny glitch brought the Toronto Stock Exchange to a halt in late February 2000. There is order of a higher kind underlying the electric revolution. New order can be seen in the shift from market capitalism to network capitalism. Owning stuff that quickly loses value through obsolescence is less desirable than owning intellectual capital, that is, ideas, with no inventory but electronic files. People don't want things so much as they want the experience of being in these shoes, leasing this car, impressing those discarnate colleagues that employ them.

A special kind of order can be found even in the apparently random dripping of a faucet, in the dispersion of ink droplets in water, or in the rhythmic interplay between radio waves and planetary orbits. Chaoticians have developed techniques, such as fractal geometry, for actually "seeing" a configuration of infinity and for measuring extremely broken and irregular figures.

The increasing demand to represent the world and nature more and more wholly — in ecology and economics, for example — has drawn many scientists into the sway of chaos theory simply because it is a way to deal with the real world more in terms of its actual structure and behaviour. In the past, scientists have had to deal with the non-linear complexity of the natural world either by approximating it roughly with linear equations or by ignoring the complex whole and concentrating as specialists on bits and pieces of reality.

The most remarkable and fundamental discovery of chaos theory is its ability to discover higher and more holistic states of order that are actually, against all expectation, structurally relatively simple. As well, chaos significantly eliminates uncertainty in our knowledge of natural dynamic systems. Communication theory represents a special case of chaos.

Chaos theory, in making it possible to perceive and measure the wholeness of extremely large dynamic systems, discovers its own kinds of elementary patterns in what appear to be highly complex and disorderly arrays. The force that pulls these patterns together is called a strange attractor, which, as described earlier, refers to an organizational principle that is delimiting, not absolute, but simple enough to be imaged. For example, the chaos of weather behaviour is bounded by a strange attractor called "climate." When one digs deeply enough, the behaviour of any person can be perceived as bounded by the strange attractor of "personality" or "character," and so on.

Chaos, the new reality of a more holistic science, is extremely useful everywhere it exists. After *Hamlet's Mill*, it has become the new linkage between science and mythology.

Chaos, Wholeness, and Electric Mythology

Our inheritance from science in this century has been a profound uncertainty about all human and natural systems. Chaos theory works differently by operating in a direction opposite to the established techniques, helping to explain what were formerly thought to be the most hopelessly chaotic areas of mental and material behaviour. Chaos is the science of wholeness and electricity drives it. Certain patterns crucial to the perception of reality are only possible through electric power. Where we could only see chaos before and have had to ignore it in our calculations, we now have a chance to produce a more holistic science. A key example of this new capability is the profound understanding of ecological relations between living forms in water and the complex activities of turbulence in water flow. It may soon be possible to bring dead waters back to life with such knowledge. We are beginning to think of the environment as a natural gestalt.

In his famous Princeton lectures in 1966, Wolfgang Köhler, one of the founders of Gestalt psychology, was commenting on some hidden laws of human perception.

> When physical systems or human perceptions are given time and
> other opportunities to do so, they change in the direction of greater
> simplicity or regularity.[24]

Gestalt psychology deals with wholes, broad patterns drawn together from several normally separated categories — physics, physiology, chemistry, and art, for example — always striving to configure results that take into account the hidden context of all that which is generally out of awareness in ordinary human perceptions; for example, a book seen against the hidden ground of literacy and print technology, or mass media understood as functions of the electromagnetic wave spectrum.

Taking our lead from the observer-oriented approach of relativity, through media training, we are beginning to understand the necessity to create more integrated, comprehensive patterns of awareness in order to simplify the complex world that electric process streams at us. Our real problems can no longer be solved by expertise from a simple, single-disciplinary view. Large patterns that contribute to overall solutions must be sought. But can computer technology produce real solutions to problems that once defied our limited specialist knowledge?

No computer has topical knowledge (like a diagnostician's hands on a patient's body), which operates like a sixth sense, with more variables than any computer can copy. Life has the aura of its transcendent elements, which computers lack. Lewis Thomas puts it succinctly:

> Even when technology succeeds in manufacturing a machine as
> big as Texas to do everything we recognize as human, it will still
> be, at best, a single individual. This amounts to nothing, practically
> speaking. To match what we can do, there would have to be 3 billion
> of them with more coming down the assembly line, and I doubt that
> anyone will put up the money, much less make room. And even so,
> they would all have to be wired together, intricately, and delicately,
> as we are, communicating to each other, talking incessantly, listening.
> If they weren't at each other this way, all their waking hours, they
> wouldn't be anything like humans, after all. I think we're safe, for
> a long time ahead.[25]

The search for the hidden ground in communications is a quest for mythic awareness, which is essential to understanding what is really going on in the world. The accurate interpretation of data requires a deep understanding of contexts. Contexts are derived from mythic roots. All mass media offer this kind of challenge to the user. One cannot grasp the meaning of any event without a strong understanding of the hidden effects on perception of the structural form of the medium itself.

Television, a habitual form of perceptual training, is the hidden ground for most of contemporary culture. It is an in-depth education in chaotic disconnectedness. In spite of its apparent complexity, TV is a living mythic structure when understood in terms of the primary characteristics of electric process. Myth is a psycho-spiritual device for collapsing vast amounts of time and space into simple dramatic unities. This is precisely what television does, collapsing or imploding information into simple filmic representations. In this way, the medium is transforming the globe, its satellite form being the primary factor in the realization of globalism. This gain is a mixed blessing. Globalism is divisive. Local identities bridle at the transformations insisted upon them by global values. Violence is often the result.

The rational chaos created by TV viewing increases our unconscious sense of the world as being random and meaningless. Beyond rational considerations, the technology itself is still essentially myth-making in its treatment of the real conditions of time and space. Just consider the out-of-awareness juxtapositions of program contents with commercial advertisements. Infamous cases of thoughtless and moronic juxtapositions abound. At one point in a Holocaust program depicting emaciation and extreme starvation, the network broke away abruptly for a dog food commercial. Sensitive human dramas are often interrupted by loud, crass furniture or appliance ads that border on puerile idiocy. We all experience this everyday, but we also assimilate such disjunction in rational thought processes so that we hardly notice anymore that the desultory lack of focus in TV broadcasting is habit forming. This habit may best be observed in our random romp around the total channel array, cruising between seventy and one hundred channels that deliver the type of programming that leads us to feel "there is nothing on."

The Internet is also a seemingly chaotic array of barely classifiable items, arranged as a web-like structure of many intersecting lines of interest. The dynamic, non-linear nature of the Internet is somewhat belied by the attempts to categorize the material into coherent files — the series of search engines, for instance, that operate in a simple logical way to introduce the user into labyrinths of byways and surprise encounters. The Internet is chaotic because it is electric driven, and electric process is dynamic, non-linear, chaotic, iterative, and instantaneous, all characteristics of mythic structure.

Increasingly, we need artistic capabilities in order to pattern our understanding. Our "museum without walls" — a world where, according to Malraux, art and the consumer world have collided and merged — demands artistic response from us in designing coherence out of an uncertain and confused world. Neil Postman quotes George Bernard Shaw in *Quintessence of Ibsenism* on the refining function of art on sensibility.

> Art should refine our sense of character and conduct, of justice
> and sympathy, greatly heightening our self-knowledge, self-control,
> precision of action and considerateness, and making us intolerant
> of baseness, cruelty, injustice, and intellectual superficiality and
> vulgarity.[26]

It is a commonplace that there is something eternally child-like about actors and artists; both attempt to create and hold on to alternative worlds of the psyche, which negate the real world. But being actors and artists, they must impinge on their freedom to criticize the diminishing of life through the control of perception. Every good artist is an outlaw, a Billy the Kid, who won't grow up and conform to conventional views.

> The radical anti-intellectualism of the via negativa expresses
> the effort to break out of our normal conceptual framework and
> "become like little children." It is akin to the reliance on the
> "foolishness of God," that shortcut to the understanding of
> Christianity, of which St. Augustine said enviously that it was
> free to the simple-minded but impossible to the learned.[27]

Although Polanyi doesn't pursue the point, this breaking out from one's conceptual framework implies a movement over to the other side of being, a return to percept. The cognitive dissonance is between breaking things down in order to understand smaller and smaller parts and pulling things together — analysis, in opposition to synthesis — in order to stress wholes over parts. And it is the distinction that McLuhan marks as the essential difference between machine process and electric process: *matching* versus *making*.

Following the negative way may result in epiphanies of insight that transform consciousness into higher states of awareness. Clearly, we need a theory of inhibition to guide us over this new and rough terrain.

> The mechanism by which a negative theology opens access to the
> presence of God is applicable here to a process of artistic creation.
> But the negation of familiar meaning may go beyond this. It may
> usher us into the presence of nothingness. Sartre's *Nausea* contains
> the classic description of this process. It is a generalization of the
> technique for rendering a word incomprehensible by repeating it
> a number of times. You say "table, table, table . . ." until the word
> becomes a mere meaningless sound. You can destroy meaning
> wholesale by reducing everything to its uninterpreted particulars.
> By paralyzing our urge to subordinate one thing to another, we can
> eliminate all subsidiary awareness of things in terms of others and
> create an atomized, totally depersonalized universe.[28]

This self-alienating process comes close to the actual conditions we bring upon ourselves when we accept the redundant urgency to consume that marks the overloaded advertising world. Ads are pervasive, their images and sounds repeated endlessly until we want to protect ourselves from the beating our psyches are forced to endure minute by minute, every day. "Coca Cola, coga cola, coga gola, cogogola, gogogola . . ." Otherwise, we become nothing more than mechanisms of response to this onslaught.

> In this depersonalized universe the pebble in your hand, the
> saliva in your mouth and the word in your ear all become external,
> absurd and hostile times. This universe is the counterpart of the
> cosmic vision, with despair taking the place of hope. It is the
> logical outcome of utterly distrusting our participation in holding
> our beliefs. Left strictly to itself, that is what the world is like.[29]

We need the courage to abandon the conventional values of the fragmented world view of industrial man and his myth of progress, and to adopt the negative posture of seeking right-feeling through the in-depth scrutiny of one's direct experience and a reversal of our role as consumers. One can achieve mental freedom in the experience of wholeness, which expands consciousness. If one trains one's sensibility always to perceive the hidden ground of events, one may acquire enough genuine human experience that life can become transcendentally positive.

> Chaoticians in medicine have discovered that "some degree of chaos seems to be necessary for the healthy functioning of the heart as it is for the brain."[30]

Perhaps the most fundamental discovery linking chaos to bodily processes is that "the level of brain function seems to be intimately linked to the degree of chaos in brain waves."[31] The formula representing this action seems simple enough: higher stimulation equals higher chaos; lower stimulation equals lower chaos.

Since television viewing severely reduces the healthy stimulations of high beta-wave activity in the brain, we should expect that the patterns of chaos in healthy brains are missing in television viewers, and there is strong evidence that they are. Studies conducted at the Australian National University in Canberra by the Emerys, a husband and wife team, determined that television viewing reduces cognition to low levels and thwarts learning, in the normal sense of material being subject to conscious recall.

> The evidence is that television not only destroys the capacity of the viewer to attend, it also, by taking over a complex of direct and indirect neural pathways, decreases vigilance — the general state of arousal which prepares the organism for action, should its attention be drawn to specific stimulus.[32]

The Emerys display their findings in a "Summary Map of Relativities for Radiant and Reflected Light Perception."[33] This chart shows the slowness and relative speed of brain-wave activity given specific tasks. The results, when compared across several other investigations, are clear: all perception attending to television viewing is considerably slowed down, whereas watching reflected light, from film to book reading, produces significantly faster brain waves. The powerful tendency of television to shut down all fast-wave activity, which is associated with general attention spans, leads the Emerys to declare that, in their well-tested, scientific opinion, "television is a maladaptive technology"[34] — one that significantly reduces the individual's capacity to learn or discern environmentally.

The Emerys' tests, along with those of their colleagues, also clearly show that there is an extremely important perceptual difference between television and film as visual media. The reflected light of the film allows for a much higher state of cognitive awareness than does television. It remains to be seen just what effects projection TV has on brain-wave activity.

The most intriguing finding of the Emery study has to do with a watershed change in memory. Because of the pervasive and intense use of CRT technology, mainly in computer VDTs and television screens, the Emerys sought to investigate the technology's effects on learning. Their studies found that in respect to CRT learning, "There is more forgetting than remembering [involved] and the a-conceptual knowledge so afforded is testable only by recognition not recall."[35] This amounts to a revolutionary shift in perceptual values and thus in the learning skills of all children.

The other CRT technology that alters children's perceptual habits is the video game. The virtual road test, which simulates highway conditions and then some, places the user as an element within the system. As we try desperately to hang on and avoid lethal violence in the life-ending scenarios, we learn to be fast and brutal in order to stay virtually alive. How could this training fail to change the perceptions of the young users?

The Emerys' report further confirms the findings of Walter Krugman. Krugman analysed the reduction of brain-wave dominance from beta downward through alpha to theta and delta, which is associated with the growth of passive inattention during the use of CRT technologies. Krugman observes that "[t]he continuous trance-like fixation of the viewer is then not attention but distraction — a form akin to daydreaming or time out."[36] It is in this way that media function to simplify perception and attention. And for parents who might be interested, the Australian study also gathers data on the high incidence of TV and video epilepsy.

Time out is a phasic state that exhibits a certain amount of mental disorder and confusion. The noted Russian psychologist A.R. Luria comments on these "special states of the cerebral cortex (e.g., inhibited or phasic conditions)"[37] and associates them with language difficulties. The Emerys, conducting experiments based partly on Luria's findings, see these effects relating to television use, which is a prolonged phasic state resulting from that maladaptive technology.

Paul Rapp has "monitored the brain waves of epileptics and has found that they become dramatically less chaotic during a seizure."[38] Clearly, in some cases, a lack of chaotic activity in the brain is a signal of malfunction. The evidence is becoming conclusive, through the work of investigators like Krugman, the Emerys, Luria, Peper, and Mulholland, that while watching television, the process of dynamic, alert interaction with reality is almost completely eliminated.[39]

Habitually shutting down the verbal and analytical functions of the mind is bound to result in a flaccid, inarticulate, and uncritical mentality that refuses to distinguish between subtleties. Children raised on a high diet of TV exhibit all these characteristics and others just as alarming. These allegations regarding the effects of our favourite medium can now be supported with evidence.

PET and MRI scans clearly show that the brain is "turned on" in different areas depending on the activities one is performing. This light show, then, gives a picture of brain states related to specific activities. By watching the light travel, we can see that sight takes place at the rear of the brain in the occipital lobes, while hearing occurs further forward. Speaking resides more forward still, and conscious thinking occurs in the cortical frontal lobes.

This neat array of complex brain modalities also involves the specializations of left and right hemispheres of the cortex. Verbal activity and analytical capability, for example, light up on the left side of the brain. Musical and integration skills produce light nodes in various places on the right. Television viewing leaves the left hemisphere almost in darkness. Magnetic resonance imaging and EEG techniques, too, give us mesmerizing pictures of the brain's dynamic actions. These techniques show that verbal centres shut down and all lively brain activity is severely reduced in response to TV watching.

Given all its effects on the brain, TV does not appear on the whole to be particularly good for maximizing the uses of that organ. This is not a matter of good or bad, but it is a situation requiring new thinking. We must consider the perceptual and cognitive changes implied by such a profound revolution in training the senses to use the brain.

Images of Myth as Chaos

The confusion and disorder created by image proliferation — inherited primarily from our advertising technologies, particularly television — increases our sense of the world as being random and schizoid. It is not hyperbole, however, to suggest that we have become addicted to these images. We need them in order to make consumer decisions, but the need is imposed.

> As the Chinese adage warns: "He who demands visual clarity in all things may lack knowledge."

Most people get their information from television, without understanding the medium's characteristic distortions. Consequently, we may all lack knowledge in ways that are profoundly damaging to social and political coherence.

Now, in the early moments of this new millennium, a general sense of values and institutions in disarray is sweeping over our confused expectations. The electric revolution has created conditions of extreme disorder and anxiety for all aspects of health. Electric conditions eliminate the past and replace it with nothing stable. Should we perceive our present condition this way? And worse, are we too spoiled and insulated by affluence to understand real adversity?

It is clear that we are living in a world that is passionately seeking a new way to order itself. So far, only money seems to command our devotion. In all aspects of human endeavour, we have to look deeper if we are to avoid the dissolution of the best that our world has achieved.

The sciences, especially biology and physiology, are turning to chaos theory because it produces deeper insights into processes in which very small events, once believed to be negligible, actually produce extremely large effects. What were once thought of as pathological, erratic, random behaviours in the functioning of the human body are now understood as "normal" chaotic irregularities, exhibiting a special order that allows for more sensitive and effective therapies. And since overloaded information systems are in critical disequilibrium, they represent chaotic conditions for which there can be a new and higher order of organization. This is hopeful. Culture itself may be a self-organizing system of destabilizing fluctuations, thereby producing the energy to flip up into higher states of existence. A mysterious tendency to general order permeates chaotic systems that are too complex for us to make sense of by ordinary means. When random events are extended to extremes, the mythic properties of the strange attractor are revealed in a clear picture of coherent substructure. Everywhere chaos exists, strange, self-organizing lines of dynamic structure can be found. As one investigator puts it: "Chaos is ubiquitous; it is stable; it is structured."[40] Are there principles of self-organization deep within the cultural chaos our technologies have created?

Electric Process, Resonant Bonds, and a Net of Mythic Power

Electric process transforms the world. Now, information from a breathtaking array of categories can be assembled electronically for the solution to even our most pedestrian problems. The Internet could become the biggest think-tank in the world.

That said, solutions to complex problems are always less comprehensive than our problems demand. Every solution is compromised by the small parts that are left out. As years go by, iteration of the tenacious aspects of our problems converts them into big future problems.

On the heels of small mistakes follow large mistakes, a process implicit in the exponential growth of information.

As the pulsing envelope of information surrounds the earth, we begin to realize that all the information in the world is available to anyone at any point on the face of the globe. Our communication reality is a living hologram. The resonant energy of the noon news broadcast from Rio de Janeiro exists in my study in Toronto, as do most of the broadcasts from around the planet. All that resonant energy welters invisibly in my little study; I could turn it all on if I wanted to and if I had the right receiving technology. We usually fail to seek entertainment this way, but, increasingly, business transactions are using just such connections to pursue profits in the post-market economy emerging from the Internet.

With so much material affluence and sophisticated technology, how are we actually worse off than before? The suspicion that time is decaying is one of the oldest ideas of humankind, almost as old as our worship of fertility. Electric process eliminates real time as a factor in communication and creates new roles for psychological time. Space also is eliminated, as any long distance telephone call, or Internet connection, exemplifies. Stress results from such dislocations in basic perceptual values. And appeals to former golden ages or preternatural states won't do.

As each point on the globe becomes integrated into the network of all broadcast information, emotional, social, and political waters are muddied. Electric process makes anywhere a centre and no place marginal. Local cultural ego begins to burgeon globally, precisely when the guarantees of local cultural autonomy are being eliminated by the values of global free trade.

Resonant bonds create a whole new sphere of interplay between events and between people who are connected only by media articulations of the electromagnetic wave spectrum. This gives rise to an abstract sociology in which people no longer have anything bodily to do with each other. Events at any point on the globe can influence events at every other point without anything other than virtual contact. Consider the global television coverage of the Olympics: all local coverage features local athletes in a grand global competition. All coverage is chauvinistic on the global stage. The power to dominate coverage and sell it to other countries clearly is where the money and power lie. Still, while the content of the Olympics is something to be seen, we no longer believe what we see.

Dumbing Down and Electric Decay

Electric process requires increasingly authoritarian strategies in order to manage the decayed public consciousness it has created: strong feelings cut off from careful thought. The turndown in the intensity of experi-

> We may be experiencing a fundamental deteriorization of the quality of experience generated by global electrification.

ence made necessary by an environment overloaded with information results in a diminished appreciation of all our senses. We alternately overstimulate and inhibit ourselves in order to feel strongly, or dull our sensitivity to moments overloaded with refined and detailed perception.

Post-modern, value-free behaviour is increasingly at odds with our most cherished civilized values: truth, justice, honour, love, peace — categories now relativized almost out of existence. We want something better than the downgrading of the human condition that we are presently witnessing.

Our sensitivity to truth is Teflon-coated with layers of information. Nature, so far, has survived our technical abuses in the pursuit of escalating wealth. But in our time, it has become paralyzingly clear that our ravage of the globe must stop, if we are to continue surviving physically. We must also survive mentally, and spiritually, in more than the parochial, religious sense. As all but the worst culprits are learning, we threaten our world with extinction. Insidiously, the human spirit erodes, impoverished by our addictive dependency on consumption and its increasingly corrupt delivery system. In North America, our affluence has ripened into cultural obesity. Cultural decay, like any mental illness, reduces the quality of experience and subtly dehumanizes everyone.

An impoverishment of meaning is implicit in electric forms because their contents are mainly images. The image actually cuts one off from deep, penetrating thought about a complex event. Our world is one in which meaning has been rationalized into simple graphic terms. Our graphic philosophy declares that "what is, is, and here's a picture of it." As ads have shown us, graphic controls can hide deep malfeasance through the subliminal exploitation of children, Aboriginal peoples, and other nostalgic characters, and in general are dishonest to true perception.

Ironically, the electric technologies that we hope will save us are the agency of the force that diminishes the quality of the best things and slightly improves the quality of what is worst. While admittedly bringing some awareness of Picasso into the lives of tens of thousands of viewers at least this once, Harry Rasky's valiant PBS program on Picasso, though excellent in TV terms, seriously reduced the significance of Picasso's work by missing the meaning of his work in a larger context. In the same vein, *All in the Family* unintentionally gave us a somewhat ameliorated view of bigotry and prejudice, and many bigots were among the show's most loyal fans. One could argue that Norman Lear's brainchild, in trying to debunk intolerance by stylizing it comedically, actually contributed to making it more widely acceptable.

We want good things, of course, but mass culture reduces our ability to distinguish the good, from the mediocre, from the bad. The majority follows the ad pitch for mass improvement by cheap newness and facile trashability. Under mass conditions, most of us do what we are told, consume what we are made aware of, and wear signs of allegiance to our favourite products on shirts and labels as though we belonged to some club or cult or consumer army. Our hope in doing this is simple enough: the realization of fantastic identification through consumption.

> The massive homogenizing effect of global satellite culture destroys local culture and establishes the dreary sameness of transnational corporate identity.
> But people will kill in order to retain or regain the myth of their identity.

The decay of human standards is stimulated by the electrification of information. Televangelism is an example of the moronic devaluation of the theological. Worry about literacy and civilized values washes like an oil spill onto the beaches of tradition. Social entropy, the running down of human institutions into randomness and disorder, threatens families and friends. Eternally hopeful, however, we sense that a new age is being born, that a deeper, finer order is emerging from within this chaos.

A new medium produces important psychic and social changes and gives us a completely novel way of looking at the world, adding yet another dimension to our increasingly whole picture of reality. Any new technology changes our position

> The true contents of any medium are the unique sensory effects contributed to the story by the medium.

in perceptual space: consider how exhilarating it was to experience earthrise around the moon, which television made possible while we sat in our easy chairs at home. That gorgeous blue, green, and white ball — our earth — was seen for the first time as though we were on the moon. Supersonic transport gets you to France in five hours; skidoos put us far out into frozen land, where we couldn't go before for fear of freezing to death; VCRs let us go back to the cottage this winter and see what we were doing last summer; and virtual reality puts us in the hunter's shoes while we stalk a large-antlered buck on a screen with an electronic rifle in our hands.

The true contents of a medium are the new sensory effects that become part of the way the medium allows us to experience our stories. Since the content of any new medium is another medium, there is a sharp contrast at play between the sensory effect of the internal medium and the new one. When you are watching a film of a novel you have read, you will be sure to sense the difference between the book's detailed landscape description and the wordless, smooth, fast pan shot of the same terrain.

Normally, we perceive without thinking much about how we do it. This is necessary in order to produce the life-supporting sketch of the most urgent lines of action impinging on our survival. Our lives are strung out between two poles: whole, or tacit experience (the somewhat chaotic awareness of the world as a kaleidoscopic sensory flux), and the need to order our perceptions with explicit knowledge (rational, logical analysis). Being explicit in our knowledge requires that we get rid of whatever part of experience does not accord with the idea of reality that we are constructing with our perceptual theories and biases. The ways in which tacit and explicit knowledge interrelate varies from culture to culture.

One cannot posit pure concept or pure percept, except mystically, as essences. In reality, perception and conception interplay and affect each other like infinitely regressing reflections in culturally distorted mirrors. Media, however, eliminate this process and establish a worldwide sameness in approach to reality. Local cultures become the retribalized contents of global corporate culture, which allows the locals to seem like their old selves but still share in the benefits of the new economic order enveloping the earth. Canadian Aboriginal institutions better their economic condition at home by making legal appeals to the world court.

We are not benignant Buddhas sitting out life in a spiritual high. Our immediate concerns are always for survival: food, space, sex, and economy. We put strict limits on experience in order to develop our sciences and technologies. Suppressing tacit experience is fundamental to the Western commitment to technical values. We are trained not to notice that these values deliver stress and anxiety disguised as comfort. We typically filter out those experiences that don't further the technical agenda.

> In electric culture, "life is lived mythically and in-depth."

Can mass media articulate the archetypal truth that underlies all art? A film of *The Odyssey* is the experience of *The Odyssey* as film. Homer's epics, rendered in bardic voice or in print, are inexhaustible. Even as a very well-made film, however, the story, reduced to a surface of allusive images, is trivialized by the medium's technical limitations. But those raised on film may not notice these losses. Production values in film seriously erode the possibility of most films being capable of rising to the level of art. Too little is left to the imagination. Great films are great because they manage to remain archetypal in dealing with the deepest symbols of humankind.

> High visual definition pre-empts deep thought. Low-order visuality emphasizes thought.

Auditory perception leaves the user's imagination relatively free to visualize internally, privately. An intense multi-sensory experience, say a film, is an interpretation of events that pretends to reality. The film creates an illusion of narrative perception, even though the film itself is not structured in this way. Still, the illusion of integrity remains strong.

Films get progressively more ephemeral at the story level, while technically more impressive. The thunder and lightning of production values eliminates our need for nuance. Cynical producers churn out sequels and take-offs, trusting the uncritical nature of a film audience trained perceptually to ignore the subtleties that thought introduces into life. One medium is more capable of representing clear, accurate, insightful perception than any other: the phonetic alphabet. This record of talk feeds the individual's inner eye and private voice. Language is an ancient system of communication that is perfectly balanced to avoid a distorted ratio between ear and eye, and between thought and feeling.

The technology of electric media, however, requires a sharply diminished linguistic dimension. The isolating coldness of the visual abhors a strong linguistic base. Effective film actors, for example, react gesturally and keep their lines to a minimum. They prefer to react. In novels, heroes can talk; villains are the talkers in film.

Without language, we are left with mere impressions, strong and satisfying as those impressions may seem. We are becoming habituated to being less thoughtful "feelers," prisoners of our crudest drives, running the gamut of redundant passions as we travel the Möbius strip of media feedback loops.

It dosen't seem to matter any longer that our stories have become plotless patterns of electric, technical effects. Production values in film give us thrill technology and no reflective, thoughtful commentary on the human condition. The implosive pressure from electric process to go fast and furiously forward gives us stories that are bloody and violent instead of peaceful and spiritual. While an exploration of values can be found here and there in certain movies, the overall tendency in contemporary films is to eliminate lengthy scenes, cut back on dialogue, put in more reaction takes, and make the camera replace words so that situations can at least seem to have depth.

Quite probably, as Mircea Eliade insists, story is an irreducible form.[41] We must have story as we must have food or sex or technology. Electric process, on the other hand, tends to dismember narrative, replacing it with symbolic associations that only seem to have an integral surface. Archetypes are no longer exemplary models but degraded clichés of use. We remain ignorant of archetypes as psychic forms, stories that can grip an entire culture — the dream of flight, intergalactic travel, deathlessness, the direct experience of God, and so forth. Our quality of life is reduced by this debasement of story.

It is also only by story that we learn to remember the past; without story, we have no past. Electric media trivialize the past through their superficial, technical distortions. History becomes virtual, a pseudo-event, like an advertisement for a real event that never happens. Electric media supplant most myths with the march of progress and the evolutionary story of gratuitous consumption.

What we are most ignorant of, most changes us. And what we miss changes us, too. Electric media tend, by policy, never to upset anyone. All media have structures that leave out important aspects of real perception and thought. Consequently, information and contexts must be taken in from several media in order to create more holistic and more stable views. Perceptual blindness comes from devoting most of one's attention exclusively to a single medium. The dynamical action of the future always resides in our ignorance. Ignorance is where the action is, since what we don't know leaves us in wonder, and wonder, as many believe, is our finest trait. What one knows is a mask to cover one's ignorance. The excitement of discovery has a large ignorance component.

The preservation of the integrity of one's inner life, in the face of the homogenizing effects of mass media, pits the individual vision against the prefabricated view of the media Cyclops. Inhibiting one's awareness by adapting consciousness to the facile cartoons of media finally becomes a personality disorder.

The medium that is least inhibitive to the development of depth understanding is print. You can't train a philosopher on videotapes (though psychiatrists use them clinically). The most important human endeavours must be rooted in print in order to fight the controls on perception imposed by electric media. Film and television, as recombinant media, have absorbed print while relying on it. This makes print the internal manager of outer conditions. Everyone knows this little inner voice when troubled or reading. All the images we take in must come with a name in order to enter memory.

This dislocation between inner and outer modes of experience is a fundamental fact of consciousness. These two spheres of mental awareness are mutually exclusive realities, brought together in the complementarity of personality. They are forever in conflict, but this is usually a productive tension; the disparity of realities creates the possibilities of imaginative projections, such as art, science, and religion.

The desire to project inner states onto outer environments is the primary fact of the evolution of human culture. In its finest form, this bipolar separation, this field of imaginative force, creates the drive for artistic expression. Art marries the disparate spheres of inner and outer; it is the best index we have of the whole of inner experience in reaction to the external environment.

Art produces a state of psychic resonance between outer structures and inner reactions. The "finer" the art, the more perceptive is our understanding of our times. The cruder the medium, the more the same questions will go on artlessly without answers. Media are not mirrors, as the producers like to suggest, but the directors of the lives of the imaginatively bereft.

The mass media contribute to the decay of mental life by emphasizing gratuitous sentimentality and adolescent views of events. The media's attitude toward violence is hypocritical in entertainments that actually make cowardly victims of us all; they exacerbate social and political unrest by turning everything into theatre, just by virtue of the presence of their cameras. They alter our perceptions so that we project media values, not reality, and thus create deeply confused relationships between individuals and their environments. Perhaps most significantly, media build up insuperable quantities of information, which require inhibitive withdrawal from the lively world.

The Cultural Surround: From Tribal Circle to 60 Cycle

> Either we continue to allow technology to surround and smother culture for fun and profit, or we learn to surround technology with cultural values in order to preserve the general quality of life. Is that the deal?

Mythic time is cyclical, while history is a rising line across the graph of time. Mythic mindset requires that everything be done exactly as before, by memory. Historical time demands literacy. Electric culture exists ambiguously between these two modalities. The more our environment falls under our technological control, the more paradoxical is our relationship with that surround. This situation has been likened to the peculiar relationship that grows up between a jailer and his prisoner.

It seems as though the more control the jailer exercises, the more
a strange kind of perverse love, a love that thrives on injury, grows
between him and his charge . . . The prisoner often becomes the
stronger of the two . . . So we, as we control the environment, have
gradually become the victims of our own control. The role of cycles
in our lives, being natural, should be a joyous source of strength.
Generally, however, we do not acknowledge their existence at all,
and when we do, we see these cyclical changes as impediments to
our efficiency.[42]

Technology has its way with us when we become surrounded by it; we become prisoners of its efficient regularities. Natural cycles, like circadian rhythms or hibernation, have been extirpated by our slavish devotion to technology. In spite of all the apparent advantages of technology, its lethal sameness envelops us, eliminating human values in the interest of the technical surround. When the industrial revolution, with its factories, railroads, and tumescent cities, surrounded nature, putting the squeeze on populations to move from the bucolic slough to the industrial slum, artistic response came in the form of Romanticism and landscape art. Such art was meant for cities where nostalgic views of a simpler life focused on a noble past, which was as fictitious as any manufactured version of human events can be. An abandoned nature became the content of urban reveries, a nostalgia that greased the grinding machinery of city slums.

When electric process surrounded industrial technology and its mechanistic mindset, the machine itself became an art form. Second-hand shops sprang up everywhere to sell the past as artifact. The abstract, invisible world of electric process brought in an abstract, confusing art that was completely severed from connections with nature. Picasso, Klee, Mondrian, and the other magi of sight focused not on the atavistic subject matter of the Romantics, but on the structure of perception itself.

With "resonance" and "field" as the dominant acoustic metaphors of electric process, visual values lose their primacy. The world becomes more like Malraux's "museum without walls" in which art is multi-sensory, pervasive, uncontained, and exists in forms that are difficult to display in a gallery. Art as a specialist category is obsolescent, just as any category has decreasingly meaningful significance. Like the mosaic structure of the television picture, problems, too, have become mosaic, requiring inputs from an array of sources. Process supplants product, even in art; Warhol's films, for instance, have zero content — they might show nothing more than a man sleeping on a couch.

In a sadly neglected little book, *The Parable of the Beast*, John Bleibtreu outlines our encroachment on the mythic domain of mind.

> The paradox of twentieth century science consists of its *unreality*
> in terms of sense impressions. Dealing as it does with energy
> transformation and submicroscopic particles, it has become a kind
> of metaphysics practiced by witch doctors and alchemists. It is not
> at all odd then, to discover that the closer we come, via the scientific
> method to "truth," the closer we come to understanding the "truth"

symbolized in myths and ritual practices concerning the habitation in the flesh of knowledge and understanding.[43]

Physics has taken science out of the realm of the visible into acoustic space. We exist in information nets where everything happens at the speed of light. It is no longer meaningful to speak of cause and effect in respect to electric events. It is possible in reality to divine a single cause for several effects (a power outage), or several causes for one effect (a holistic analysis — chemical, genetic, social — of a suicide). Mechanical models no longer serve us well, even to get practical work done. Even building a bridge today requires a computerized approach. Look for *process patterns*. An electron is no longer considered a thing but a process. And an idea is not a definition but a pattern.

In the Age of Print, with its visual bias, seeing was believing. But images are no longer knowledge, nor is ours a visible science any longer. Modern physics has eliminated such naive approaches to nature. Quantum science puts us more in the position of medieval man, whose belief in the everyday intrusion of supernatural, invisible forces meant he could not simply trust his visual sense. Likewise, the powerful, invisible forces of electric process press persistently on our existence. Granted, images are everywhere. Their function, however, is not to clarify meaning but to manage perception to specific ends. We have thus come to suspect the visual, literally turning the world on its ear. Even our astronomers *listen* with radio telescopes in order to *see* farther into space.

Today's science lives with uncertainty. Ambiguity and paradox have re-entered conscious awareness and undercut cultural faith in absolutes. Like medieval man, we are recognizing the power of the invisible — that the principles of underlying structure (that is, the effects of media on perception) aid us most in understanding electric events. Uncertainty and statistical probability have replaced the old, positivist certainties of the nineteenth century.

> A new surround, or technological environment, is first seen as a powerful threat to our knowledge. As McLuhan noted, old environments become passive containers; new environments are active processors that change values and perceptions.

The printed story surrounded the teller-of-tales; the city surrounded nature; the movie surrounded the novel; television surrounded the movie; and holography will surround television. In short, systems enlarge by establishing new outer-boundary controls.

Cultural awareness must grow at a faster rate than technology. A new control boundary is imperceptible to anyone within the old system. A medieval man, for example, living in the psychic space of a geocentric worldview, cannot cope with the new surround of the Copernican, heliocentric view of the universe. He is helplessly lost within an obsolete structure of reality. Our present condition is similar: we are living through the paradigm shift from the nineteenth century industrial metaphor of machine process to the surrounding new paradigm of electric process. One cannot inhabit two different worlds with a peaceful mind.

The new, surprising, unknown, and startling comes into awareness from the periphery of vision. The fixed stare centres on details at the expense of perceiving the action at the visual edge, which is always in rebellion against the centre. A new surround is a cultural edge phenomenon, out of awareness except as a general impression of motion, signalling a threat to the centre of perception where there is no movement.

A new surround, or paradigm, negates the old certainty — that which is clearly seen at the centre of vision. Though perceived as a negative effect by those possessed of the fixed cultural stare, the surround, as an anti-environment, takes on the positive role of supplying the critical "nay" to the outmoded affirmations of the old paradigm. Such shifts in the vision of reality inevitably produce emotive turbulence and intellectual uncertainty.

We have learned, particularly through the work of Harold Innis, Lewis Mumford, and Marshall McLuhan, that we alter the environment by technically extending our bodily and mental functions. A car extends the body, the computer the central nervous system. Such extensions alter the interplay or ratios between the senses and produce new perceptual patterns. Our reality, for example, is conditioned by the imposition of cinematic structure on our perception, particularly in regard to one's image of oneself. Everyone is "on camera" and dresses for the part.

The real and the filmic have become inextricably linked, often producing confused personal perceptions. The hidden ground of the mass media's technical effects changes the way we experience just about everything. As the telephone demolishes space, it diminishes the longing due to separation; the radio makes it possible, just barely, to endure traffic; and contemporary movies wholly exploit the human emotional system virtually with technical film effects.

Beyond these well-known features of media life, we need to consider the new ability to simulate whole sensory modalities in virtual space. Can technology and love be synthesized in a new dimension of human experience? And now that biotechnologists can wire the interior functions of the cell, what messages will we impart to the newly enslaved cell? These electric changes are not trivial. We are experiencing a shift from the dominance of literate values and information content to the values of electric process, the integrating, simultaneous and decentralizing patterning of global communications.

Electric conditions often overload the sensory apparatus. The surface of any array of information is chaotic until it is perceived as a whole, integral, pattern. A cocktail party, for instance, has a deep structure not quickly or easily perceived, which begins to insist itself on awareness as the party presses on. This perception of unity by pattern requires an investigation of the underlying structural principles in which each of the parts of the pattern participates. Much of modern art works this way, from Picasso to T.S. Eliot. Now, life for the ordinary citizen demands the same awareness of structure and deep content. The parts of the pattern are not causally linked, but are more like particles in an electromagnetic field, aligned by invisible forces and connected by resonant frequency rather than simple, physical means.

The psychological resonance of symbolic structures becomes an aspect of everyday communications. The CNN format — mollifying, yet comprehensive — is a resonant global structure that conditions our perception of the news. This presents us with an entirely new way of thinking about relationships. The revolutionary significance of electric process as a conditioning surround can be better appreciated when CNN locks onto some obsessive programming, like a famous trial or a deadly plane crash. Just being there with a camera produces endlessly intriguing programming.

All the senses but touch are located only in the head. Touch is the mythic envelope that contains the other senses.

Sensory Ratios and the Mythic State of Mind

The mass media of communication are intense sources of sensory stimulation that trigger particular mental states. Smell is nostalgic; the ear, our dominant hierarchical sense, is the time-binding organ that lets us think; the eye deals with space and drives us to action. Taste is largely smell. And touch, the master sense, is chronicled throughout most of Greco-Roman mythology, from Sophoclean incest taboos to Leda's ravishment by the swan of Zeus. There are no independent senses, only a sensorium of continually changing relationships. *Each reorganization of sensory ratios produces a distinct state of mind.*

Media enter the senses directly to operate as electronic brain stimulators. Electric media set up patterns of electromagnetic resonance that produce in the brain specific states of mind. Media produce effects that condition perceptions, which are translated back into program contents. In this way, content is always subservient to media form. Film, for example, significantly simplifies the intricacies of plot, while television absolutely trivializes it. As plot disappears, the medium is increasingly capable of impressing on the user the effects of its form. And it is the form of each medium that establishes a specific state of mind in the user.

Several years ago, using surgically implanted radio-sensitive electrodes, Jose Delgado, demonstrating for a *Life* magazine photographer, stopped the charge of a raging bull instantly, simply by switching his radio-control dial to the passivity centre in the bull's brain. Dogs can be made viciously angry one moment and, with the flick of a dial, passive, happy, hungry, or sexually aroused in the next. We do something like this to ourselves when we use different media, which become stimulators of emotional states.

Such experiments have been going on for more than fifty years. The procedure is now being used to implant brain regulators to alleviate the horrors of Parkinson's. This is just the latest in the parable of our self-engineering. Human genes spliced into pigs produce much leaner bacon. Whether or not eating that bacon is a subliminal act of cannibalism is harder to say. Human genes implanted into sheep and pigs are producing organs for transplant that their human recipients won't reject. The species barrier is all but eliminated. Smarter chimps? What couldn't we do with them? Some municipal bureaucracies may be interested.

Dr. Penfield, the great neurosurgical pioneer in this field, was able to demonstrate how inexhaustibly whole our experience is. By probing certain brain areas, he brought remarkably intact memories into conscious recall in some patients, down to the most minute detail. This result tends to confirm that human experience is taken in fully, including the vast area of rich detail that does not register in consciousness.

Surgical implantation and manipulation are not the only methods of brain control available to us. Interesting effects can be created through the application of extra-cranial stimulation. Deep sound has been used for this effect. Bridging the gap between severed nerves may very well turn out to be a matter acoustic resonance. Our response to the intense environmental pressures on our senses is to cut back sensitivity. The media must thus heighten the stimulation — short of implanting electrodes in the brain — in order to get the desired response from us. It's a vicious spiral that emphasizes thrilling production values at the expense of humanizing contents. As Neil Postman suggests, we may be *Amusing Ourselves to Death*.

Although the neuroelectrical vibrations of the human brain are in the extremely low frequency (ELF) range, they are susceptible to reinforcement by electric stimulation and feedback. Biofeedback experiments, for instance, have a significant enough effect that this technology has successfully regulated the heart and other bodily processes. States of mind are associated with specific EEG wave patterns. All along the spectrum, from beta through alpha, delta, and theta — that is, from high-alert wave patterns to sleep patterns — the emotional system is strung out, wave length by wave length.

Radio, television, film, and the telephone each produce a distinct electromagnetic effect. Radio is operative in the medium to medium-high frequency (MHF) range; television goes from the top of the MHF range to the very-high frequency (VHF) (along with FM radio) and ultra-high frequency (UHF) ranges. Like a chord in music, resonance between compatible frequencies is likely. The electromagnetic arrangement of a particular medium has the effect of rearranging the ratios of the senses.

I know from monitoring the question of the deleterious effects associated with VDT use that there are serious problems generated by the use of that technology, which is not fundamentally different from television itself. Let us at least see what is happening and be honest with ourselves about what we find. For example, Dr. Ross Adey at UCLA has shown provocatively that exposure to ELF electromagnetic energy alters the capacity of calcium to safeguard heart function.[44] Many heart patients now are prescribed calcium channelers. He has also discovered that the low-level electrostatic charges that build up on cell surfaces alter the rates of mitogenesis, the rate of cell subdivision. Thus ELF sets up what appears to be pre-cancerous conditions of cell division even at these "harmless" 60 Hz levels. [45]

The next time you have been watching television for a while, turn the set off and immediately begin reading. You will observe that the eyes will not yield to the demands that reading makes. They lack focus and tend to roam about, relatively incapable of producing the voluntary action of linear movement that reading requires. Nor is the mind in the correct state to easily take in the meaning of what one is reading.

The alpha domination of brain-wave activity resulting from television viewing has to be intensified to beta dominance in order to read properly. It is clear that shifting from one medium to the other is considerably more demanding than it would seem, as anyone walking out of a matinee movie into a bright sunny day will discover. There may be a close link between states of mind and the differing resonant states of media.

I remember, a few years ago, a psychiatrist related a story about a home for criminally violent girls in which the television played an important role. The girls were dangerous to themselves and others, and required strict and forceful supervision. When television was introduced into this situation, the girls fell passive and attentive. No violence occurred during television time. It started up again as soon as the electronic pacifier was turned off. The television clearly quelled their psychotic behaviour.

Environmental consultants often startle workers when their analysis of the workplace turns up a deep-seated annoyance with the intense, but inhibited, monotone buzz of the fluorescent lighting. Sixty cycles, in the range of low B-flat, is the mind-stultifying music that tracks the day of the office worker, though unremarked by those involved in the design and use of the workplace.

> Telephone presents a low-definition auditory stimulus that always prevents correct visualization of the other party. Telephone all but breaks the connection between ear and eye.

We know also that a static-electric generator is capable of altering the negative-ion concentration of closed environments, and that this technique appears to contribute positively to the well-being of the office worker. We are just beginning to investigate these subtle but powerful electromagnetic forces that operate on humans to change their mental states. Some, like Cleve Backster, even suppose that human mental states can influence plant life and growth.[46] But these are extremely subtle forces compared to the powerful effects of our dominant media.

In eliminating visual cues, the telephone is a very unnatural mode of communication. It works best between persons who already have a kinesic or facial experience of each other, who are on fairly intimate terms. The demand for intimate involvement in the telephone situation even makes it difficult, though not impossible, to vent anger. Telephone is a mask — that is, you can't be "seen" when using the medium. The timbre of a caller's voice can intimate a strong, but unspecific, image, though the caller's true appearance may be nothing like the suggestive sound of his or her voice. In casting for phone sex voices, for instance, the timbre and tone of the voice should create a mental image for the client like the voluptuous women who people the TV ads. But since it is impossible to correctly visualize over the phone, it is easy to fool the caller.

Visual depth was added to film when the medium moved from "silents" (with orchestrated, external sound) to photoelectric sound-tracks. In the same way, the strong visual stimulus of a photograph tends to beg for acoustic enlargement. This characteristic of the photo-graph is best evidenced in the poster art that advertises movies, which tends to focus on action images — big action generally equals big sound. In the family album all the "snaps" bear acoustic resonance for the family members who are familiar with the times recorded. A family photo album is as much a soundscape as an image gallery.

The video display terminal of a computer moves from eye to ear. The operator must be able to produce that all-important inner voice that "talks" the information being processed. The VDT is most stressful and damaging to those who are dealing with silent mounds of unintelligible figures, or who process a language with which they have little or no inner-voice contact. The least damage is done to those who use the com-puter for creative writing, in which the inner voice is strongest of all.

Literacy demands a specific arrangement of the senses, one funda-mentally different from the organization of the senses required by non-print media. Other media, such as film, radio, and TV, stimulate one sense more than the rest, which changes the synesthetic arrange-ments among the others. Print is a visual code for representing sounds; we read a page of print as a system of visual cues for sounds, which require a reconstruction of the whole experience being communicated.

Private sensory data and personal thoughts fill in this holistic structure. Electric media are not looped in this way.

The most useful way to rate media effects is by observing their effects on the word. New media add changes to language that weaken its power to deal with the complexity of human experience. Yet they also supply a vernacular vitality to language by using it as it is lived. The problem is that this vitality is useless except to those who already have a strong traditional sense of the functions of language.

It is instructive to perceive what happens to the word as it is assimilated into each medium. In films, dialogue is kept to a minimum, and acting is highly kinesic, largely made up of facial reactions. Syntax and vocabulary become simplified in the extreme. Paralanguage predominates in order to convey as much emotion as possible, without using a lot of complex language. Think of Marlon Brando as Stanley Kowalski calling "Stella," shouting with Slavic voiceset.

The telephone twists, extends, and tenuously stretches language. The hemming and humming, the truncated grunted and nasal "filler" reduces language to its minimal role in communication. One can get by with a vocabulary of between 500 and 700 words and still use the telephone quite adequately for general purposes.

Radio, of all electric media, leaves language most intact. It is still possible to program drama and literature on radio, as the Canadian Broadcasting Corporation has done continuously over the years. But in sponsor-dominated radio, language has been removed, except for diskjockey patter, in favour of the musical recording.

Since electric media are recombinant forms, the radio has made a return to voice in its merger with the telephone. Phone-in shows, especially national and world-news round-up shows create a new verbal radio that is bringing listeners back in large numbers. Listeners were always there, no doubt, but their radio programs functioned as a mere ground — acoustic wallpaper. With talk radio back, listeners in surprisingly large numbers are once again becoming directly involved with the medium.

"Regarding the fullness of my human experience, what is lacking when I use this medium?" This is the question that is most useful in the perceptual training required for survival in an environment overloaded with information. Knowledge comes at the point of recognizing what is missing in any experience, especially mediated experience.

Under pressure to ignore what is missing, the course of least resistance is to just let it all happen. The vigilance required for the maintenance of perceptual and intellectual freedom starts with learning how to get the true picture of things and events by investigating what Edward T. Hall so aptly labels the "out-of-awareness aspects of communication."[47] Selective habits of perception help us to artfully construct the patterns of meaning necessary for personal survival in the face of the endless onslaught of consumption-biased media.

Such virtuosity in understanding the profound effects of media on human processes is essential to mental and spiritual survival. The damned will have to live in a cartoon world of vacuous plenty, feeling "well informed" but oblivious to the terminal decay of the environment, unable to rise up the slippery slope of self-delusion that Dante used to punish the worst sinners in his hell.

The Janus View: A Complementary Look Back at the Future

Janus is the perfect god for McLuhan's rear-view mirror. He is the god of beginnings, but especially of auspicious transitions. He oversees the movement from the old to the new. He is Januarius of the year and Janitor, the doorkeeper from one side of things to another. Above all he mitigates changes dealing with chaos. What a god for the new millennium. Like us, Janus simultaneously looks back at what has passed for reality while experiencing the unreal feelings of a new, incoming reality. The duality of human experience is always emanating from the split between thought and feeling. The past, laden with feeling, is the record of our unique embodiment; the future, full of thought, threatens to eliminate the special identity we have made out of that data. We spend much of our lives reconciling this division.

> Looking at starlight, we see the past and present reconciled.

The need to reconcile both the wave and the quantal characteristics of light is the paramount example of the necessity and practicality of bringing two modes of mutually exclusive experience together. This is definitively mythic in the most practical and realistic sense. There are many other examples of the need for reconciliation in experience, because everything is grounded in its opposite: love in hate, hunger in satiety, good in evil, and inhibition in projection.

The split in ourselves projects ambiguities into the real world, which have to undergo inhibition in order to appear objective and solid — that is, in order to get the work done that allows us to remain in historical time and progress. Otherwise, we would become aware of the myth that we are living, and our vision of reality would collapse into spiritual quietude.

> Cultural objects mask their mythic grounds. Each object is both itself and something else living on the edge of meaning.

Complementarity, the reconciliation of mutually exclusive aspects of reality or what Oppenheimer called, "this immense evocative analogy,"[48] occurs quite naturally in any experience that includes both the interior and exterior aspects of events. A complementarity of the simple and the complex forces us to recognize two modes of perception simultaneously. The complex physics that leads to a nuclear bomb results in the spectacularly simple eradication of an entire city and the mushroom cloud in the mind.

"From the outset the principle [of complementarity] was recognized as one of potential humanistic reference."[49] It is good to remember that the opposite of a great truth is not necessarily a great falsehood, but perhaps another great truth.

Pressure on all humanistic ideals occurs when the belief in idealistic perfection is abandoned, a result forced upon us by our inheritance from physics. As de Broglie warned:

> If we insist on perfectly exact definitions, and, at the same moment, a completely detailed study of the phenomena, we find that these two notions are idealizations, the probability of whose physical realization is nil.[50]

An environment severely overloaded with information, much of which travels at the speed of light, is an environment increasingly simultaneous in its actions on people. There is little or no time to react to informational events in such a world, no time to take time and care with things. We become automata of the environmental system of media relations.

Yet many still cling strenuously to the simple ideal of alternation, the idea of one thing after the other. Alternation is the mentality of sequencing that is appropriate for Newtonian mechanics, but not for electric process. In order to maintain the ideal of sequence — which is applied not just to work but to life in general — we must massively inhibit complementarity. Complementarity defines the ambiguous coexistence of the seemingly mutually exclusive ideals: simultaneity (all-at-onceness) and alternation (one-at-a-timeness).

Even if it turns out that we have been mistaken in stressing these ideas of ambiguity (relativity, uncertainty, incompleteness), they have been part of the general revolution of ideas in our time and have had powerful effects. After all, the falsifiability of scientific theory makes most of it transient, or at least forces some of its ideas into narrower and narrower special-case contexts. Nevertheless, none of it can be dis-invented. The world we live in has been shaped by these ideas and the inexorable effects of electric process.

Even if the sanguine implications in the Theory of Dissipative Structures of Ilya Prigogine and his followers confirm the anti-entropic view of life on earth, and even if this has universal significance and replaces the deep pessimism of uncertainty, the cultural damage has been done. The need for repair is the work of the next hundred years. We have come close to being overwhelmed spiritually by the implications of particle physics and the Rutherfordian, atomic view of reality. Floyd Matson states the case as well as anyone.

> For a problem of "uncertainty" or "indeterminacy" arises, in
> whatever field of knowledge, from the presence of a degree
> of complexity and subtlety which renders the subject matter
> recalcitrant to the keenest apparatus . . . that can be brought
> to bear in its analysis.[51]

Tantamount to announcing the end of scientific progress, this peculiar view of material behaviour, which has been forced upon us by physics, has also invaded our studies of human behaviour. For all of the knowledge that it holds, medical science, for example, has become fraught with uncertainty and is at best a probabilistic science that finds it more and more difficult and unsatisfying to deal with the individual case. Iatrogenic (doctor-caused) illness is presently the number three cause of illness in the United States.

Niels Bohr, the father of complementarity, sees the problem of lack of certainty as pandemic to all human thought. Since we now know that initial conditions in any experiment are infinitely varied, we are left to determine the limits of certainty in our scientific work. Beyond a certain point of practicality, the usefulness of the illusion of certainty ends.

> The very fact that repetition of the same experiment . . . in general yields different recordings pertaining to the object, immediately implies that a comprehensive account of experience in this field must be expressed in statistical laws.[52]

This may not be true. In chaos theory, the absolute inability of any scientist to reproduce exact initial experimental conditions precludes gaining certainty, but at the same time exposes the possibility of attaining only a complex, dynamic tendency to certainty — that is, a strange attractor. Meteorology is constantly attempting to bring practical, regularized, dependable prediction to weather, and on the local level must fail to do so, because chaos makes little differences that produce gigantic changes in global weather activities, which in turn change all local weather systems.

Probability, as a technique, enhances the scientist's ability to predict material behaviour. However, the effects of probability can undermine a society's health. Probabilistic social sciences are hardly more humane or accurate than governments, which move on a wave of pollster's data, without principle, toward self-perpetuation.

The desire and necessity to live in a world of institutions based on the principle of causation — and the hard, unambiguous facts that flow from this bias — has to be reconciled with the indeterminate thrust

> Applied to human affairs, probability enfranchises a behaviourist view that predicts on the large scale, but which is powerless to deal adequately with the individual case.

of the rest of the world, which is caught up in the transformations of electric process. We must, it would seem, adopt the Janus face, the face of the guardian of the gate who understands life in the rear-view mirror, whose vision favours neither past not future, but requires wholeness and reconciliation — a vision that is structured like an electromagnetic field in which every point is affected by every action, anywhere in the field.

Having an overview of the constantly changing configuration of the field of reality leaves us far better prepared to survive endless change than does the specialist's blindness to holistic vision. Janus, who appears to be the antithesis of wholeness, suggests an irresolvable war between reason and feelings, but is in fact two parts of a divided whole, not unlike the divisions between the hemispheres of the brain. The reconciliation of these two modes of experience is essentially a spiritual matter. Until we achieve the spiritual strength for such an integration, we will continue to resort to inhibition, which allows the suppression of the one mode of experience in the interests of the other.

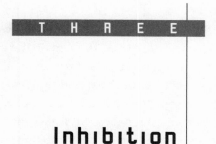

Inhibition

IN *THE PARABLE OF THE BEAST*, John Bleibtreu tells the story of one of the most inhibited creatures on earth. "The cattle tick is a small, flat-bodied, blood-sucking arachnid . . . It emerges from the egg not yet fully developed, lacking a pair of legs and sex organs."[1] In this form, it begins to mature into a tick until, eventually, through several moultings, it acquires its missing parts and is "prepared to attack warm blooded animals."[2]

"The eyeless female is directed to the tip of a twig on a bush by her photosensitive skin, and there she stays through darkness and light, through fair weather and foul, waiting for the moment that will fulfil her existence."[3] Incredible as it may seem, ticks in test situations have waited for this moment of communication with a warm-blooded animal for as long as eighteen years![4] Such a host sets off an alarm for the tick, "the scent of butyric acid," a substance present in the sweat of all mammals.[5] The cattle tick is unaware of everything else in the world but this action, in which she consummates her existence in one wild, blind leap through space. Throughout its lifetime, the tick does not move or eat or defecate. "The metabolism of this creature is sluggish to the point of being suspended entirely."[6] The sperm she has in her also waits to burst into life, which it does when it receives a little blood sucked from a mammal host. Eighteen years is both a lifetime and just a moment to this peculiar creature, who dies as soon as she gives birth.

This is "literally senseless existence."[7] All creatures inhibit their surround in order to stay focused on the purpose for which their lives were designed. *Homo sapiens* is somewhat like this as well. While the tick was born this way, we have had to develop just such a strategy to protect against being overwhelmed by information.

The environment is information rich; there may be too much information. Increasingly, human beings appear ill suited to the perpetual intake and retention of the extravagantly burgeoning amounts of complex data. In order to survive this deluge emotionally and intellectually, we have begun to invent ways to ward off the chaotic effects of the media-driven waves of information that daily crash over the seawall of our conscious defences. We want to simplify our lives. To do so, we unwittingly produce massive inhibitions — with the aid of media — that desensitize us to the fullness of life.

This strategy of selective ignorance is habit forming. Cut off by a reluctance to stay fully open to events, we become decreasingly capable of functioning in our own best interests. We turn to masochistic and suicidal activities: drugs, alcohol, crazes, raves, religious fervours, social non-commitment, lotteries, general dropoutism. And, incessantly, we watch television or sit for hours in front of a VDT. Cathode-ray technology guarantees the dominance of low-level feeling. Thought is almost filtered out.

Once we inhibit our instinct for survival by desensitizing ourselves to meaning, our world takes on a cartoonish simplicity in which thought is systematized for only the most elementary recognitions. Thus electric process empowers the debasement of cultural life. We risk becoming enslaved to mass media. The sundering suction of the maelstrom of mass culture pulls down everything in its whirl of random debris. How are we to survive?

From the inhibition research of Georg von Békésy we know that desensitization is the surest way to save ourselves from a complete schizophrenic breakdown in the face of this communications inundation. Reducing the sensitivity of the receiving organ, the sensory apparatus itself, saves us from having to stay alert to the assaults of the informational environment.

In order to effectively inhibit our connections to the world we must:

(1) shorten attention spans, (2) scuttle detail, and (3) reduce awareness to minimal perception or (4) watch a lot of television and (5) sit for hours in front of a VDT. This desensitization occurs at work and at play. Naively, we insist that nothing will go wrong as we deliver whole generations of infants into the grip of this sensory bias for inattention.

Voluntary attention is the alert mental state created when we work. It is the attention required for fine work, like reading or measuring — work that engages the sequential, logical operations of the mind, demanding finesse, persistence, or precise perception.

> Consider two kinds of attention: voluntary and involuntary; one is simple, the other complex.

Involuntary attention, as part of our evolutionary inheritance, is the faculty that allows us to correctly infer threats or actions in the general environment. We select just those minimal aspects of any situation, which tend to occur in the periphery and not the focus of attention, that may be dangerous or of interest to us. Humanity has survived by using this instinctual, involuntary attention, which is built into our perceptual systems as part of unconscious adaptation.

> After centuries of the literate bias of voluntary attention that built rational, scientific culture, electric process returns us to the primitive, involuntary bias of acoustic values.

In reading, the eye moves with a high degree of voluntary control over the line of print, working hard to persist in this unnatural action. The natural movement of the eye is involuntary. The primary function of vision is to be a wide-roving, minimal reader of the environmental scene, always alert for danger and secure retreat. The eye leaps about with apparent haphazard action looking for only the most critical clues to events. The TV tube is retraining primitive eyes. All of the non-specific data from the total scene registers on the brain, but not at a conscious level.

Voluntary attention aids conscious awareness and enhances our capacity to interpret complexity, whereas involuntary attention is a survival mechanism that allows us to ignore the distracting complexities of information in a crisis. There are other inhibitions that are not useful for our survival. This type of inhibition persuades us to reduce our engagement with life. We are slaves to historical time and its linear continuity; our attention from the earliest years has been fixed on logical, sequential forms. Educationally biased, we ignore too much information about the human condition. We rely too much on the official historical record and ignore the achievements of great but unheralded individuals. The whole of black history, for example, has only recently been recovered and established. Education, in an effort to become job training, has become training in what not to observe. Our community colleges train young people in a skill, but neglect the literacy and overview that make success in any field worthwhile.

The graphic revolution has had the overall effect of cutting us off from full involvement with the whole, balanced sensorium. Seeing has overdeveloped our sense of voluntary control over experience. Acoustic values in the forms of live music, psychiatry, religion, and voice mail are becoming our common obsessions. Electric culture returns us to the dominance of involuntary attention. Television trains the user to sample its pictures quickly, picking up just enough information to make correct, simplified determinations of "what's on." This training also teaches the user to ignore detail, and may have something to do with the fact that thousands of little mistakes have entered our lives.

> All of the information from our experience flows through us, but, because of inhibition, most of it doesn't register in consciousness. Where does it go?

How do we learn to ignore so much of the rich supply of information that is streamed at us through all the media of communication? Do we simply select what interests us and ignore the rest? Does that protect us from what we ignore? In the thirties, forties and fifties, Wilder Penfield, at the internationally respected Montreal Neurological Institute, investigated the role of the hippocampus in memory mechanisms and discovered that all perceptual experience is actually saved.

Our sensory lives remain with us forever in some form or another, and can be retrieved by the right stimulation. In spite of Penfield's work, it is difficult to appreciate the fundamental change in the mind's information processing activities that has occurred as a direct response to an environment overloaded with electric information patterns. We build conscious memories of past experience by selecting that which accords best with our self-esteem. The rest we bury in a shallow trench barely covered by the silt of forgetfulness.

Selection is the essence of communication. Communication theorist

Colin Cherry provides this powerful insight into the communication process:

> All the various statistics of language relate to our powers of predicting what a person is likely to say, in certain defined circumstances — *but when he says it, then he communicates with us only by virtue of departing from these predictions.*[8]

Our expectation of what might be said relies on our guessing how much news — that is, the unexpected — will be part of the exchange. If your pastor tells you to "f-off," that's news; if the boy on the corner offers this advice, then it is merely a redundant cliché. Any statement, then, should be considered a simple representation of a much more complex set of information variables.

In an environment overloaded with information, the selection process increasingly shows irrational characteristics because it is adulterated by preconscious negative fragments, which we must try to inhibit. We each have a secret identity fed by these rejected fragments of preconscious, subliminal experience. Each of us becomes a self built of random psychic pieces, playing multiple roles. Unlike the contents of the unconscious, this insistent psychic material can be called up into consciousness by our own efforts.

This is what it means to say that we live "mythically and in depth,"[9] as McLuhan first observed of electric culture. It is having to cope with large amounts of emergent preconscious materials filtered out of experience, which can then unexpectedly emerge into consciousness. There are many cases on record of people lapsing irrationally into movie-of-the-week responses to real events. Millions of people, with real identities hardly richer than their T-shirt allegiances, wander about aimlessly, driven by the psychic materials lodged just below consciousness.

> The pain and anxiety of living in a world supersaturated with information requires some form of inhibition.

We are taught in school to reduce awareness to simple, cartoon-like structures — the lessons. This conceptual training conditions us to ignore relationships that complicate the idea of the lesson, which is usually a simple theoretical application isolated from reality. In this way, we can produce some desired action based on a minimally correct understanding of events. The big lesson of replacing reality with virtual abstractions begins in the pre-school years with media. Education superimposes theory on experience, and that body of theories becomes a lesson in how to experience. Once we have learned germ theory, our experience is thoroughly conditioned by a certain apprehension regarding the invisible aspects of health. The principles and definitions invoked live in the lesson's carefully defined context. But no definition eliminates all ambiguity. As soon as one defines something, exceptions come to mind and narrow the basis of the definition.

Education, Jacques Ellul warns, is little more than "pre propaganda";[10] it establishes the mental habit of sequential, logical order that skews our lives positivistically, in direct opposition to our emotional needs. In contrast, electric realities, approaching the speed of light, completely alter the meaning of sequence. There are no steps in instantaneous communication. But there is almost certainly an imperceptible chaotic order behind the apparently random pattern of information overload. Banner ads on the Internet present an apparent randomness to the user, but in fact these ads are selected and placed with scientific care.

Inhibition: The Power of the Negative

An optical illusion is a special case of perceptual ambiguity that exploits the normal relationship between a figure and its ground, that is, positive and negative space.

One of two possible figures in an optical illusion must be suppressed into ground, out of immediate awareness, in order for the other figure to be seen. The process is easily reversed, so that the ground suddenly flips into figure the moment the first figure is sufficiently suppressed. This flipping of positive and negative space is a paradigm of communication in which the relationship between the medium and its message takes on special significance. Twentieth-century art has been playing with this ratio for years.

Modern art has moved along with existentialist philosophy towards the exploration of increasingly radical negations. Surrealism distrusts all meaning and so does modern poetry. It regards easiness as vulgar and intelligibility as dishonest. Fragmentation alone can be trusted;

only an aggregate of fragments can carry a meaning that is wholly
ineffable and protected thereby against self-doubt.[11]

Michael Polanyi's argument in his *Personal Knowledge* does not particularly consider the integrative effects of electric process on the structure
of meaning. The fragmentation of knowledge into artificial categories is
a pre-electric condition that contributes to the "easiness" and "intelligibility" that traditionalists desire. Our problem is now one of trying to
deal with the profusion of interrelationships that result from the integrating tendencies of electric media, which create large scale patterns of
meaning that, at the same time, eliminate the general validity of simple,
linear definitions.

Electric process forces information to flow across media boundaries
— film, telephone, fax, TV, VDT, VCR, CD-ROM — creating great difficulties in focusing meaning. If we want to understand the "radical
negations" Polanyi is concerned about, we need expertise in dealing
with the underlying structure of meaning — that is, the analysis of contents in relation to their medium. The revolutionary theme of negation
is the result of the proliferation of commu-
nications technologies and the awareness of the role of media in relativizing
meaning. In our desire for clear understanding, we tend to inhibit awareness
of the medium and to remain focused on
media contents only — for instance, the
program we are watching.

> Francis Bacon, the father
> of modern science, was
> negative about the
> benefits of method
> in learning.

In *The Communication Ecology*, Barrington Nevitt comments on
Francis Bacon's distinction between "aphorism" and "method":
"Aphorisms, representing a knowledge broken, do invite men to inquire
farther, whereas Methods, carrying the show of a total, do secure men,
as if they were at farthest."[12] The traditional use of the open system of
aphorism for stimulating logical inquiry is being replaced by the false
completeness of methods, which rely on theory and its linear diagrams.
The facts and evidence of method render unnecessary the learner's
involvement in the process of learning through conversation and
debate. Now everything can be laid out on paper, including instructions
that tell you how to process information according to method.
Aphorisms intensify insight through the attempt to reconcile paradoxes

(e.g., "freedom is a special form of slavery"), but methods promote the bias of the reductionist, or specialist, world view, which has prevailed in modern science and in our lives at the expense of the resonance of the whole human condition.

Nevitt outlines the conditions leading to the cultural transformation in which paradox — positive and negative merged — was degraded in the interests of the growing illusion of clarity demanded by the biases of empiricism. He cites one of McLuhan's favourite commentators, Rosalie Colie.

> Degradation of paradox is one result of a revolution in thought which valued clarity and exactness above the tricky duplicities of comprehension induced by paradox. In *The Dialogue Concerning the Two World Systems*, Galileo's Simplicio points to the dangers involved in favouring "words" over "things" as guides to truth: "Once you have denied the principles of sciences and have cast doubt upon the most evident things, everybody knows that you may prove whatever you will, and maintain any paradox."[13]

A spokesman for a world in the full flush of scientific certainty could make such a statement as Simplicio's. We no longer can. The sureties of science have been overwhelmed by the insubstantiality of matter. Positive/negative and either/or are now transformed into both/and and digital ambiguities. Regarding meaning in science, as in any other metaphysical discipline where interpretations vary, contexts are everything. The slogan "atoms for peace" is certainly an intriguing paradox that begs considerable discussion and transcends the methodical policies of any Atomic Energy Commission. Under the conditions of functional paradox, both positive and negative forces merge; each becomes a function of the other like time and space in Einstein's view.

After three centuries of our assimilating the myth of scientism (the belief that eventually science will answer all our questions), electric process has reversed this secular hubris and retrieved paradox from its early Renaissance storage. Electric media inspire paradox and return us to an aphoristic bias, which favours organic patterns over linear models. Bohr's principle of complementarity, which recognizes the necessity to investigate mutually exclusive modes of behaviour in matter, makes it clear that we get our most important work done, even in physics, in a frame of reference dominated by paradox. Quantum theory itself is based on the paradox of complementarity, in which light is seen as having both quantal and wave character-istics. Paradox can marry positives and negatives into complementarities: some things can be true and not true at the same time.

Every paradox is a symplex.

In philosophy and religion, the world has become fully paradoxical. The problem in these crucial areas is to successfully inhibit paradox if we want to keep it simple. Despite its convoluted the-ologies, religion is the world of the simple, while philosophy is that of the complex. The theology that emerges from this conjunction has always been one of primary symplexes. The Bible, which has allowed us to talk simply about a Christian God, is at the same time inexhaustibly complex as an anthropological document. Electric process enhances the simple and therefore supports elementary religious views. But phi-losophy's new task of negating all of the logical principles on which rational thought was based has made its work all but impossible.

In its quest for accuracy of statement, philosophy has tended to become mathematical in its precision. However, the irreconcilable para-doxes that have come into this field have made the futility of such an approach apparent. For example, the long-standing Law of Non-Contradiction (A is A) is contradicted by complementarity, as Korzybski has shown: no A is all A. The positivistic functions of modern philos-ophy have been particularly under assault from the post-modern bias for self-referential textual limits that negate tradition. In other words, the conditions surrounding the writing of any philosophy make it unique and thus all philosophies become special cases. This whole post-modern approach itself becomes a paradox. The question that is at the heart of this paradox is whether we can learn anything if we can't learn everything about some thing or event.

Our inhibition of the awareness of paradox in our lives is fairly effective and allows us to get on with the business of earning a living and raising a family. The trick for us is to avoid falling between two psy-chological stools: living in an obsolescent environment while working in another that negates it.

People once had dinner parties. Not every lunch was devoted to

> **Does electric process depersonalize us sufficiently that everyone becomes partly a negative social force?**

business. Now, everyone is working very long hours and few people have time to visit socially. These same people, however, have four or five hours a day to give to viewing television or computing an ersatz social life through e-mail and chat lines. We seem to have become somewhat desensitized to the need for other people.

Friendships now seem more difficult to maintain. I have "close" friends whom I see only once or twice a year. Somehow we manage to remain close, but we don't have the time to maintain the connection on a more intimate basis.

Society as a whole surely suffers from this tendency of our environment to split us apart. It is hard to get people to come out for things, whether they are art or politics. It is as though anything deemed by our media gatekeepers to be not important enough to report on is simply not important. Whatever else this says about us as a society, it certainly shows that we have changed. And it seems to me that we have changed negatively.

Electric process, in creating global relations through the great informational envelope that surrounds the planet, has inadvertently inspired powerful and frequently violent local reactions to corporate marketing. It appears that even here, locally, each individual is pushed to behave like a foreign culture and become a small and negative node of resistance to global marketing power. But if the price is right, assimilation doesn't take long and chauvinist interests die a quick death. Besides, the

> **Electric process inhibits access to the fullness of experience.**

giants allow for some local ownership and that is locally mollifying, as Wal-Mart and McDonald's know. Consumers, it seems, have no time for each other. We buy alone.

I learned at an early age not to talk to anyone while watching a movie. That rare individual who did talk during movies risked the stern hiss of censorship from those sitting nearby. Similar conditions prevail, ironically, in the family room in front of the television. Most media completely sever intrusions from other modes of communication: witness the effects of a Walkman, a computer, or even the humble telephone. When fully involved with an electric medium, one does not want to miss a single facial twitch, a nuance of attitude, an intimation of tactility, or any dislocation from the alpha state. All else is cut off in this persistent and formative training that we receive from our popular media.

The first effect of electric media is this in-depth training of the user in sensory inhibition. The media have created entirely new sense ratios between perception and conception, which emphasize simple feelings and subdue complex thought. The evolutionary function of inhibition to aid survival by focusing attention has been subverted by electric process, which conditions us to use inhibition too extensively in warding off the complex effects of information overload.

Nobelist Georg von Békésy, in his physiological study of inhibition, concludes that "survival requires that we discard the unimportant portions of . . . information."[14] Importance is a value. What is unimportant information? In the end, there is only one criterion: the information that is important promotes the healthy survival of mind, body, and environment.

Inhibiting the perceptual freedom of people on a grand scale, mainly through advertising and other media uses (e.g., what's *not* on), may not promote the health of society. All information influences human well-being; it shapes us, and so, the world. Whatever damages one's vision

> Some information works against health and survival, and aims merely to deliver audiences *en masse* into commercial hands.

of reality is harmful first for the body. This is not a matter of moral debate, but a measure of the sort of inhibited thinking that is still part of modern medicine. The passing paradigm of mechanistic thinking is still clashing with the emerging paradigm of electric process. In *The Turning Point*, Fritjof Capra cites Lewis Thomas, who puts the dilemma succinctly.

The mechanistic view of the human organism and the resulting engineering approach to health has led to an excessive emphasis on medical technology, which is perceived as the only way to improve health. Lewis Thomas . . . is quite explicit about this in his paper "On the Science and Technology of Medicine." After his remark that medicine has not been able to prevent or cure any of our common major diseases over the past three decades, he goes on to say, "We are, in a sense, stuck with today's technology, and we will stay stuck until we have more scientific knowledge to work with it."[15]

So it seems that technology itself is inhibitive. The entire auto industry stands to confirm this role for technology. Our perceptions are linked to our technological aids. Shifts in technology are so swift, costly, and, in some cases, radical that they outstrip the individual's capacity to adapt to frequent change. As for the cost of constant obsolescence, society's ability to pay for these changes is finite.

The body's intake of information is on the same order of importance to survival as the intake of food. We metabolize information; it changes the way our bodies work. We ingest it, break it down, and store it as energy. We are even more ignorant of the actions of information on the body, however, than we are of the actions of memory on life. Memory informs the body and inhibits our free action. And as everyone knows, the powerful, salubrious effect of the mind in cases of illness is all but legendary.

Although we are processing sensory experience every moment, we seldom have conscious awareness of our senses sensing. Typically, we ignore the functions by which we take in information. Should we be able to tell if our senses are malfunctioning? It's a mystery, for example, how the inner ear can inhibit the sound of the heart beating. If it didn't happen, we would never sleep. In this way, inhibition serves us as nature intended.

The knowledge that we must inhibit internally as well as externally lies in our cells. Though it is rare for this neural system of inhibition to break down, it does under certain conditions. Insomnia and anxiety are often associated with episodes of "hearing" one's heart beat. The ear can be heard hearing after a long exposure to intense noise. The eye can see itself seeing usually under extreme light conditions. Rock concerts afford ample opportunities to play with the perceptual values of inhibition. Deep perception is always marginal.

> As a mode of interchange with our surroundings, information literally sustains life and ensures our survival; information can also be destructive, making life more precarious.

Because of the unrelenting pressure from all media to take in more information than we can possibly deal with, lethal levels of stress, as Hans Selye has eminently demonstrated, mount up to threaten the stability of our health. Some people, especially those who work with computers, break down completely and cease to function in their own best interests. They manifest disturbing symptoms of depression and general maladaptation to the information environment, and often require radical therapies.

The formless glut of impression that flows from all electric media overwhelms our coherent sense of reality. The confusion produces a sort of schizophrenia — an inability to maintain an integrated personality — and impresses discontinuous effects on one's identity. This amalgam of reality and fantasy adds multiple-role tensions to the specialist notion of a single self. As well, some people fear that they will lose control and allow suppressed psychic contents to emerge into conscious life.

Daily, each of us toys with the extended identities which are associated with product consumption: one moment you're the captain of a yawl with the right kind of lip balm, fighting the elements off Cape Hatteras; the next, a star in the right sunglasses who receives an orgasmic wave of adulation from a shrieking throng of fans; or better still, a great athlete with the right foot powder, breasting the tape for gold or winning for a beer. You're a mountain climber, an astronaut, a diver, a dreamer . . . all the flashy multiple roles of the schizoid ad world that massage the psyche into buying the right stuff.

This mosaic of fragmentary lifestyles hardly aids the development of an integrated personality, which has little to do with an array of consumer desires and the associated goods. Such short bursts of attention entrench a lack of completeness and thoroughness in thought. Ideas, like ads, become mental cartoons. Thinking becomes a threat to comfort: complex, time-consuming, and dangerous in its potential to disturb the fragile balance of an overextended self-consciousness.

Simply put, we likely become what we behold. Witness the recent case of a fourteen-year-old boy who murdered a seven-year-old neighbour. The boy carved off the child's flesh in order to collect body fat, which he drank believing that the fat would make it possible for him to fly. Preposterous as this sounds it is precisely outlined as a possibility in the movie *Warlock*. There are many cases on record of such unreality seeping into our lives. Through media technologies, fantasy is invited into the world. Electric media allow us to rehearse and give structure to irrational futures.

A Modest Correction to Norbert Wiener's Notion of Information as Ordering Neg-Entropy

There is a paradox in the clash of cultural values with those of information technology. Information has long been defined as negative entropy, the ordering effect of culture on nature. Information is the primary human activity of creating meaning to fight randomness in the world. In short, neg-entropy simplifies the complex too-muchness of the experienced world through islands of evolving knowledge. Information, however, always achieves the state of overload — an ultimate complexity that demands an ever-increasing facility to simplify. That's why cartoons and animatronics have become so popular; these forms of representation radically simplify and allow us to survive being overwhelmed by the demands to know something about everything. Negative entropy, that is, communication, always strives failingly for wholeness of expression.

The more pressure on a complex system to become ordered, the more it tends toward minimal correct inference (MCI). Simplicity is obviously a stripping down to bare essentials, but it is also the practice of leaving out. Leaving out, refining to essentials, getting to the core, the gist, the heart of the matter — this is the objective that drives all cultural and scientific activities. The practice of leaving out, in fact, could be a useful definition of art, but it operates against Weiner 's notion that all communication is a metaphysical good.

From Rune to Cartoon: The Fundament of Inhibition

Often in communication, it is what has been left out that is most important. Communication is the art of creating meaning by selecting what to leave out of the record of one's experience. As we know from inhibition studies, we never notice that we are purposely diminishing our awareness to keep life simple. What one says is only meaningful when measured against other ways of saying the same thing. Clichés are verbal cartoons. "I love you," he says, when he actually means, "I'm twenty-nine, bored with bars and my own cooking, starting to lose my hair, and since we have a few things in common, why not try marriage; we can always get a divorce." Her "I love you" may mean, "I've had the career and it's not all that it's cracked up to be; I'm looking for security and I want to have a child because I need the experience of motherhood for fulfilment; you're not my ideal mate but I've tried living-together arrangements and they're unsatisfying and lead nowhere."

These I love yous are complex and paradoxical. The wedding that follows is an array of predictable simulacra. As Jean Baudrillard has established, since there is no non-paradoxical truth to their I love yous, the simulacra are everything. Taking a page from Korzybski, Baudrillard asserts that "the map precedes the territory";[16] in fact, the map invents the territory. Inhibition eliminates ground in order to restrict awareness.

Real communication uncovers the hidden ground of the unspoken, or suppressed, parts of the message — that's what courtship is for. Everyone learns very early to inhibit this real communication and to express something that is acceptable enough to the other parties that one will get what one wants from the communication exchange.

Inhibition is the primary leaving-out process whereby communication is made possible. In our informationally overloaded environment, we soon become habituated to seeking no more than the minimally correct inference in any situation, especially in situations where there is little motivation to communicate at all. This is often true in the workplace, where, with the introduction of computers, there is too much information of very little value, and the overwhelming need is to eliminate it. In the face of this low-level semantic death by information poisoning, this is plain survival.

The Cartoon Effect

When a minimal correct inference (MCI) is formalized as an image or a cliché, the result is a cartoon: a groundless figure for which we need not supply an interpretive context. Similarly, it is in the nature of electric communication to promote crude, one-dimensional thought in a multi-sensory form.

> Because we consciously perceive less than ten percent of the visual information per second on a TV screen, it is a medium that trains us to prefer the minimal correct inference (MCI) over the detailed and fully realized event.

The tendency of electric process to stress figure at the expense of ground was first noticed, even before the turn of the century, by artists. In general, the overall characteristic of modern art has been to eliminate figures, while becoming increasingly theory-bound in an attempt to get the viewer involved in the hidden ground of aesthetic ideas.

The artworks attempt to be concretized percepts, which the artists are required to explain by concepts. Much of our Western art over this past century approaches minimal visual figuration, with some of it so stripped-down that there seems to be almost nothing there at all. A colourful wash? A few vague markings? A work of genius? How can you tell? The general public remains perplexed by much of our most touted art. Without figures in their art, the unthinking are lost.

The biological Law of Least Energy tends to keep things simple and works against the complications of over-cerebral approaches to human problems. Keep it simple, we say to ourselves; complexity is the enemy. Under electric conditions, the cartoon, like the Gothic rune, feeds us with a sense of the secrecy of wide, tacit knowledge.

The cartoon enhances the importance of ambiguity by using metaphor, paradox, and pun. It is a form that transcends the one-dimensionality of our acquisitive technocracy and the humourlessness of the computer, which lacks a threshold of ambiguity tolerance. The cartoon allows us to piece together important parts of a problem in the simplest and, often, most powerful fashion.

Television is a medium of cartoon simplicity. At the content level, the cheaply animated video is the perfect programming form for television. At the technological level, television, by virtue of its crude definition and simplicity of composition, is hardly more than a cartoon. The only meaningful difference between reruns of *The Flintstones* and *CNN News* is that the animation is better on *The Flintstones*.

A cartoon projection likely connects with the inhibited materials of the preconscious dimension of the mind better than any other medium. Its humour, grounded in grievance, vents preconscious negative tendency with a miniature catharsis. As well, since the cartoon is sub-syntactic, it stores best in the preconscious. No elaborate linguistic transformation is required in order to liberate the powerful ambiguities of the cartoon.

> The need to reduce all complexity to MCI is growing at a rate at least as fast as the increase in available information.

Television appears to have trained us to become addicted to the MCI approach to information. We now consume enormous amounts of information in MCI fashion. We recently have seen a huge growth in the sales of non-books of raw data: books of lists, digests of every sort, almanacs, books of record achievements, books of firsts, books of places, comprehensive compendia of sports stats, an encyclopedia of every TV show that ever aired, and even blue books are making a comeback. What is so attractive about this kind of material that millions of people find it irresistible?

All such books are one-dimensional; they supply a sense of extreme precision and apparent order in an uncertain world. There is little ambiguity in any such book; all the data are uninterpreted because they are meant to mean only one thing: most home runs, the first locomotive, the richest man. These are facts, and we have been trained to think that facts have meaning. Precisely at the time in human history when the Age of Specialism, with its credo of facts, is over, facts become a sort of art content, an amusement.

These books, presenting data cartoons, are *high context* forms of information, often approaching zero in their capacity to mean anything. *Low context* materials, such as difficult literature or philosophy, increasingly become pushed to the periphery of general awareness and tend to be the preoccupation of elites. At the centre, the mass media present crude, trivialized analogues of reality that are actually uninterpreted data cartoons of real events. The processes that give rise to them are ignored.

The part that is missing in a cartoon allows for strong psychic resonance. The simple figure focuses attention on the fact of how little is required in this medium for a strong sense of understanding. The need for filling in that the cartoon presents elicits strong involvement from the viewer. What one fills in is under better control in this medium than in any other.

One never misses the satirical point that the cartoon shapes in order to stimulate insight. The power to inhibit contrary argument and focus on a powerful generality is characteristic of the cartoon. These are images that pre-empt abstract investigations of ideas. They effectively inhibit awareness of complex processes. They are pure figure.

The cartoon effect enters the realm of language in the form of the acronym and the logo: IBM, CBS, NCR, NRA, Sci-Fi, TGIF. T-shirts with cartoon advertisements for rock bands, resorts, cities, and the like, or simplistic social commentary, are a seemingly permanent fashion. Many of them are obscene if one understands how to supply the missing context.

The acronym is a verbal cartoon that is also a symbol. NASA means a great deal more than just its name: the Space Age, flights to the moon, the shuttle, life on Mars, exploration of the solar system. The purpose of any acronym is to provide a foolproof method of gaining MCI in the face of the complex world of corporate images, committees of government, and informational complexes in general. We have learned to read newspaper headlines like: "Snafu in GOP Demos AIDS Bill," but the need to do so has escalated, and with the pressures of too-muchness from electric process, the cartoon effect in communication has permeated all mass media.

Look at the want ads in any newspaper: "1 Bdrm. bach. nr. sbwy. N. Tor. rply Box 123 P.S. 69." The cabbalistic vise that electric process puts on language is abetted by the high cost of advertising, whose code of imploded inference has become conventionalized in our communications.

The more that information is converted by MCI to cartoon effect, the less sensitive we are to detail.

The result is a sort of perceptual fundamentalism that reduces the likelihood of our ever having enough information or whole enough patterns to understand events at the level of process. As these runic tokens are increasingly employed, language loses its rich etymological resonance and becomes stilted and static. We are adrift in a sea of information, but not much of it will slake the thirst for creative innovation.

Electric process configures by means of mosaic form. The television screen is a mosaic of points of modulated light. Mosaic form operates by juxtaposition. Each part in a mosaic affects the meaning of every other part, though none are connected by continuous lines, only by lines of inference.

Mosaic is the antithesis of cartoon.

In a mosaic presentation, the viewer works to create figures by juxtaposition out of a complex ground. The viewer of the cartoon sees only the figure and doesn't miss the ground. In a mosaic, as in a pointillist picture, the figure is drawn out by meshing together the independent parts. In a cartoon, the figure/ground relationship is severed, and the cartoon works only if the figure elicits grievance — the key to humour — from the preconscious ground. A cartoon tends to suppress alternative views, while mosaic is all relationship and multiple views.

As relationships between things grow, the organic, open system of knowledge thus created requires an understanding of wholes. Electric process creates an ecology of information that far transcends the rigid positivistic forms of knowledge we inherited from the previous centuries. Almost none of our significant problems can be resolved by one specialist discipline. Information is now assembled from a wide swath of relevant fields and formats. This is a trans-informational age where real survival depends on coping with complexity, a fact that inspires the majority to inhibitive strategies in order to avoid the overloading of the sensory apparatus and the mind's normal processes. But for those few who can take the changes full in the face . . . well! That will make news.

Entropy, the decay of closed systems, is an idealization. It is unfortunately not generally understood, even by some scientists, that all systems, at least to some miniscule degree, are in reality open systems and thus interdependent. An infinite number of interrelations exist between all systems. There is always a detectable environment adulterating perception. Gravity always tugs a little, and matter, even something as simple as water, may have memory traces. Even under the strictest scientific conditions, an object under scrutiny is adulterated by photonic energy. Light is never absolutely negligible, any more than the colonization of the human cell by independent families of mitochondria is a negligible aspect of the racial story of DNA.

> The total effect of information production across all media is the creation of a complex psychic disequilibrium.

At the present time, all media bear traces of all the other media. The interplay between media creates a very complex interplay between senses, so that writers are thinking about TV and film when they are writing, either deliberately or out-of-awareness. Some films, like those of Bergman or Fassbinder, deliberately evoke bardic storytelling in a novelistic context; some lawyers talk in such a highly literate style that they seem to visualize the copy while they hear themselves speak it. All media appear to be merging into one multimedia form, just as the technology for recording information is also merging into one final, perfect form.

The creation, preservation, and transmission of information is only theoretically governed by the rules of negative entropy (the ordering of random chaos by creating meaning). In the dynamic flow of information, interactions are relationally random and infinitely complex. Infinitudes of complexity always outstrip meaning. As such, the creation of meaning only enhances and extends the complexity of chaos. Chaos itself becomes a new paradigm of order as the war between entropy and meaning winds down.

The attempt to characterize information by the theoretical consider- ations of heat physics, as Norbert Wiener[17] and many others have done, may well now be an obsolescent analogy. Information, and the way we deal with it in mass media, can pollute, destroy, and severely dis- order life.

An Adaptor Steps the Power Down

Adaptation is a "process in living systems for the reduction of the effect of a stimulus. It is mainly a progressive loss of sensitivity during a period of stimulation."[18]

The more intense the stimulus, the more effort we make to adapt less painfully to it. A teenager with a five-hundred-watt stereo amplifier adapts to the very intense bombardment of pulsed air on his ear by giving over huge amounts of his own energy to counterbalance the stereo system. The process dulls his hearing sensitivity, even unto deafness or temporary auditory closure. This adaptation to the point of numbness is a form of sublimation. "The sim- plest way to get rid of information is to reduce the sensitivity of the receptors."[19] In the long run, overstimulation destroys sensory acuity.

We easily adapt ourselves down to lower levels of sensitivity to evade the continuation of painful overstimulation, thereby losing the ability to perceive broad patterns of meaning.

The eye, especially, is highly adaptive. It is a common assumption that the eye sees with constant linear acuity. Upon closer investigation, it is easy to discover that this is not the case.

> In normal use the eyes are rarely still for long. Apart from
> small tremors, their most common movement is the flick from
> one position to another called a "saccade."[20]

The well-known phenomenon of saccadic activity is readily apparent if one is reading when tired or bored, or if one is reading exceptionally difficult material. The eye is under maximum stress to force its fixating, jerking way along the lines. Under these conditions, the eye makes an increasing number of "mistakes" by flicking about over the page as though the page were a whole picture.

> Saccades usually take less than a twentieth of a second, but they happen several times each second in reading and may be just as frequent when a picture or actual scene is being inspected. This means that there is a new retinal image every few hundred milliseconds.[21]

This somewhat frantic, ongoing attempt by the eye to assemble and continuously reassemble the image that it is presented with is an example of our complete unawareness of inhibition. Instead, we harbour the illusion that our vision is smooth and uninterrupted.

> Such eye movements are necessary because the area of clear vision available to the stationary eye is severely limited. To see this for oneself it is only necessary to fixate on a point in some unfamiliar picture or on an unread printed page. Only a small region around the fixation point will be clear. Most of the page is seen peripherally.[22]

The fovea of the human eye, a central portion of the retina densely packed with sensory cells, allows for high degrees of focus, a principal need of human activities that require finesse.

> Only in the fovea, the small central part of the retina, are the receptor cells packed close enough together (and appropriately organized) to make a high degree of visual acuity possible. This is the reason one must turn one's eyes (or head) to look directly at objects in which one is particularly interested.[23]

As we know, when we look at an object, the eye jumps about the image with saccadic leaps and does not make a smooth transit around the boundaries of the image. Von Békésy assures us that there is good reason for this: "The retina seems to lose its 'pattern recognition ability' quickly if the pattern is maintained on one portion of its surface."[24] If one forces the image to stay on one portion of the retina, the image begins to disappear in a few seconds. Von Békésy puts it flatly: "Under ordinary conditions the continuous movements of the eye prevent loss of our visual sensations through adaptation."[25] The eye sees best by roving about and resisting long, fixed focusing on single objects of attention. People in face-to-face conversation always play a facial dance of looking away and back. The reason for this is to keep the sharpest image possible of the respondent on the retina. The tendency to adapt to images suggests that ads or announcements must be constantly more ingenious to gain and hold attention, which is constantly adapting to the original stimulation of the original format of the ad. This phenomenon may also account for why our cities are so full of visual garbage.

Inhibition through adaptation can easily lead to boredom, since so much of the low-level stimulation of advertising and shopkeeping presentation is perpetually going stale. Unconsciously, we learn to reject the organized stimulation of only a short while ago. Our obsession with the novel, the eternally modern, also derives at least in large part from this general aspect of perceptual life.

I have many times in my life suddenly become aware of a store or architectural novelty in my neighbourhood, which for years I have completely ignored and missed "seeing." Such perceptual events are, of course, not uncommon, even if the reasons for the inhibited object are darkly out of awareness.

Boredom: The Sloughed-off Environment of Self

Inhibition starts as an unconscious need to dull the senses when they cannot cope physiologically with the glut of informational stress from the immediate environment. Our bodies know that they shouldn't adapt to constant discomfort, but our technologies induce us to cooperate. Mental health is threatened by overabundance in any sphere. Smoking, drinking, and drug use are habits of dulling awareness and pushing reality away; even too much good health seems a liability to some people. There are deprivations associated with affluence. Convenience and comfort are purchased by dogged devotion to an expanding income, which guarantees escalating consumption. The stress of having to pay attention to work in order to facilitate inhibitive comforts is a fundamental irony in our way of life. These costly benefits of the good life can become an intolerable curse. A yawning, unspecified hole in the heart develops. Not able to clearly perceive the losses we suffer, we want more than a few nice things and easy money; we want the best of everything, now.

We inflate what we consume with illusions of connections with higher than human powers, analogues of the afterlife. From Wonder Bread to wonder drugs, from washday miracles to miraculous cures, everything in media life is "amazing," "fantastic," "sensational," "fabulous" — the dross of Madison Avenue spritzed with a lacquer of superlatives.

The characteristic psychological state of a well-inhibited personality is depression. Boredom is the beginning phase; pathological inhibition, the end. Boredom is an incipient state of depression in which one develops the habit of resisting stimulations to lively response. Boredom is the ultimate form of self-indulgence: cutting oneself off from oneself in a sort of sensory suicide. The busyness yardstick of business involves a frenetic persistence in avoiding self-encounter.

This flip, or reversal, is the ultimate effect of extreme inhibition: the mass of inhibited material gains the upper hand in the psyche and overpowers the established order of the reality that has ensured

> All this non-sense involved in denying our humanity mounts to a point of critical mass. We live with the fear that such a personality will flip into its opposite without much warning. Boredom thus becomes mania.

survival to this point. There are two sides to boredom: it is not only the effect of fending off stimulation, but also results from having stimulating experiences cut off by autonomous systems.

The more highly ordered a system is, the less open it is to human involvement. The completely self-ordered or automated system exists apart from any human interaction. Using such systems makes the user subservient to the device. The ancients knew that the person who uses machines becomes mechanical in mind and spirit. Having a technique, as Jacques Ellul observed, is to mimic the automated; it's a way to get work done and remain inhibited. We all must do this if we live and work in the world.

Our domination by computer and television technology ensures that, to some appreciable degree, our responses become programmed. The preconscious contents that govern our actions bypass the value system entrenched as consciousness. Because much production requires only low-level human involvement, work flips into information processing.

To become secondary in importance to the programs of autonomous systems is implicitly boring. Being cut off from the mental activity of thinking about how to do a job removes all human pleasure from work. The boredom of being a mere activator of programs reduces imaginative interplay, the one indispensable aspect of enjoyable work. If, as N.O. Brown suggests, "the cessation of work is hell,"[26] then the cessation of imagination in work is surely purgatory.

Rejecting States of Mind

> In *1984*, Orwell foresaw a society in which a systematic elimination of information was necessary to ensure governmental control.

We urgently need to eliminate massive amounts information. Remarking on the degree to which the over-richness of our informational environment prohibits fuller awareness and more holistic perception, George Leonard advocates developing awareness of the total human biofield.

> As it is now, our perception of biofields comes up against the sternest censorship. Thought control, the kind we imagine for ourselves in the most frightening fiction, is already a reality. Indeed, thought control is the most pervasive fact in our existence, and possibly always will be.[27]

Leonard is not talking about brainwashing and totalitarian governments; rather, he is referring to the phenomenon of inhibition, the inescapable perceptual filter built into the human organism to aid its cultural survival. He is also remarking on our cowardly desire to be spared understanding and evade the very negative effects of being overwhelmed by the full complexity of reality. Taboo subjects must remain hidden from public view — like the question of how so many Nazi war criminals were brought into Canada and the United States in a clandestine fashion after the Second World War by those governments. The sex trade in Third-World children is a taboo subject that may soon emerge into daylight. Our mental survival depends on complacency and a carefully selected rejection of much that the media environment pushes at us.

This question of survival is real and is based on scientific grounds. We reject certain information because we must. Our nervous system is constructed so as to make the perceptual environment simple enough to be manageable.

The most crucial function of the human central nervous system is rejection. Around 100,000 separate bits of information start toward our brain every second. If all of it arrived, we would go instantly mad. A number of neural mechanisms, particularly the reticular formation in the brain stem, act to screen out all but a small fraction of this information — that which is needed for bodily survival plus that which is decreed as relevant by a particular society. We cannot overestimate the quality and quantity of the perceptual material which could reach our conscious awareness, but does not.[28]

In addition to adaptation, compensation is an important aspect of inhibition, and an effective "method of eliminating unwanted information."[29] Compensation operates by cancelling equalized sensory inputs, which prevents the overloading of the higher centres of sensation with unimportant information. The hearing system abounds in such events. Very little ambient environmental sound is crucial to action or survival, and is cancelled out or strongly inhibited by "normal" perception. Silence can be deafening; when noise abates, we become suddenly aware of all that we have been inhibiting.

Waking Dreams

Media feed characteristic mental states and move us through altered consciousness imperceptibly. We inhibit awareness of dreams because of their surreal complexity and don't care to understand them. When we try to remember and recount a dream, it emerges as a simple cartoon sketch. In fact, there is a variety of important mental states that can be monitored by EEG measurement as Rod Gorney suggests in *The Human Agenda*:

Dreaming was discovered to be a fundamental physiological process related to other bodily rhythms and essential to health. Various stages of sleep, alertness, drowsiness, relaxation, and boredom have been distinguished by the EEG personalities or independent dominant qualities, with those who think visually as contrasted with those who think in sounds, movements or textures.[30]

The visual/passive, acoustic/dominant split is one fraught with significance in an environment controlled by electric media for the advertising of both consumer products and political images. But, let's look at the problem of the organization of the brain.

In 1967, Georg von Békésy revealed an old debate in physiology, one that still rages: what he calls an "enduring controversy" that "has to do with localization of neural activity in the brain. At one time it was held generally that localization in the brain was not specific but that different areas may be involved from time to time in a given kind of activity. The present trend in brain theory has moved away from such 'mass action' and toward a high degree of specificity."[31] None of this is new, but it does reveal the futility of either/or thinking.

Why are we afraid of the possibility that things can be both true and not true at the same time? Your medication may be an effective pharmaceutical, or you may be getting well by placebo effect. Every disease, although usually only considered physically, also has a psychological component. The stars that you think you see now can never truly be seen now; that is an illusion of time and space. The light that comes to your eye varies greatly in age, some of it taking aeons to get here. Some of the heavenly bodies that you "see" have died many years ago, but their sourceless light is still arriving here. Think that computer "literacy" guarantees a progressive future? Or that this documentary film reveals the truth about this Aboriginal group? All such propositions are true in one context and not true in another. Much of electric culture operates like this.

An area of the brain that is registering near-idle activity is an important component in a pattern that shows another area raging with neuroelectric energy: the localization is a function of the general configuration of brain areas. When the verbal centre, or Broca's and Wernicke's areas, are lit up with gamma illumination in the act of reading a difficult text, the apparently dormant other areas are significant by their inactivity. One must understand how the complex whole can be coexistent with the single point of information, just as cloning is based on the possibility of replicating a whole organism from a single cell.

> In considering various interpretations of the brain's bimodal activity, we discover a fundamental complementarity: there is both mass action and specific location in brain activity. In fact, the brain seems more a hologram than anything else.

I remember hearing from a fairly dependable source, a professional anthropologist, of a case in which a patient had his verbal centre destroyed in a car accident while in London. A speech pathologist was brought in from a local university to see if anything could be done to retrain the patient to speak. Against all expectations the fellow began to recover his speech even though his verbal centres were severely damaged. It was ascertained that the man began recovering his ability to speak by using another part of his brain. But his speech returned with his original Brooklyn accent — quite different from the educated London accent of his speech therapist. This presented all involved with a marvelous enigma. Is the brain holographic, possessing full capacity at every point in the brain?

Karl Pribram studies this complementarity between brain function and the hologram. Through his controversial work with monkeys implanted with monitor electrodes, a new theory of how the brain processes visual information is emerging. Pattern recognition "feeds forward" from the inferior temporal cortex and the posterior striate cortex. These impulses are integrated in the visual colliculus and the geniculate nucleus. What this means for the interested amateur is that Pribram is actually saying that vision is an assembly, not a copy event. A complete pictorial copy of an object is not stored intact somewhere in the brain. Rather, a number of disparate inputs from various regions of the brain assemble the picture in a mosaic fashion — simple little pieces juxtaposed in a complex pictorial pattern of relationships.

Projection

Years of careful experimentation in the extremely difficult area of sensory activity have disclosed at least one solid propensity of perceiving organs: the strong tendency to inhibit simultaneous stimulations and to "funnel" a complex stimulus toward a central or localized area.

> The projection of sensation outside the body is still a mysterious business, one which is crucial for life. Von Békésy is succinct: "The funnelling of sensations into a space outside the body is an important feature of neural funnelling, for it controls practically all our behaviour."[32]

It is easy to test this "funnelling effect" simply by putting three sharp pencil points together on the forearm. The three points will appear to a blindfolded subject to be one point. The threshold of the funnelling effect can be determined by spreading the points gradually until they are felt as more than one. It is not abnormal for a spread of as much as three inches to still appear as one point.

> It is apparent that the lateral inhibition that occurs in sense organs
> is not the straightforward kind that we find in muscle systems. The
> lateral inhibition of sense organs is actually a funnelling action that
> inhibits the smaller stimulus effects and collects the stronger effects
> into a common pathway.[33]

Funnelling of nervous sensation is the assimilation of several separated points of stimulation into what is perceived as one stronger stimulus. This is the core of the inner/outer paradox of human perception. Historically, from Bishop Berkeley on, we have wanted to know where the act of sensation fits into the question of objective reality. Without knowledge of the interrelationship between inhibition and projection, this remains the most basic question about perception. Von Békésy again:

> We see by internal sensations on the retina and in the brain but
> we project the object correctly in space. As in hearing, we can locate
> sound sources correctly in space although we hear internally. This is
> basic to survival and even to all general movement and activity.[34]

Just as we take in multiple stimuli, not sufficiently separated, and read them as one strong one, so the funnel effect in an obverse manner results in a conic location of objects and sounds in space. We will attribute more sound and sight to an object that has startled us than is actually appropriate to it. The aural and visual modes of perception are interplaying most strongly in this fundamental relationship. It is much easier to locate an object in the environment visually than acoustically. The aural mode is powerfully internal, and evokes strong emotions that add to the perceptual act. The visual mode is much more neutral, especially without sound, and allows us to easily detach ourselves from the thing perceived.

> This matter of external projection of vibratory sensations seems
> to be strange and hard to believe . . . Every well-trained machinist
> projects his sensations of pressure to the tip of a screwdriver, and
> it is this projection that enables him to work rapidly and correctly.

For most people this projection is so common that they are unaware
of its existence.[35]

As obvious as this example may seem, one must consider other more
penetrating uses of this faculty — for example, in the projections
involving the mass media of communication. This focusing of attention
into space is too complex to yield a coherent theory of perception. All
we can know is something about the dynamic interplay between the
internal and external processes of inhibition and projection.

Von Békésy's studies in the physiology of inhibition have produced
an extremely useful insight into these forces. He says precisely that:
"The more we are trained to project external sounds outside the body
the easier it becomes to inhibit internal bodily noise."[36] Mental health,
then, requires the projection of inner states. A society that has developed the intractable habit of projecting inner life into television and
film entertainments, as well as the telephone, computer and radio, is a
society with a deep need to re-sensitize its inner life; we need something other than media, which are virtual and do not help to quell
internal neurotic noise.

Moment to moment, there is always too much information for the
senses to handle. This is the normal state of affairs. Because of the introduction of electric process into all aspects of contemporary life, the
growth of the amount of information that we are required to inhibit has
increased beyond the limits of assimilation. We survive this onslaught
by developing our abilities to select what is important and by squelching
what is relatively trivial. Without an extremely refined faculty for
inhibiting information flow to the higher centres of consciousness, each
one of us would be overwhelmed and all ability to act would be lost.

Life requires inhibition, but is it a faculty that can be overstressed,
one that can function too well? Are we protected from harm in the
inhibiting activity?

It is well known that we are not able to observe continuously or
even to think continuously. We do these things in certain intervals
of time that may be called "temporal quanta" or "the conscious
present". From the point of view of electrophysiology, I have always
been interested in these momentary lapses of consciousness in
which momentary reductions of the magnitude of sensations occur.[37]

This self-referencing "hiccup" of inattention has intrigued scientists for years. The little interruptions in focus indicate another possible inhibition mechanism of significance to perceptual studies: *holographic rhythm*.

With Pribram's holographic model of the brain,[38] it seems likely that its localized linear functioning is rhythmically balanced with a holistic faculty for periodic overview. The brain, in short, if left to function freely, is, to use Fuller's term, comprehensive — balanced rhythmically with both detail and overview. The freedom to be concerned with detail is never let to interfere with the general tendency of the brain to maintain awareness over the dynamic overview of the large forces in the environment.

Von Békésy has detected just such a rhythm in brain function, but insists that time is a basic element of perception. "There is the possibility also that the electrical activity in the brain is not continuous, that there is, rather, a periodic scanning of the entire cortex."[39] But for now, in his opinion, it appears that the safest conclusion is that sensory perceptions tend to break up into "small discrete periods of time." Von Békésy develops this point concerning "time blocks" with a statement that should be of interest to teachers of reading.

> In speech there is a definite tendency to break the discourse into certain chunks, and try to recognize the chunks as units, disregarding the fine structure within the chunks."[40]

Although there is no one correct way to teach reading, it appears that the "chunky" method promises better results than methods that take one word at a time.

Von Békésy regards the actions of vision as a complementarity, rather than a hologram. Like the behaviour of light itself as both quantum and wave, the voluntary, fixating jerks that occur in the action of reading every line of print are balanced against the strong tendency of the eye to resist such linear attention. The natural action of the eye is to rove widely over any visual field, but when something of importance is discovered, attention to that detail must prevail over the involuntary scanning.

Paradoxically, as has been discussed earlier, the roving of the eye is essential for sustaining the image strongly on the retina. Though fixating locates the crisis or the point of interest in a visual field, frequent interruption of the fixed image must occur in order to avoid the fading of the image on the retina. This paradox of stasis in kinesis is technically exploited in film, where the correctly timed sequence of still pictures creates the illusion of perfect motion. The eye thus has its roving role altered to movements within the cinematic framework, and can completely inhibit the environment of the interior of the theatre.

Reading requires intense focus. This habit tends to decrease the alert, general scanning that insures survival against threats in the environment. The absent-minded professor, crossing the street rapt in thought, is a case in point. Regarding survival potential, one is left to speculate what the long-term effects of subverting a prime evolutionary function through the overuse of a single medium might be.

The computer picture presents the eye with a radiant-light equivalent of the paper page. This is the reverse of the light-reflective printed page. MRI analysis shows clearly that the two different methods of reading register in different locations in the brain. The VDT picture of a page encourages the eye's natural tendency to rove widely, and defeats the attempt to maintain voluntary control over the word-processing activity.

> Word processing by computer produces a complex conflict between the printed page and the video display terminal: an electrically pulsed, radiantly lit picture of a printed page.

Saccadic activity, the visual leaping about and refixating of the eye, does not seem to interrupt the general effect of experiencing smooth continuity in the act of seeing. The jerking of the eye is essential to highly focused seeing.

> Most people are either unaware of their own eye movements or have erroneous notions about them. Far from being a copy of the retinal display, the visual world is somehow constructed on the basis of information taken in during many different fixations.[41]

Ulric Neisser offers a simple, yet instructive experiment to demonstrate this visual construction. Ask a person "How many windows are there in your house" or "How many chairs do you own?" Rarely does one have a ready answer. An "internal representation" has to be visualized; that is, an orderly series of new visualizations must be constructed as one goes around the house in one's mind. The diminishing distinction between seeing and imagining suggests a similar process in both acts. It appears that "mental images are constructs and not copies."

In vision, we are at first minimalists, quickly taking in just enough to make a correct inference when sizing up the situation confronting us. As discussed, the process of vision operates by extremes of inhibition; we leave out details not immediately needed to make an instant, correct response to potential environmental threats.

This inhibitory action is fundamental to the act of reading, as H.J. Chaytor, one of McLuhan's teachers at Cambridge, has observed in his fine study on the perceptual shift into print culture.

> If we take a line of printed matter, cut it lengthways in half, that
> the upper half of the lettering is exactly divided from the lower half,
> and then hand the slips to two friends, we shall probably find that
> the man with the upper half will read the line more easily than the
> man with the lower half.[42]

Chaytor is here pointing out the simplifying efficiency of the action of vision as applied to reading, in leaving out much that is not crucial to quick minimal perception.

> The eye of the practised reader does not take in the whole of the
> lettering, but merely so much as will suggest the remainder to his
> experienced intelligence.[43]

When we read, we are in fact engaged in a very complex activity.

> When we read, the visual image of the printed word-form
> instantaneously becomes an acoustic image; kinesthetic images
> accompany it, and if we are not reading aloud, the combination
> of the two produces 'inner speech' . . . both inner speaking and
> inner hearing.[44]

Awareness of this complex process is almost completely inhibited. The shift from the auditory mode to the visual is subliminal. The experience of language in our culture is one in which "silent" reading severely proscribes the perception of the acoustic values implicit in speech, if not eliminating them altogether. Chaytor exemplifies this action by the case of a man hearing an unknown or foreign word: his first question is, "How is it spelled?" or "What does it look like?" One always spells one's surname these days; we do not trust the other's ears, or our own. "Such is the consequence of association with print; in printer's ink auditory memory has been drowned and visual memory has been encouraged and strengthened."[45] But Chaytor, though perhaps right for his times, has neglected the effects of electric process.

Since we are moving massively into assimilating electric word processing into our lives, we should know what the perceptual effects of such an important change in habits are likely to be. For one thing, as discussed earlier, reading from a VDT is not the same as reading from a printed page.

Literacy rates appear to have fallen off across the general population, especially among younger generations, who have become used to electric forms of information. As *Endangered Minds*, Jane Healy's heralded inquiry into the current educational crisis, showed clearly (if disturbingly), children are losing their capacity to process verbal and mathematical information, and have reduced general cognitive capabilities as well.[46] The falling scores in American proficiency tests — including the powerfully influential SAT — confirm the observations of the schools regarding the decreasing verbal competency of North Americans. Though the proliferation in contemporary testing styles that gauge levels of literacy makes the issue too complex for a simple cause-and-effect understanding, television and the perceptual modality it engenders may be the culprit. One fairly pervasive habit among parents is the use of television to narcotize the noisy kids and bring peace to the household. Two things are happening here: (1) the child is zoned out of the reality of its environment and is being trained in TV perceptual values (i.e., inattention and anti-social attitude), and (2) there is no interaction linguistically with a native-speaking adult. As Healy has shown, the science in this area of early development shows fairly clearly that if language tracks are not laid down in the early months when the brain is forming physically, the child will forever lack full language development.[47]

Cultural Lag as Inhibition

Print doesn't destroy story, it simply guarantees that stories develop literary characteristics. Film doesn't destroy the novel, it only guarantees that the more complex, uncinematic ones won't be widely read, whereas movie-like novels sell massively. TV doesn't destroy film, it only guarantees that films become more like TV.

> McLuhan first observed that new media transform and inadvertently inhibit the effects of older media.

No culture is aware of its own lag in seeing the real effects of such transformations. Print, as we know, effected a radical change in perceptual values throughout the western world. The content of the first books to come off the early presses was printed versions of earlier manuscripts: *The Shepheardes Calendar*, *Book of Hours*, tales in the aural mode, and devotional utterance arrested visually on the printed page.

Printing transformed aural culture into visual form by splitting whole perception apart in new ways, by separating, for example, words and music in song. The old poets loudly protested the poem frozen on the page in print as a barbarian novelty. Poetry thus devalued by print made way for a deluge of prose, and music became orchestral and precisely scored. The troubadour was banished to the music hall. The old forms were quickly obsolesced under the pressure of the new innovation of print technology.

Chaytor discusses the lag, or dislocation, between printed and spoken language, and points out how this disparity in development has resulted in the disaster we know as English spelling.

> Script and, to a far greater extent, print follow and do not anticipate the development of the spoken language; they preserve archaicisms and are chary of admitting neologisms; they help the development of a literary language and style which is often far removed from current habits of speech . . . School instruction starts with the book and the book's orthography is regarded as a kind of legal code against which there is no appeal. Meanwhile language develops, and sounds change, but "spelling" remains fixed . . . with the result that English orthography is now the despair of Europe . . . The fundamental reason for divergence between spoken and written language is the

fact that a visual image is more lasting and more readily appropriated than an acoustic image.[48]

Chaytor goes on to say that whenever spoken language is at variance with written language, it is usually the written form that prevails as authoritative. This entrenches the habit of cultural lag, and makes formal language a good deal more complex than ordinary speech; witness any legal opinion or theological argument.

A more contemporary divergence in media forms sees the traditional book clashing with the e-book — an electronic version of a book accessed by a handheld LCD reader. Some hyperbole is circulating in computer engineering circles to the effect that the paper book is moribund, dying out, and will soon be replaced by the electronic version of the book. Sitting on a plane or bus you can act on the slightest whimsy and call up any book you can think of from an electronic library, and if you have not started with the right book, you can ramble through an unlimited number until you get one you like.

The argument supporting the continued use of the paper book is complex, but one insurmountable fact militates against the e-book — you cannot read it. Not at any length, that is. The Emerys and others have shown convincingly that the brain, when stimulated by a cathode ray tube or its LCD cousin, is lit up in non-verbal regions. The e-book involves not reading, but watching lit icons. The informational experience of the latter mode is so significantly different from the old book that a comparison is not illuminating.

The dissemination of information has moved from the rumour mill to the pamphlet, the pamphlet to the newspaper, the newspaper to radio, radio to television, and television to the Internet. Each of these once-dominant news forms, which powerfully commanded its audience with a high degree of credibility, has obsolesced into an easily ignored format. The newest form seems far more advanced than the older, slower forms. Today's newspaper appears to be retarded as it covers yesterday's TV news. The question of "how" the news is covered seems not to matter much, since nobody remembers the news anyway.

> The assimilation of the new requires the inhibition of the old. With each new form of communication our need to inhibit the old increases.

As we are increasingly assaulted by media with novelty, our

expanding capacity for the "new" develops into an addiction. We relinquish our hold on the broader cultural pattern and salivate for the next toy designed to make our lives more convenient or entertaining. We hang in the wind like a gizmo mobile, twisting on the end of an advertising gyre. Just the experience of confronting the new is enough to consume our energies wholesale. Our inhibitory tendency, however, prevents us from making much more than cartoons of what we watch. Old-fashioned, real news, which always had a difficult time holding a large audience, has, as we know, been transformed into entertainment. Everything is snipped up into brief sound bites of thirty seconds or less, so that complex issues are presented to the inhibiting viewer as a minimosaic of barely rational associations — hardly an in-depth analysis. The infamous sound bite is the news equivalent of a cartoon sketch.

Most contemporary cultures are in the process of translating themselves into media forms. Going to Hawaii is not to arrive in Hawaiian culture but to become an audience for the Hawaiian show of the obsolete Hawaiian culture. Iraq monitored what was going on in the Gulf War from CNN coverage, mainly by Bernie Shaw; he was the lone American allowed to stay in the country, because otherwise Iraq would not have known anything about how the war was going, or how the rest of the world was seeing it. Under such conditions, the experience of culture itself becomes vicarious. Direct experience is minimized; everything is on tape, or CD, or film, or in a coffee-table book. One does not have the experience itself, but rather a mediated version of the event. Even sport has become nothing more than a sporadic series of replays, requiring no attention from the user.

Museums and galleries regularly rent portable cassette players with taped lectures to accompany important international art shows. What the untutored aesthete learns from the elementary lesson on tape is to see as he or she is told. The much more difficult job of learning to see for oneself is avoided; the gallery experience can be both taken in and inhibited, just like TV news, so that few people can recall it. Real life is supplanted by its mediated version, which becomes the actual experience of those who allow themselves to be "colonized" by the networks. Life is forced to imitate not art, but media representations of the real. Mass culture, the fountainhead of adolescent banality, becomes the instructor of cultural behaviour. The older forms of culture take on socio-economic rarity.

Memory, as it selects what to retain, leaves out the negative so far as possible. Memory designs escape from the negative, transforming perception of the past into palatable half-truths. As children of our own psychic landscapes, we do not easily give up our tenacious grip on that aspect of our identity. We preserve our early pasts in allegories of pleasant misremembrance. So we fictionalize our pasts and travel with light memories into futures requiring strong self-esteem. This is all as it should be, one might argue, if it weren't for electric media.

Mass media, operating like a surrogate memory, allow the user to escape from the power of the personal negative by burying that disturbing material in the preconscious mind. Media inhibit even the most pressing negatives and turn the mind toward forgetfulness. The real desire for change, even revolutionary zeal, becomes absorbed by media into a mass culture laboratory, which turns such legitimate aspirations into simple-minded plots for binding commercials together. Again, the Gulf War was, in some ways, designed and directed by the Hill and Knowlton ad agency.[49] Coverage of the war was sponsored. The Big Three networks followed the ad agency's advice, and the war was brought to a speedy, well-propagandized conclusion.

All media are extended technologies that manipulate memory so that it loses its power to alter culture in any significant way. Memory becomes the memory of old media, the redundant message of the product redundantly consumed.

The Bushmen, Inuit, or Papua New Guineans cannot survive radio, film, and video. These are forms of awareness that are obviously lethal to any culture of perpetual dawn. Oral cultures perpetuate cyclical time and depend on memory. Each generation emulates the past, simulating the ritual continuation of their forebears. They are cut off from the linear progression of historical time. The action of electric media on such peoples is the elimination of their experience of the world, which is validated by reading nature. In one generation, they are severed from a culture that has been evolving for millennia. The tribal identities of preliterate peoples are effectively negated by their entry into electric culture. They are required to inhibit who they once were. Soon, they are merely figures without a cultural

> Culture is memory under pressure from technical change. Media envelop culture, wrapping media values around cultural values.

ground, lost in a jungle of information, often murderously bent on retrieving their lost identities.

A peoples' inhibited past can be retrieved as art content by setting up a simulation of who they used to be. Although this strategy usually results in serious social and political trauma, it is happening everywhere in the world. Aboriginal peoples who were once confined to a limited awareness of the world are now worldly bureaucrats, lawyers, and politicians, arguing that dominant governments give them back their territorial and property rights.

We both romancticize the past and take it quite seriously in trying to find justice for those wronged by European invasion. We have a love of the pioneer spirit, which hardly tells the truth about how it actually destroyed so much that it came in contact with.

This habit of mind can be seen in the way we accord art status to any old object: furniture, butter churns, copper tubs, old bottles — all symbols of harder times, romanticized into objects of snobbish appeal. These objects fetch high prices, regardless of how junky and useless they may actually be. Surrounded by environmental forms that trivialize the work of the human hand and accentuate the values of informational play, we seem to be expressing a need to sensitize ourselves to the human scale these objects reflect. We learn to remember the past inaccurately. We surround ourselves with the cultural detritus of a past that was little like our nostalgic and simulated reconstruction of it.

Trashing Experience for Expedience: From Percept to Concept

Direct experience, the percept,* is always richer than any theory that attempts to interpret it. Percepts encourage imaginative departures from the norm. Concepts* produce narrow values and enhance the predictability of behaviour.

The conceptual, when formulated as theory, is always, in the long run, at odds with direct perception. When a concept has been internalized to become part of one's perceptual bias, it becomes an inescapable filter on direct experience. Conceptualization encloses life and dimin-

*As these terms are being used here, concept refers to the total mental impression resulting from perceiving. Concept is the theory-bound idea of a class of objects resulting from their combination. Percepts spring from life contacts, while concepts are abstractions usually devised in solitude or under laboratory conditions. Observing a kangaroo is a percept; the Theory of Evolution is a concept.

ishes awareness of the whole complex of reality, yet allows us to do useful work. Percepts are more directly linked to the unutterable, ineffable complexity of life, and guide us in overview. The percept is essentially liberal, open, and tolerant of paradox; the concept is conservative, legalistic, scientific, and demanding of law and order. In reality, these biases operate simultaneously, together creating complex cognitive tensions beyond the domain of theory — in politics and economics, for example. A total reading of the political moment through media, economy, and social conditions, as well as certain intangibles, should impinge on government in conceptualizing a specific policy initiative.

Actually, we have neither unadulterated direct experience nor wholly conceptual mental capabilities. I had a professor who once showed us just how advanced we were in our modern awareness by asking the seminar, "What time did the sun rise this morning?" "About six-thirty," someone said. "And what time will it set this evening?" "About eight-thirty," came the reply. "You see," the professor said, "we still live in a Ptolemaic universe." Our perception of the sun's behaviour was clearly at odds with our concept of the Copernican, heliocentric universe. Our beliefs are founded on the narrow base of simple appearances. Our true feelings are resonant with direct experience.

The multi-sensory media of electric process can simulate a total perceptual experience. Someone else's simulation of a percept — say a filmmaker's concept of the experience of a dream — becomes an element in how our actual dreams take place. The two realms of experience interpenetrate and deeply affect each other. To some extent, the conceptual side of life almost eradicates our conscious awareness of how percepts work as whole, comprehensive, emotional, psychological entities. Emotional life inevitably becomes partially fake through conceptualized feelings.

We learn to inhibit those perceptions that transgress the accepted view of civilized order. With electric culture, however, the old pattern of civilized values is subverted. The delay or inhibition of satisfaction, which is the foundation of civilized society, is not only obsolete, but also economically opposed to the all-at-onceness of electric form. Electric process thrives on immediate, multi-sensory gratification through consumption and the massive extension of credit.

Inhibiting The Insight of Limitation

> We have been well trained to expect exactness in all things, if not in ourselves.

At the root of the myth of exactness lies an unconscious preference for mechanical time and space — a perceptual inheritance from the last several centuries. This hangover continues into the Computer Age, in which the appearance of exactitude is electronically part of everything we do on the machine. The weak link in all of this, however, is the human factor. Subliminally, we know there is very little hope of ever finding a way to communicate exactly what we mean, even in conversation. While we accept these failures in human communication, we are almost totally intolerant of computer-generated mistakes — faulty programs, electronic glitches — all the ways mistakes can, and do, enter into our communications by computer. This raises the frustration level of communications in our time to a very high pitch. Nevertheless, as communicating creatures, we spend most of our lives inhibiting the sad facts of inexact transfer of meaning, as though the hope springs eternal of meeting that one special person who will understand us perfectly.

> Personal communication depends on a complex web of tacit agreements, wherein certain limits to understanding each other will be ignored.

Every human perception is a universe of interrelations. Even the person we love the most remains a relative stranger to us. True, nobody can afford to think like that — we have practical work to get done. We must inhibit the perception of our real intellectual and emotional limits. Sanity requires it. To be forced to give up the power to inhibit recognition of one's real limitations is a crushing blow to a healthily functioning ego. In ages past, there were enforced recognitions of one's limitations everywhere in one's life. Now the unexamined life is de rigeur.

The perceptual biases of all electric media contribute to the inhibition of the insight of limitation. Print, on the contrary, extends our knowledge of our limitations, because the precision that language applies to life and the subtlety of its discriminations increases the scope of self-knowledge through education.

Too often, social and political criticism pits limitation against limitation. The limitation of what the authorities know and can't say confronts the limitation of what the citizens have been propagandized to know by media sources. We have been carefully trained not to think like this. Such limitations to the truth are circumvented by acceptable means that allow the citizen to avoid looking stupid and for the establishment figure to look honest and sincere. This inhibition implicit in contemporary government is wearing thin, and may be one of the main reasons why one hundred million enfranchised voters won't even bother to vote in the next US election. If getting re-elected is the most important job of a politician, then the media people, who take in massive amounts of money in re-election advertising campaigns, want first and foremost to avoid displeasing their sponsor through news coverage. Every effort is made to suppress awareness of such crucial hidden grounds. But many voters seem to be getting wise to this venal game.

Eventually, with effort, one becomes skilful in recognizing and discarding the imperfections and failures in systems of thought. Interpretations of even simple events vary. Language issues uniquely from every mouth. The habitual falsity in our observations and statements of fact are neatly suppressed under a weight of rationalizing concepts. We cannot communicate exactly because our limits vary and beg not to be recognized.

What we utter is a mythic construction that tells not about things and events, but about ourselves and the structure of our consciousness. If one's consciousness is well-built, reflecting useful knowledge about the structure of events and behaviour, it should win out over foolishness and frenzy. Only a healthy culture can sort these values out in public life.

Still, we cling tenaciously to our need to be exact, which is a measure of our fear of the non-mechanical, other side of things. The illusion of exactness comes directly from the unity of thought of which every consciousness is comprised, or thinks it is. We continually sift the environment for assimilable pieces that are consonant with our sacrosanct unity of mind. Everything else is tossed onto the slag heap of awareness — the preconscious.

Inhibition as a Positive Negative

> Communication travels in waves, rhythmically arranged to impress messages on senses. All organic matter communicates by expressing complex arrangements of action and inhibition in its growth.

Organic actions, the increasingly complex interplay between living elements, appear as a building up to higher and higher states of meaning. Simple cells agglomerate, communicate, reproduce, and project themselves into larger, more complex units of life. They have a powerful, inner-directed tendency to grow in the force of their activities. But this is only half of the picture; another equally powerful force prevents this growth activity from outstripping all limits.

Like the systolic and diastolic rhythm of the heartbeat itself, inhibition (shutting down) operates in a precise balance with its opposite, induction (opening up). Not nearly enough is understood about this rhythm of life, this induction and inhibition.

> The essence of rhythm is the alteration of tension building up to a crisis, and ebbing away in a graduated course of relaxation whereby a new build-up of tension is prepared and driven to the next crisis, which necessitates the next cadence.[50]

While this may seem as obvious as the tension/release mechanism of sexuality or the systolic/diastolic pulse of the heart, the crucial point here is the dynamic reversal implicit in the movement of energy — rise/fall, on/off, positive/negative, and so on. This dualism is not vitalistic, but as mysterious as symmetry and as mundane as an energy wave.

> If the series of actions thus engendered consists of alternating contraries, such as rise and fall, push and pull, suction and expulsion, and each element in spending itself prepares and initiates its own converse, the resulting rhythm is a dialectic.[51.]

Like mirror opposites, these two forces, positive and negative, constitute a complementarity, a mutually exclusive set of cases in which each opposite is the source of the other's existence and rhythm of growth. At base, we are dealing with the "basic pattern of life," DNA language in its most rudimentary form of expression. Implicit in every moment of material life is the ability of the living part to reverse into its opposite. Paul Weiss has summarized the inhibition action.

> Briefly, each organ or each cell type produces inhibitors of its own growth, and the total concentration of these in the circulation comes into equilibrium with the productive or generative mass to produce a steady state.[52]

This equilibrated pattern of conflict and resolution in organic matter appears to establish an essential paradox, an ur-grammar that enfranchises all language rather than all conflict in human growth.

The function of inhibition in the body has its parallel in the mind. Since inhibition is a "covert" activity, however, it is difficult to study scientifically; the study of the mind, too, does not yield verifiable data. We look instead for patterns of meaning that reveal the action of inhibition.

Inhibition is the formative mechanism of the interior processes leading to communication; its external antithesis, its induced form is projection. Inhibition is like forgetting; projection is a construction rather like memory. The two together produce utterance.

As discussed earlier, internal processes select certain figures of information and funnel them into exterior space. Internal processes are quieted by projecting them outward. There is a relationship between the need to de-stress the organism and the particular materials that are projected outward. Projection, the fundamental urgency to communicate, taps off the inhibited negative tensions of the preconscious, thus reducing the danger of a sudden and destructive reversal of mind.

Paradigm Flip and Inhibition

Once the model of a specific world view has been established, all perceptions that don't support this model tend to be pushed into the background or eliminated. Though science proceeds by selectively ignoring events that do not reconcile with existing theory, events finally force a breakdown in theory that results in a breakthrough to a new paradigm. Such revolutions often have accidental beginnings, since those in specific fields tend to keep a tenacious

> In spite of the useful views it supports, a scientific paradigm is a method of ignoring certain perceptions. A paradigm is a special case of inhibition.

grip on the old paradigm. Doubt is born when exceptions to theoretical rules increase.

Floyd Matson reminds us how partial our scientific rationality is: "The great change (in physics) was brought about, as Einstein had noted, by Faraday, Maxwell and Hertz — as a matter of fact half-unconsciously and against their will."[53] The unconscious recognition of the flip potential in any paradigm is like the growing seed of a brain tumour that eventually consumes mental organization.

> In 1873, proceeding from the ordained mechanical premises,
> Clerk Maxwell ended up with a set of equations (the electro-magnetic
> theory) which clearly repudiated those premises and cast doubt
> upon the entire foundation of Newtonian mechanics. Even then,
> many leading physicists rejected Maxwell's conclusions because
> they could not be rendered visible and substantial in terms of a
> mechanical model.[54]

Having suffered through several decades of intractable ignorance among some of his most powerful and "knowledgeable" colleagues, Maxwell was forced to recognize the truly inhibitive effects of scientific determinism on their vision of science and reality.

> If . . . cultivators of science . . . are led to the study of the
> singularities and instabilities, rather than the continuities of
> things, the promotion of natural knowledge may tend to remove
> that prejudice in favor of determinism which seems to arise from
> assuming that the physical science of the future is a mere
> magnified image of that of the past.[55]

Theory resists change, but at certain points in cultural history too many discrepancies collect, and theory can no longer be stretched to cover phenomena that do not support its principles. The mechanistic view of substance and connection entirely shifted in the face of a force field that is totally connected and has no substance.

> The Newtonian principle of action at a distance, which lay at the
> heart of the mechanistic world view, was inadequate to account
> for the interactions between fields of force demonstrated by the

equations of Maxwell, in which the electromagnetic field could exist as a wave independent of the material source.[56]

This vision of fixed relations signalled the end of the mechanistic paradigm and machine process as the dominant form of informational structure.

The inability of scientists to "see" what Maxwell had discovered — many of them world figures like Lord Kelvin, the famous British physicist and one-time president of the British Royal Society, who, in 1900, asserted dogmatically that "X-rays are a hoax"[57] — was a massive inhibition that resulted from paradigm blindness and insensitivity to change. Even at this high level of serious inquiry — perhaps more so at this level — the need to ignore or trash certain percepts is indispensably important to the maintenance of the old paradigm. The individual's conscious unity of mind is exactly analogous to the function of a paradigm, which is to eliminate unwanted information that might upset the established equilibrium in a particular view of reality.

In the case of Maxwell, many great scientists simply got stuck in the old paradigm and couldn't break through their own self-imposed inhibitions. They simply could not perceive that many of their cherished beliefs were no longer "facts," and that they had to move beyond the mechanistic notion of action at a distance to a new, more complex metaphor of field effect: electromagnetic resonant connection.

Similar inhibitions mount up and cut us off from the fullness of experience. Only when one is questioning perceptions are breakthroughs not only possible, but likely. Still, when sufficiently inhibited by old ideas, we become quite numb to the new. As we age, the inevitable puerility of the new and the stable sameness of the old opens deep conflicts of preference in many people, and can easily motivate inhibitions.

Succumbing to the Numbing

To "see" requires interpretation, and that involves ideas about the real world. One also has to understand the structure of the informational process in order to break through to the out-of-awareness dimension of any event. The assault from too

> When the senses receive more information than they can process, inhibition eliminates all threats to the balance of consciousness. We miss more than we notice.

much information, however, has the physiological effect of numbing, or desensitizing, the sensory apparatus. Eyes, overstimulated, begin to lose their sight; ears processing too much sound go deaf; an itch unrelentingly relieved by scratching becomes painful. All pleasurable sensory experience is momentary. Know when to quit or the senses will do it for you.

A desensitized society — and it seems clear to me that ours is increasingly becoming one due to the effects of mass communication — may not be wilfully insensitive, but the effect is the same. In our society, which is overburdened with information, we simply cannot produce sufficient energy to remain sensitized to all its problems. In fact, it appears that our motivations are quite the opposite. As the range of awareness expands, driven by anxiety to cope, the depth of our understanding becomes increasingly shallow.

> The onslaught of mass communications, especially television, makes you do nothing about everything.

The requirements of the mass media for endlessly escalating amounts of information make it seem like every problem known to humankind is being exposed and attended to. What actually happens is that the flush of superficial interest in one social problem or another quickly dies, giving each "cause" a transience similar to the fading of the evening news. We become used to gorging on pizza while watching news images of starving children. The people on the receiving end of the TV tube try not to inhibit the endless appeals for active commitment to alleviate starvation and disease. Nevertheless, in the interest of some degree of sanity, the numbness must settle in.

The degree of social interaction required of us daily far outstrips our capacities and time. The movement of many people over to the right of the political spectrum may have something to do with the endless, impossibly escalating demand for social sensitivity. We have all become victims of overstimulated social concern. When we're asked to do too much all the time, we do nothing, and rationalize the decision. We project our social and political malaise into anti-social and undemocratic forms. Our lives are lived increasingly in negative response to the burgeoning forces of technical innovation.

Anti-Environments: The Creative Negative

An anti-environment is a perceptual order of things that runs counter to conventional modes of thought and action. Foremost and principally, an anti-environment results from any technological extension of inner states, electronic or pharmaceutical, into the existing environment. The Impressionist, Dadaist, Surrealist, punk or

> As McLuhan observed, new technologies, including media, create anti-environments of psychic and social awareness.

rave movements are anti-environmental strategies. In this sense, artists are outlaws. These creatively negative forces counter and destroy the remainder of the civilized past.

In media life, establishment values are always under attack in the interests of change. As anti-environments, media carry the strong appeal of inhibitory pleasure. Cities no longer produce cultural order; they are, rather, centres of profitable chaos.

I have never forgotten the marvellous image Quentin Fiore contributed to *The Medium is the Massage*. It was a powerful statement through the medium of sculpture: a giant, twenty-foot-high reclining woman, with knees up in coital position, receiving visitors from a long queue in front of her through a ten-foot-high vagina. The gallery line-up was remarkable — conservatively dressed businessmen reading newspapers, women in pill-box hats and smart suits, all looking somewhat bored alongside others equally unexcited, waiting to return to the womb.

As Freud suggests in *Civilization and Its Discontents*, the womb is "the first lodging," the archetypal home.[58] This revisiting of this gargantuan womb-as-house had all the patina of Gulliver's dangling dalliance on the giant bosom of the Queen of Brobdingnag. Art is always anti-environmental in this way, offering a reprieve from the mundane. Through these fun-inspiring, anti-environmental effects, we gain the power to deal with the forces of conflicting and obsolescent demands on our lives. Media thus deflect us from our concerns with reality.

Events in the world today, however, confirm the negative function of anti-environments as controls for our perceptions of real events. Even the worst news comes bracketed in the mollifying art of commercials that say, sub rosa, "Everything is all right." Romanticism was an answer to the waning punctiliousness of the eighteenth century, but the same

> Anyone who insists on remaining innocent of the effects of electric process is bound to become increasingly alienated from existing patterns of social change.

Romanticism can be retrieved today as an obsolescent, nostalgic aura to enhance sales in TV commercials.

The shift to the political right all around the world seems to confirm the probability of alienation. Law and order, and rationales for a pullback from social responsibilities have come quickly into effect, not only in North America, but around the globe. New environments seem, in the early stages, to be a threat; at the same time, old environments increasingly seem irrelevant to current needs. Change is always reactionary, but what happens when change is speeded up to the point where everything is obsolescing all the time? We experience a profound loss of identity — and extreme violence as we attempt to retrieve it.

Identity is hardest to preserve at the highest levels of affluence. In North America, people earning cyber salaries don't know who they are any more than the electrified Third-World tribesmen who have been forced to forget their past. Like a tribe that fears neighbouring tribes, these infocrats live in gated communities, futile palisades against social reality. The people of the Third World need to know that to regain their identities they have to maintain a strong sense of who they used to be.

The transformation of politics into theatre amounts to entertainment,

> Under electric pressure, government and theatre have merged. People amuse themselves to death with media in order to deflect their attention from the awareness of their robotic lives.

designed to convince public consciousness that nothing has really changed, nor needs to be changed, that the old verities are still potent. All the while deep changes are creeping in as the hidden ground for the paradigm shift into global reality.

Whether one points to Afghanistan, Kosovo, Slovakia, Chad, Pakistan, Sri Lanka, Chechnya, Kashmir, Palestine, Ulster, Iran, Iraq, Scotland, Chiapas, Quebec, or elsewhere, cultural theatre is paramount in local struggles for autonomy. All such exploitation of regressive awareness for local political or social gain is completely ironic in the face of the actual emergence of global consciousness.

It is precisely the divisive nature of global consciousness that accounts for the violent retrieval programs of frustrated localities.

Electric process flips everything onto a planetary scale through information technology, the true collectivism of our times.

There's a little Luddite in each of us, a desire to see human beings triumph by trashing sophisticated, robotic machines. The violence of video games confirms this, along with the increase in vandalism and the defacing of public property. Our feckless crying out against the monstrous, cannibal effects of electric power, which devours time and fractures peace of mind, is diffused in the swirling winds of inexorable change. In the long run, we have no alternative but to inhibit our awareness of the robotic slavery that is engulfing the world.

Getting back to cultural basics seems to be an attractive answer for many people; it is a conservative, reactionary response to electric complexity that is completely inhibitive. Ironically, the more global our reach is, the less global our compassion. The costly generosity of old-time liberalism may be dead forever as the industrial world becomes massively pensioned off while millions elsewhere starve. The imbalance ought to breed terror in our hearts.

The world is a network that anyone with courage and overview can co-opt. Managing the effects of media is the first business of politics; everything else is secondary. The new anti-environment of

> Terrorism is the politics of electric process.

electric process has completely changed what some thought to be the eternal verities of the American political process. The creative strategies for the management of public consciousness for political ends gave birth to the media kingmaker, the director of the imperceptible hidden ground of the new politics. The business of keeping the public focused on political figures and having them ignore the hidden ground of the private-appointed government — where the permanent power resides — is becoming an extremely complex and costly, yet unavoidable, enterprise.

The demands of the anti-environment require new strategies for directing public attention. Crises are faked to feed power. Modernism is an old strategy denoting cultural panic in the face of new environments. The faster electric values are brought to bear on everything from morals to high fashion, the faster things appear to change and become modern. Such a strategy makes everything, morals included, almost instantly trashable, since the new "new" is just around the corner.

The obsolete survives by inhibiting threatening change. After all, we need to protect our high cultural investment in specialism and the fragmented, categorical systems of order on which our institutions are based. We trade off whole life for the narrow benefits of specialist affluence. People seem never to tire of watching the parade of vaunted experts march into the quicksand of their own ignorance of paradigmatic change.

All anti-environments bode creative negative change. At the interface of the old vision of reality and the new one, where the potential exists for everything to flip into its opposite, there is a powerful static of paradox, ambiguity, and general confusion. Our world disintegrates; the old paradigm — the industrial world view — becomes visible, and attracts the attention of the majority, who call for specialization precisely when specialization can no longer do the job. The invisible, electric dynamic of the actual environment is lost on the majority, leaving the inhibited world to go out of synch with the new forces that determine its actual destiny.

Overview — the capacity to project on a large, complex scale — empowers electric elites, most of whom are very young and post-literate. Only very small elites can stay abreast of the complex, high-speed changes effected by electric process. Boundaries dissolve, and classifications and categories "reamalgamerge"[59] into new, more holistic units. There are no more experts who can do it all; now everyone has some expertise. It is ironic that this future is always already present, yet the majority is completely helpless to recognize this invisible anti-environment. *The future is the tacit present.*

Each of us, as an ersatz specialist, becomes addicted to vacuous arrays of data. This pursuit of trivial data takes our attention away from our serious lack of interpretive skills, including those few who should possess overview.

This epidemic lack can be seen as a linguistic failure. Language learning is extremely serious business. A young man whose range of response to that which displeases him is located somewhere between the word "bullshit" and some other unoriginal obscenity does not simply have a vocabulary deficiency. He has a perception deficiency. He cannot distinguish between degrees or kinds of displeasure. He must somehow have his consciousness raised. He must be persuaded that he is missing something.

Such a young person may be said simply to lack art and the refinements in sensibility that alone make intelligent judgment possible. But along with the classics, education specialists have trashed the serious study of art, thus closing the door not only on the past, but on the future as well. Under the conditions in which our hypothetical lad is left to live, life appears to him to "suck." He may be right, if one considers that a teenager is a person who acts like a baby if he's not treated like an adult.

Popular culture is the laboratory of emergent futures. Those whose job involves imposing obsolescent views — heads of corporations, politicians, teachers — are most threatened by and vulnerable to serious cultural change. Universities and scientific trusts often stand in the forefront of resistance to inevitable change. One need only recall Lord Kelvin asserting that "[r]adio has no future," or Sir George Bidell Airy, Astronomer Royal of Great Britain, scoffing at the computer as "worthless," or even Dr. R.A. Millikan, the 1923 Nobel winner for physics, suggesting that "[t]here is no likelihood that man can ever tap the power of the atom"[60] to understand the inhibitions of the great and powerful in the face of unwanted change. The list of such *faux pas* is dismayingly long.

> In a period of paradigm shift, the most powerful forces of cultural change are most invisible where vested interests in previous perception are greatest. Institutions are always playing catch-up with real change.

Education lags behind reality, and children know it. They sense that their real education is taking place in the streets, in video arcades, at raves, and at home. The schoolroom lesson seems increasingly irrelevant to them. The teacher/pupil relationship becomes adversarial, counter-productive. Any school that attempts to train a child to perceive only in terms of concepts, ignoring the rich perceptual ground of the child, is doomed to fail.

In the case of education, the general environment is seen to be functioning as an anti-environment to the schoolroom. Teachers know it and try to remedy the situation by bringing in media to bolster the lessons of learning. This approach is not much different than handing out tranquilizers to the class. Even "enriched" curricula mean only more concepts and further abstractions, which ignore the percept in the formative experience of the child. As the Japanese seem to know best, education must include some significant *doing* or it will fail to be first rate in its effect on students.

In the transition from an old to a new environment, we suddenly gain awareness of the old forms. At a time when the Age of Specialism is over — our current situation — the leaders of our institutions are discovering specialism and trying to change our universities into job training centres. We are introducing team medicine into hospitals and spending millions on a grid of community colleges in which the number of graduates already far outstrips the available jobs. All this because of a weak, linear vision of "progress."

> Commitment to the ideal of progress guarantees the destruction of the earth because it is based on waste — material waste and the waste of human imagination.

Evolving stability is created when ecology is balanced with economy. True progress must marry human hearts and hands. In a world governed by statistical generalities and mass production, we can no longer afford the luxury of ignoring the exponential chaotic effects of all the concomitant little exploitations around the globe. Beyond the despotic hallucination of policing good ecological behaviour, people must undergo a visionary change.

On a larger scale of immanent disaster, one can see the inveiglement of whole populations into consonance with the ideologies of the global market economy. These obsolescent ideas, which forever promise economic salvation, are what Barrington Nevitt calls "anesthesia for further surgeries"[61] — they operate on the power of people to order their economic lives independent from the destructive corporate mania for mega-growth.

In today's information environment, the "invisible hand" that controlled yesterday's market equilibrium has become conspicuous by its absence. By anticipating national controls at electric speed, international financial operators have reversed government intents, thereby intensifying the disequilibrium of market economies everywhere.[62]

A great part of the garbage created by the global market economy is human. It is much cheaper to pension people than to employ them. The loss of lifetimes of expertise is nothing to such an economy that is in a state of total confusion about what to do with people who are displaced by automated systems. What remarkable, negative social forces have coagulated out of the global complexities of transnational corporate greed and malfeasance.

Inhibition and Projection

Films are emotionally powerful influences on social climate that achieve their effects through certain simple manipulations of reason and logic. Once Hollywood decided to abolish the death penalty, it was just a matter of time before public sentiment shifted in that direction. A series of films

> Communication is the result of a complementarity between inner (complex) and outer (simple) modes of experience. This mutually exclusive activity is rationalized by electric media.

that were shattering indictments of the death penalty were made with the biggest stars for the largest audiences. The same was done, for example, with divorce, race, sexual mores, and ecology. The deeply inhibiting inner life of common social climate can only be overcome by projections of alternative views, which, after time, become consensual. The only other way to effect such changes is by violent means, as in Afghanistan, Iran, or Palestine.

Probably more so than any force for racial equality, television simply and effectively focused on the injustice of discrimination. In spite of very deeply held contrary views in the American south, that social climate was changed significantly simply by putting the camera on the face of bigotry.

In the early sixties, a large group of Canadians were demonstrating in front of the American Embassy in Toronto, which at that time had a meagre and relatively passive Caribbean black population. Local media went to McLuhan to get his explanation of why these white, middle-class Canadians were doing this. His response was to remind these reporters that because of TV these people "feel like blacks." He was referring to the coverage of police dogs attacking fire-hosed blacks in Little Rock. Because of television, with its strong emotional bias and ability to make anywhere everywhere, these young people could "feel" powerful, virtual empathy for these unfortunate fellow human beings.

Mass media are projective technologies. The mystical impulses of imagination, when concretized as architecture, for example, set up a clear separation of inner and outer — though all linkage is not lost, as Ruskin's famous treatise on Gothic form confirms. One can perceive, as with music, certain large lines of the cultural image formed by the amassed artifacts of any culture. This is not sure knowledge, but an indicator of a general type. We can get the right cultural "feel" of things and places from such artistic projections.

Though we know very little about the process of taking in tacit, whole experience, it is clear that at every moment of perception the human sensory apparatus is selecting and rejecting certain elements. The question of where the rejected information goes and what it does when stored is almost entirely open. We know far too little about the preconscious mid-ground between the unconscious and conscious domains of the mind, but we do know that the rejected materials are not deeply repressed; they can be called up into consciousness by ordinary efforts of the individual. That is not true of materials lodged almost irretrievably in the unconscious, where they can only enter the glare of conscious light by quite extraordinary and usually indirect means (typically by the interventions of a psychotherapist or otherwise through dream analysis). The more we safeguard our sanity through a rejection of parts of experience, the more such inhibition diminishes our humanity. The projections of media are sourced mainly from the preconscious, although true art tends to touch down into the unconscious. This is a scale of possible relations in media and not absolute categories.

> In its simplest form, inhibition is a basic evolutionary advantage that allows the individual to select instantly only those elements of perception immediately essential to survival.

In the more complex environment of electronic urban society, inhibition still functions to focus the individual, whether one is crossing the street in dense traffic or fighting the constantly fading attention at a video display terminal. This stressful focusing and refocusing increases one's desire to inhibit the complexity demanded by electric media.

The richer the environment with informational content, the more impermeable the inhibition filter required to continue functioning. The habit of mind thus induced, one which simplifies and ignores aspects of the environment that are judged of little importance or of too great a complexity, creates a situation in which overview becomes an increasingly rare facility. But overview, which grasps complexities on a large scale, is precisely the ability most required for survival in a global environment.

Without overview there can be no workable social or political structure to our actions. Sending donations to the world's starving is an act fraught with this sense of futility. Our simple sense of wanting to get food to starving children is laughably inadequate when compared to the actual complexities of local rivalries and their heartless agendas. Efforts in these areas are doomed to fail without a world view capable of projecting global solutions. If most large charities spend almost twenty dollars a month to account for twenty dollars a month, then what does giving mean?

"Education is pre-propaganda"[63] — lessons in what to ignore, what to inhibit.

Education reinforces the natural tendency of humankind to inhibit the intake of information. *The lesson is a set of instructions on what to ignore.* By selecting a principle, theorem, or issue to be studied in isolation, a lesson simply reinforces the reductionist fallacy that nothing is connected to anything else in ways that could usefully influence the step-by-step analysis of one thing at a time. So the indictment of specialist education proceeds. In fact, we need knowledge of the thing both *in situ* and in the lab. It is in this contrast that the larger view is born. But specialism blinds us to larger vision.

It is true that electric process has made us aware of entirely new skills required for productive functioning in the abstract world of information technology. Pattern recognition replaces reliance on simple visual modelling. The pervasive element of uncertainty introduced into all human endeavours as a metaphysical negative, inherited from particle physics, together with overload conditions, has eliminated the omniscient expert. If we try to account for many things happening at the same time, we are forced to consider vastly more complex and dynamic patterns of awareness.

Computers ideally only simulate our rational, conscious side. The trouble is that the computer functions as a linear, logical, one-dimensional processor of information, and does not have the ability to represent the metaphoric ambiguities implicit in the unreconciled opposites of human imagination. The computer is a technological answer to the need for a tool to facilitate the reconciliation of the opposites of the specialist and generalist world views. The one-at-a-timeness of computer functioning, even at electric speed, is not structurally capable of simulating the all-at-onceness of human perception. Computer education is, then, training in how to inhibit the wholeness of human vision.

> Inhibition biases the complementary relations between tacit, whole experience and the explicit projections based on it.

Most electric media are structurally doomed to gravitate to the simplistic. Still, art is not impossible when the commercial constraints are removed — from film, for example. In the meantime, media reinforce the inhibitive habits implicit in the particular way that each presents reality to our senses. Simple-minded has a new meaning.

A severely inhibited personality, like the ones on the Christian right who fear dancing, may have a dangerously simplified system of mental organization, one that rejects new material as inadmissible and relegates it to a preconscious limbo where its negative effects grow. Such individuals are likely to be biased toward the "grammar" of one medium. The new illiterate is the person conversant with only electric media. Print is still the main media that promotes intellectual growth.

Any system, including the human one, when pressed to the limit of its capability, flips into its opposite. Mental breakdown is pandemic among us. Everywhere electric process has been introduced, people cease functioning and psychotherapy flourishes. Just as we once emulated machines, now we assimilate the characteristics of electronic devices. One's awareness of the speeded up transience of life takes hold when, trying to appear up to date with a teenage child, she looks at you and says, "Oh, that's so five minutes ago."

Radio Telephone: Lowering the Definition for the Inhibited

In 1922, before business had figured out how to commercialize radio, more than seventy colleges and universities had gone on-air with adult education classes that could be taken by radio for credit. Churches were also using radio to look for proselytes. Before long, the radio spectrum (from 540 to 1600 KHz) was stimulating excited listeners with strong inner imaging. The effect of radio was actually visual. Radio stimulated inner imaging through the rich acoustic detail supplied by the genius of the early sound men. Later, radio devolved under pressure from television to become merely an extension of the record industry. All elaborate show production ceased. The sound man packed up his equipment and stole silently away to the foley studios of Hollywood, where simulated track sound was a booming business and still is. The radio audience dwindled severely. If it had not been for the automobile, one wonders if radio would have survived at all.

Radio broadcasting began as an AT&T experiment in what they called "radio telephone." On February 11, 1922, AT&T put their radio telephone equipment at the public's disposal in New York on a pay-for-air-time basis. The first radio broadcast facility was set up in a narrow studio somewhat like a telephone booth.

The two media have come together again, though in a somewhat different way, in talk radio — an attempt to secure involved audiences.[64] Radio is a high-definition medium, full of information and tightly ordered to allow for intense reception, but excluding listener involvement. (The higher the organization of a system, the less opportunity for involvement by the user.) Phone-in television is low definition and highly successful in securing from the viewer an in-depth sensory involvement. In bringing the telephone to the aid of the radio, the definition of radio has been proportionately lowered so that it can compete with television, and involvement has stepped up considerably. The co-production that results from shows that have high viewer participation requires only low-order organization. In this way, phone-in radio becomes a fairly low-definition medium that powerfully involves the listener. The best radio today recognizes that the best programming transcends programming. Radio has become free-form and alive, and is far less scripted, closed, and one-way.

Everyone's opinion is solicited, though the announcers and interviewers, trained in good radio technique, die a thousand deaths when some fogey phones in hemming and hawing haltingly with inarticulate opinions. In fact, the new low-definition format is outdrawing all other forms of radio. The most popular programming is the garden show — people nattering about their mulching and misting, their spading and spraying. The future of radio lies increasingly in its ability to involve the audience imaginatively in the auditory stimulation of the human voice. Radio telephone is a new medium designed to dis-inhibit a somewhat depersonalized audience. This kind of radio is extremely popular because it makes a co-star of every listener. The radio telephone format emphasizes a complementarity of local interests and global involvement.

Talk shows and phone-ins of every kind abound, and the telephone, the lowest of the low-definition media, slows the pace of programs almost to the natural levels of face-to-face conversation. The advanced technical achievement of producing very high-definition sound is now reversed, and the crackle and sputter of low-fi voices enters the radio network from noisy phone lines jammed with eager, amateur contributors. But, overall, one gets the impression that the people are not as stupid as the broadcasters have taken them to be.

> As Marshall McLuhan would have it, the old hot radio has been cooled off by its marriage to the telephone.

The endlessly varying inputs of public opinion take the hard edge off the old closed system, and the radio becomes a central clearing-house of social attitudes. This material is often in striking contrast to what one finds reported by newspaper, even though the patterns of opinion in radio are not the product of scientific sampling or editorial supervision. Television cannot compete with this entertaining format, though it tries.

With television, one simply registers a response bred by consumer habit. A new, large audience has shifted to radio. What is this audience getting? A forum for venting their preconscious rage, while disclosing the structure of their conscious inhibitions.

Flip: Ultra-Paradoxical Response

> Any system pushed to the limits of its capability reverses into its opposite.

If a third party enters a bedroom where a man and woman are having sex, the love-making is certain to immediately reverse into histrionic attempts to recover composure. Pavlov, in his attempts to condition animals to produce predictable, automatic responses to controlled stimuli, discovered a completely unpredictable reaction in some few animals, which he called ultra-paradoxical response (UPR). UPR is the unexpected, instant reversal of the conditioned response. With an unexpected intrusion into the conditioning situation in the laboratory, the effects of positive response to conditioning can instantly flip into inhibition. The dog behaves opposite to its conditioning.[65] McLuhan has developed this idea in his *Laws of Media*,[66] whereby a system pushed to its limit reverses itself.

In Pavlov's case, the force that gives rise to the flip cannot be understood in terms of physiology alone; it is an anomalous, total reversal of the unit of conditioning against all theoretical expectations. The animal's saliva glands instantly dry up when the salivation stimulus bell is rung. Clearly, this rare but significant situation in animal conditioning can bear several interpretations, but is very like certain radical reversals in human personality.

When Saul suffers his epiphany on the road to Damascus and flips into Paul — an instant change from zealous persecutor to ardent Christian disciple — do we have a historically important instance of UPR? St. Augustine experienced what he called an "ontological illumination" and, with this flash of insight, flipped from hedonist sinner into self-abnegating saint. Or so the mythology surrounding his conversion and his *Confessions* suggests. St. Francis of Assisi underwent an instant reversal of identity as well.

History is well supplied with anecdotal evidence of this strange phenomenon. Reformed alcoholics and junkies appear to meet such a moment before becoming crusaders against their former vice. Fortunately, one is not required to believe that there is a causal link between the laboratory dogs of Pavlov and the many great personages exhibiting the human equivalent of UPR.

Contemporary culture is not immune to the effects of UPR, though there appears to be no credible explanation of the process. The source of the power of reversal can be detected in the myths that we are living, many of which are apocalyptic in nature. We live in resonant expectation of visits from UFOs — lights of revelation in the sky, technology flipped into mystery. California rumbles every day underfoot with vibrations of apocalypse; the inhibited fear of catastrophe lies like a geological fault, under mind. For the rest of us, nuclear physics bequeaths a nightmare that threatens us even in its "peaceful" applications.

On a homelier level, the spectacle of television evangelism indicates that masses of people undergo UPR experience. Like dime-store Pauls, they are converted overnight from minions of the Prince of Darkness into militant Christian fundamentalists. The overall unity of their vision of life has been reversed, flipped into an entirely different, other self.

What is this remarkable mental process? UPR is now a less rare and isolated phenomenon. Its frequency of occurrence has grown exponentially along with electric process. This splitting of the psyche into positive and negative components is a typical tactic of advertising.

The central effect of electric process on the psyche is the formation of a complementary relationship between projection and inhibition. Everything in the psyche is rooted in its complement, its mutually exclusive flip side. Just as there can be no thought of light without considering both its wave and particle properties, which are non-causally linked, so with good and evil, and the integration of the left and right hemispheres of the brain. An electron with a reverse spin is a positron. If these complementary parts meet, they self-destruct. Our lives are lived in relation to a precarious balance of complements, unrelated except as potentially annihilating psychic opposites seeking reconciliation.

Ancient humans — those who inhabited the upper paleolithic caves of southern France and northern Spain — had kinship systems, a family ethos, religion, and, in many cases, remarkable technologies. Their world view was exceptionally narrow, although their knowledge of the heavens may have been fairly elaborate, as well as their understanding of other crucial environmental relationships, like their sense of weather dynamics. These forebears were vulnerable to a nature "red in tooth and claw" and were too busy surviving to invent a culture monumental with awareness. In its most rudimentary form, the history of humankind is one of a growing awareness of the unity, in spite of the differences, of all humanity.

> Teilhard de Chardin put modern man in his place by observing that there is no essential difference between upper paleolithic man and us except in terms of the evolution of awareness.[67]

It is paradoxical, then, that we have come to a point in time in the evolution of culture when awareness, our main psychological advantage in the evolutionary plan, is being reversed by the inhibitive effects of electric process. All indications of this change point to masses of people overwhelmed by the complexity of their environments. We have a generalized need to desensitize ourselves to protect against being blown out like small amp fuses in a heavily overloaded circuit.

We live at a time when every moment is new. Tradition goes out with the rest of our trash. We are completely vulnerable to change and helpless against the new; history is such a specious and narrow category of information that we have no time or use for it, requiring as it does exponential efforts of revision on a massive scale for more holistic meaning. Our sensitivity to the inverted pyramid of history as a useful form is severely dulled.

> If electric process pushes civilized forms to the limit of their capability to function, are we approaching a cultural flip point?

Improvement in the human condition has been our struggle for the last century; this motive has surfaced to be formalized as liberal social science. We invent strategies that purport to be capable of bringing about Utopia — artificial intelligence, for example — but, in reality, we have reached a point in post-history where, because of the speeding-up of human systems by electric process, we ironically find ourselves overwhelmed by the pressure on ordinary intelligence. The past is expanding at a greater rate than our powers of interpretation and assimilation. Will we acquiesce to having electric devices do everything for us? The quality of individual life is falling off, buried under the overload of new knowledge and the implicit stresses in trying to live life in a narrative way. Life is no longer a story; it is a spiritual morph of accelerated decline.

For many, it seems that no alternative remains but to turn inward and disconnect from the random stimuli of a mindless environment that has flipped increasingly into informational conflict. The most effective strategy for evading electric hyper-activity is desensitization, the dulling of the senses that reverses the evolutionary agenda of expanding awareness.

The Hamlet Complex

It is not possible to live and progress without risking action on partially specious perceptions. The question is how to recognize that point in thought when the minimally correct inference legitimizes action. Consider the story of Hamlet as a parable of inhibition.

> One must inhibit thought at some point in order to act.

The spectre-haunted prince desensitizes himself from the intolerable implications of "correct" action to avenge his father's murder by putting on an "antic disposition." Although he doesn't act to attain revenge, he does see the problem correctly "disposed" into its proper structural parts. *Dispositio* is the second step of five for the construction and delivery of a rhetorical argument: (1) *Inventio*, (2) *Dispositio*, (3) *Eloquentia*, (4) *Memoria*, and (5) *Actio*. Hamlet is full of rhetorical references — and for good reason.

The prince has recently returned to Denmark from Wittenberg, Luther's city and the centre of Protestantism since 1517. The University of Wittenberg was the seat of the anti-Aristotelian skepticism and new dialectic of Peter Ramus, which he devised to defeat the "ancients," grammarians steeped in etymology and paradox as the inviolable fundament of thought.

Partly, Hamlet's inability to act can be seen on the grand scale of this clash between the old and the new forms of communication. Hamlet has been thoroughly schooled in rhetoric. Unfortunately, he is an unreconstructed grammarian trapped in a new paradigm designed to make the world safe for Protestantism and the new science, a mindset that could tolerate no paradox. Hamlet, unfortunately, is paradox personified.

His completely paradoxical situation drives Hamlet to contemplate suicide. He couches his thoughts rhetorically: "To be or not to be, that is the question." This topic, which dominates the play, is the first rhetorical step, *Inventio*; the subject matter for rhetorical treatment is discovered by an ingenuity that will attract the attention of, and give pleasure to, an audience. In this case, as so often throughout the play, Hamlet is his own audience. The play is built up around the tensions of action and inhibition — Hamlet's ability to act only in acting, to dramatically rehearse his duty of avenging the dead. As soon as a plan of action is formulated, the argument against it is born.

The eloquence of Hamlet is unassailable; he chooses a blinding array of techniques for framing every possible insight into his dilemma. On the one hand, for example, he compares himself to Hercules, whose labours epitomize action on the grandest scale; on the other, he tries on the persona of Pyrrhus, whose victory at Tarentum against the Romans was as costly as a defeat — a parable of the futility of action. Hamlet sees action always as a misconceived adventure, doomed to produce dire effects. The fact that he is uninhibited in this regard makes him seem crazy.

In the scene with Yorick's skull, *Memoria* dominates rhetorically in Hamlet's harkening back to former happy times. The rhetorician makes use of the faculty of memory in order to engage the nostalgic sympathy of the audience. In this case, Hamlet's memories only serve to intensify his present dilemma. Being so irredeemably split into opposites, he is indeed his own best audience. Being so massively inhibited, his inner turmoil is intensified by his inability to project.

Action, Hamlet sees, makes him a machine, depersonalizes him, and, in pursuit of the expected strategies of a traditional revenge, sets him going through the motions of sweeping his palace clean. *Actio*, the delivery of a rhetorical performance, is directed toward getting the audience to react. The pun here suggests that the act of speaking well to the audience produces the audience action of dis-inhibition. Catharsis can be seen as a tapping off of preconscious tensions. Hamlet, acting as obsolescent rhetorician, is a caution to the new skeptics who are giving birth to the formally inhibited, logical positivist mentality.

Inhibited from saying what he must to the usurping king, Hamlet, as we know, has a company of players come to the palace. He expects to instruct them in acting out; that is, to project the truth in the form of a play. (Interestingly, the palace courtier, Rosencrantz, explains how it is that the company is available for this performance at the palace by using the term inhibition in a punning manner: "I think their inhibition comes by means of the late innovation." This is a reference to the riots between the London children's companies that led to a prohibition against their playing until things had cooled down between the rivals.) The players will not be inhibited, Hamlet insists, this time in the other sense of the word. This is what makes them valuable to the inhibited Hamlet, who, ironically, cannot take any action except acting itself, creating a performance in which everything that is being suppressed by the audience within the play is brought to their attention through the manipulations of a paradox.

At the root of the Hamlet Complex lies the profound uncertainty of having a basis for action. The contemporary world, dominated by the formal uncertainty[68] that has permeated every stratum of social awareness, is living amid the mechanistic and logical rubble of the old dogmatism, inherited from the nineteenth-century scientific paradigm. In a world made too complex for easy understanding of what to do even in the most crucial situations, we become accustomed to inhibiting information and deprive ourselves of any basis for action.

Hamlet, obsessed with uncertainty of action, increasingly becomes the ghost of his father's ghost; he fades away further and further from reality until he slips into madness. He and his players are an army in the belly of a play that is a wooden horse — one that never exits to do real battle. Hamlet is inhibited by too much ambivalent and paradoxical information. As a rhetorician, he sees both sides of every question and lacks the pragmatic spirit of the new Protestant scientist who finds it easy to act ideologically, even on specious grounds. Hamlet's sense of language, his deep-dyed taint of grammarian bias, does him in.

Shakespeare's Hamlet, as a study in inhibition, is one of the most exacting of Shakespearean roles, requiring the lead to brilliantly act out the inability of a man to come to action. The audience must suppress awareness of this paradox in order to experience the play as a play. As soon as one perceives this two-level aspect of the play, one is no longer a member of the play's audience, but is instead a disinterested bystander who has stepped out of the play's magic circle of credibility, who partakes of the benefits of the dis-inhibiting effects of the play at a higher level of critical insight.

Certainly, Shakespeare desires some awareness of the play's split vision as a contrivance to show off his structural prowess as a playwright and his knowledge of the psyche. In the "play-within-a-play" sequence, Shakespeare incorporates the paradoxical device of actors becoming actors internal to the play, which gives the play a Pirandello-like insight into the illusory aspect of realism. This device invites the audience to expand their awareness of the play as play. Hamlet becomes an exercise in selective levels of inhibition, with Shakespeare manipulating figures and grounds.

The Hamlet Complex implies that we live in a post-modern world in which most of our business goes on automatically. Our ability to act within the systems that move our world is severely limited. Existential questions like "What can be done?" and "Did something happen?" are questions appropriate to the inhibited frame of mind. Not knowing what to do forces each of us to retreat and stay out of the workings of systems. Our inhibition seems justified philosophically. Action requires more naivety.

In the contemporary context, the practice of self-inhibition, which results directly from the effects of electric process and overload conditions, makes Hamlets of us all.

The Preconscious

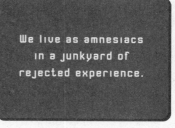

We live as amnesiacs
in a junkyard of
rejected experience.

BELIEF IN THE EXISTENCE of a preconscious dimension of mind predates modern psychology. Schelling, in *Philosophie der Mythologie*, regards the preconscious as the "creative source."[1] Fichte, the apostle of the ego, in his *Psychologie*, regards the preconscious region of mind as the birthplace of dream contents, an equally intriguing pre-Freudian supposition.[2] A half a century later, research on the preconscious appears to have been thwarted by Freud's approach. In "A Note on the Unconscious in Psychoanalysis," Freud presents a context for the preconscious:

> We learn therefore by the analysis of neurotic phenomena that a latent or unconscious idea is not necessarily a weak one. We feel justified in making our classification agree with this addition to our knowledge by introducing a fundamental distinction between different kinds of latent or unconscious ideas. We were accustomed to think that every latent idea was so because it was weak and that it grew conscious as soon as it became strong. We have now gained the conviction that there are some latent ideas which do not penetrate into consciousness, however strong they may have become.

Therefore we may call the latent ideas of the first type *preconscious* while we reserve the term *unconscious* (proper) for the latter type.[3]

It is asserted in the same essay that consciousness sets up a "repulsion" and "resistance" to penetration by unconscious forces, which is not posed against the entry of preconscious forces. But Freud's bias was to assign relatively small importance to research into preconsciousness, and to concentrate his attention on the much more intractable area of unconscious mental activity.

Freud, ever technical and mechanistic in modelling his ideas, draws on the new medium of photography for an analogy to mark the unconscious/preconscious distinction. His analogy suggests that the preconscious materials have a different kind of negativity, so that they can easily be made "positive" by conscious action and selected for entry into daylight as full-fledged ideas.

> The distinction between preconscious and unconscious activity is not a primary one, but comes to be established after repulsion has sprung up. Only then the difference between preconscious ideas, which can appear in consciousness and reappear at any moment, and unconscious ideas, which cannot do so, gains a theoretical as well as a practical value.
>
> A rough but not inadequate analogy to this supposed relation of conscious to unconscious activity might be drawn from the field of ordinary photography. The first stage of the photograph is the negative; every photographic picture has to pass through the negative process and some of these negatives which have held good in examination are admitted to the positive process ending in the picture.[4]

Interestingly, having established the metaphor of the photographic negative, Freud apparently misses the telling pun — he doesn't say anything about the tendency of preconscious materials for subversive reversal. This is not part of his conception of preconscious function. One is also left to wonder what Freud means by a "primary" distinction, given the extremely significant difference in power that he marks between strong unconscious upheavals and weak preconscious disturbances. Clearly, in our times, the power of the preconscious cannot be described as weak.

The psychic force of a domain of mind that is exponentially larger than in recent pre-electric generations is very powerful. Every year, more and more people approach the psychic breaking point, and many go beyond.

In his 1915 paper "The Unconscious," Freud describes the position of the preconscious as standing between the conscious and unconscious. But he devotes relatively little attention to this area of mind in the years to come. (Even today, it is not easy to find psychologists writing in scholarly journals who are interested in the preconscious.)

> A mental act commonly goes through two phases, between which is interposed a kind of testing process (censorship). In the first phase the mental act is unconscious and belongs to the system Ucs [unconsciousness]; if upon the scrutiny of the censorship it is rejected, it is not allowed to pass into the second phase; it is then said to be 'repressed' and must remain unconscious. If, however, it passes this scrutiny, it enters upon the second phase and therefore belongs to the second system, which we will call the Cs [consciousness]. But the fact that it so belongs does not unequivocally determine its relation to consciousness. It is not yet conscious, but it is certainly *capable of entering consciousness* . . . that is, it can now, without any special resistance and given certain conditions, become the object of consciousness. In consideration of this capacity to become conscious we also call the system the *'preconscious'* [Pcs].[5]

Consciousness is awareness, the unconscious its antithesis. Consciousness is also linguistic and semantic, making meaning out of the polymorphous flux of tacit experience. The unconscious appears to be completely sub-linguistic, expressing itself in the complex garble of dream images and archetypal forces that defy clear ideational formation.

The ambiguities of visual imagery affect the mind below the limen of consciousness. Articulated sound, as in music — for example, mindless humming — seems centred in the preconscious area. It is sub-syntactic but tends powerfully

Preliterates do not "see" their words as things as literates do. They share the many acoustic states of story and the effects evoked by the words. This is a world similar to ours, which is dominated with slogans, ad copy, and acronyms floating about in the resonance chamber of electric process.

toward meaning like a buried, half-forgotten lyric. The meaning of music, in terms of the tone and tendency of feelings, is accessible by conscious efforts. But the conscious mind always has more than a little difficulty in assigning meaning to even the simplest image, because no image is only itself or experienced in isolation; it is always something else as well.

Consciousness tends to want to confine images to single meaning, to denature them of their resonances. The dynamic and arrhythmic movement of the preconscious defies this orderly agenda. The deep, inarticulate forces of the unconscious can express a revolutionary shape through the agency of the dream, but this is by no means the only dynamic of the preconscious. Mainly, the preconscious is the domain of mind immediately involved with environmental forces. Significantly, both poetry and music are most capable of pulling all three dimensions of mind (conscious, preconscious, and unconscious) together in active interplay. Other media can do this to lesser degrees. Visconti's *Death in Venice* and Fellini's *La Strada*, do so quite evocatively, since both films simulate the poetic and the musical authentically.

Certain images connect us to the dynamic forces of the unconscious, particularly dream images. Words demand order and clarity. The balance between these two is struck best in the poetic form. Prose favours consciousness in a way that generally doesn't disturb unconscious forces. Great poetry cuts deepest of all language into the dark valley of the unknown self. Music is the medium through which all this works best.

The preconscious seems linguistic only to a primitive degree. An idea, having been rejected by consciousness, must be deconstructed in order to demote it to its place out of awareness. Preconscious materials may lack syntactic order and stylistic construction, but since they can gel into an idea and snap up into consciousness momentarily, they must exist in some primitive linguistic form — likely as paratactic fragments and phrases, a conjunctional stream of consciousness better called in this case a stream of preconsciousness. Writers like Joyce, Beckett, Pynchon, Rushdie, and DeLillo know this and exploit it.

The preconscious material is also imagistic; in a rejected and uninterpreted mass of inhibited material, ideas are inextricably linked to images. The preconscious is the balancing point between the two other dimensions of mind, a storehouse of images and language fragments that can, like art itself, suddenly gel into a structure for conscious acceptance — though this is, again like art, threatening to the mind's established conscious unity. The projections of the preconscious become a cultural retrieval exercise of considerable complexity.

Our reactions to ideas that seem genuinely new is fairly predictable. Humboldt got it right when he observed that "[f]irst people will deny a thing; then they will belittle it; then they will decide that it had been known long ago."[6] The denial phase is the rejection action of conscious rigidity; the belittling suggests that the material doesn't have the stature or structure of respectable things or ideas; and the appeal to antiquity ("there is nothing new under the sun") denotes the dim suspicion that the material comes from somewhere else in the mind, perhaps travelling through the collective unconscious.

That new assaults on the structure of consciousness — think of Picasso, Klee, Kandinsky, or Pollack — finally receive strong acceptance as cultural masterworks suggests that we are sharing in this artwork not the unknown isolated contents of the individual unconscious of the artist, but the preconscious similarities of environmentally shared experience. What is "blowing in the wind," is something that we share or fear together. Communally shared perception must previously have had an environmental form that was part of general experience. Thus "the Age demands" through its environmental influences.

> People's fears of the new probably arise from the slag heap of the preconscious, where they dimly recognize similar rejected materials in their own minds that impinge like taboos on consciousness.

Considering the metaphor of a tripartite division of mind (for example, Freud's id, ego and superego; Plato's three-part soul that comprises the rational, spirited, and id-like acquisitive element; or the recent model of two hemispheres joined by the corpus callosum), it is useful to see the unconscious as *sub-linguistic/imagistic*, the conscious mind as *syntactic/semantic*, and the preconscious as the *mediator* between these dimensions. The preconscious is an area that deals in minima: visual cartoons and preverbal stutter. The primitive condition of information in the preconscious makes it ripe for primitive, subliminal appeals.

The Subliminal Self: "Crystal Vision"

William James was a faithful member and former president of the Society for Psychical Research, which was founded in 1882 by a number of fairly hard-headed investigators of the paranormal. Their interests ranged from hypnosis, clairvoyance, and stigmatism to spiritualism, haunted houses, and automatic writing. Their initial objective was to bridge the gap between the insensitive skepticism of the scientific establishment and the pandemic credulity of ordinary mortals in such matters. *The Proceedings*, or publications, of the society still make interesting reading. One intriguing psychical peculiarity for James was the phenomenon he called "Crystal Vision."

> One of the most important experimental contributions to the Proceedings is the article of Miss X. on 'Crystal Vision'. Many persons who look fixedly into a crystal or other vaguely luminous surface fall into a kind of daze, and see visions. Miss X. had this susceptibility in a remarkable degree, and is, moreover, an unusually intelligent critic. She reports many visions which can only be described as apparently clairvoyant, and others which beautifully fill a vacant niche in our knowledge of subconscious mental operations.[7]

The use of the word "subconscious" here is telling. Freud's battle to gain control of the terminology of psychoanalysis required his rejection of terms already in use. In the famous 1915–17 introductory lectures on psychoanalysis, he is specifically authoritarian in attempting to rid his discipline of the possible mystical connotations associated with the term "subconscious" because of the Psychical Research Group.

> I should also like to hear you admit that our designations, unconscious, preconscious, and conscious, are less prejudicial and more easily defensible than some others which have been suggested or have come into use, e.g., sub-conscious, inter-conscious, co-conscious, etc.[8]

However, the strange case of Miss X., the crystal gazer, is interpreted by James in a way that gives his term "subconscious" the meaning of "preconscious." James cites an example of the habitual subconscious operations of Miss X.'s mind and offers an explanation of the process that shows it to be definitively preconscious action.

> Looking into the crystal before breakfast one morning she reads
> in printed characters of the death of a lady of her acquaintance, the
> date and other circumstances all duly appearing in type. Startled by
> this she looks at the *Times* of the previous day for verification, and
> there among the deaths are the identical words which she has seen.[9]

To his credit, James persists in seeking a reasonable explanation for this episode, though he confesses abiding respect for the mystical. Almost everyone harbours similar stories, which seem to defy rational explanation. In this case, the crystal reading is brilliantly accounted for on a psychic level much humbler than the mystical. It is found, upon further investigation, that

> on the same page of the *Times* are other items which she remembers
> reading the day before; and the only explanation seems to be that
> her eyes then inattentively observed, so to speak, the death-item,
> which forthwith fell into a special corner of her memory, and came
> out as a visual hallucination when the peculiar modification of
> consciousness induced by the crystal gazing, set in.[10]

Using the metaphor of light, James divides the mind into three. By analogy, the ultraviolet represents the unconscious and the infrared is the preconscious; consciousness itself is likened to the visible portion of the spectrum. The deep purple that shrouds the icons of the unconscious is impenetrable and powerfully retentive, giving up only impressionistic hints of its savage, polymorphously perverse condition in the form of heated dreams. The infrared, brightening night into roseate day, produces images like those seen through the scope of a sniper's rifle, where the reality of day tucked away and ignored in reduced light is made visible with a little technical effort.

The question remains: Do we take in and process all the information of general experience? Is most of the material not pertinent to our immediate point of interest disposed of subliminally by being retained out of awareness somewhere below consciousness, as the work of

Wilder Penfield and his followers at the Montreal Neurological Institute strongly suggests? It is more than possible that *traces* of all sensory experience received by an individual are retained, and that these traces reside in the preconscious. Otherwise, how would these fragments randomly drift up into consciousness from time to time?

The Subliminal Self: A Graphic Illustration

Pushing his strong scientific bent to the limit — including experiments on himself with psychotropic chemicals — William James came to believe that everyday science is always trapped in defending an obsolescent mode of thought.

Too many scientists forget that the paradigms within which they work are the result of acts of imaginative revolution that overturned an older scientific vision. That old vision held precursors as slavishly in thrall as they themselves are to their established interpretation of reality. They know this, yet, because of funding specificity and other commitments, can't easily make it meaningful without risking their material well-being.

> In psychology, physiology and medicine, wherever a debate between the mystics and the scientifics has been once and for all decided, it is the mystics who have usually proved to be right about the facts, while the scientifics have the better of it in respect to the theories.[11]

James further cites the interesting case of "animal magnetism," which led, over violent objections in medical science, to the final acceptance of hypnotism as a therapeutic practice. Hypnotism, coming down from Mesmer through Braid, came into general practice — Freud used it to some extent — and proved a considerable benefit for certain psychological disorders, though it didn't prove to be the panacea its originators had hoped. The importance of hypnotism lies elsewhere. Curiosity about this phenomenon sparked a more general interest in the dimension of mind that was articulated by hypnotic trance. Carl Jung conducted investigations that revealed a subliminal self below the threshold of consciousness.[12]

The English term "subliminal" was coined to represent Herbart's *unter der scwelle sc. des Bewusstseins* ("under the threshold of consciousness"). This mental state remains a psychological enigma to this day.

James collected accounts of unusual experiences for the Psychical Research Group, which finally altered his sense of science by focusing him on the out-of-awareness aspects of science. Calling normal science "shallow," he admits to having made his own "*salto mortale*," or leap up to a higher realm of understanding, through his own validating experiences with the supra-ordinary.

> The preconscious and the subliminal are almost exactly the same, overlapping significantly, and that dimension of mind has greatly increased in relative importance to consciousness.

I have myself, as American agent for the census (SPR) collected hundreds of cases of hallucination in healthy persons. The result is to make me feel that we all have potentially a 'subliminal' self which may make at any time irruption into our ordinary lives. At its lowest, it is only the depository of our forgotten memories; at its highest, we do not know what it is at all.[13]

James, noting how these "irruptions" seem to evade the authority of conscious organization, describes the extraordinary but fairly common-place experiences as "capricious, discontinuous, and not easily controlled."[14] One might assume, after all this time and countless studies, that the confusion James confesses to has been cleared up. That is not the case. Psychology still maintains a fairly shallow view of this determinative function of mind. "Yes, yes, the preconscious, the sublim-inal, we know all about that; they're mainly fictions from the old psychology" — so the general spirit of inquiry goes today.

The contemporary use of the word "subliminal" is almost exclu-sively reserved for reference to the effects of advertising in influencing behaviour toward specific consumption patterns. In the present situa-tion in North America, only fools would believe that they are not significantly affected by the efforts of motivational research in Madison Avenue firms. (I do not think it necessary to argue that case here.)

In discussing the effects of advertising and what he calls the "Graphic Revolution," Daniel Boorstin discovers the central paradox of the cultural shift from the "Ideal" to the "Image" through the creation of pseudo-events. Instead of trying to find the "truth," as a habit of mind, we have become conditioned to respond to mere "credibility," since a logical argument for any position can be maintained by manipulating the facts.

One explanation of increasing American interest in credibility is a simple paradox of the Graphic Revolution. While that Revolution has multiplied and vivified our images of the world, it has by no means generally sharpened or clarified the visible outlines of the world which fill our experience. Quite the contrary . . . *By sharpening our images, we have blurred all our experience*. The new images have blurred traditional distinctions.[15] (Emphasis added)

This blurring effect is the result of inhibition in the face of information overload. Can a photographic image be more than just a sign? A symbol? Only in rare cases does a photo have an interpretive context on a large enough scale to be culturally significant. The infinite repeatability of the photograph takes away the special characteristic of the human product as a unique occurrence. True, some photos tend to beg this distinction, but, in general, photos are usually confined in meaning to subjective projections of the subliminal.

Symbols have meaning in tradition, but signs must constantly be interpreted in the light of a swiftly changing environment. A certain bewilderment always exists between symbols and signs. Boorstin thinks that we enjoy this condition of impressionistic relations with our images: "The consumer cannot be wholly satisfied, then, unless he is partly bewildered."[16] So, one learns to cherish the rich fragmentary incoherence of preconscious contents and their liberating lack of integrated structure.

Advertising is, of course, our most popular reading, listening and watching matter, precisely because it transports us to where the rigidities of the real world have dissolved. As we stroll through the world of advertising, the half-intelligibility of what we see and read and hear encourages us to hope that our extravagant expectations may be coming true.[17]

Advertising is already in preconscious form. Full of verbal and visual ambiguities, advertising diddles with credibility and blinds us to truer contexts for judgement and action. In this world, the appropriate action is simply to buy. Impressions are presented through advertising that are not fully formed ideas. It is a world of garbled ideas. Advertising can be taken into the preconscious without affecting conscious screening at all.

Advertising, for all its entertainment value, is mainly the pseudo-ideational, pseudo-symbolic presentation of pseudo-events.

For a hundred years or more, the subliminal has been noticed as qualitatively different in its operations from the unconscious, yet little has been done to investigate this fundamental difference in processing information. In 1892, Meyers remarked in the February *Proceedings of the Psychical Research Group*: "The sub-

> Given the subliminal appeals in the structure of advertising, it is difficult to inhibit its intake. We are all swollen to bursting with the glut of it.

liminal memory includes an unknown category of impressions which the supraliminal consciousness . . . must recognize, if at all, in the shape of messages from the subliminal consciousness." Meyers conceived of the subliminal as closer to consciousness than to the unconscious. In fact, the subliminal is fundamentally different from the unconscious in its relations with consciousness. It is not merely a matter of a metaphor of distance. The subliminal is still accessible, its contents retrievable and under individual control. If this were true of the individual's relationship to the unconscious, we would need no psychiatrists.

Commenting further on the psychical researches of Frederic Myers, James refers to "what [Myers] calls 'the subliminal self' or what one might designate as ultra-marginal consciousness."[18] The difficulties in this area of psychology have persisted ever since, principally because we have never had a theory of inhibition. Inhibition establishes a fuller role for the preconscious as an anti-environmental defence system, which acts against the overwhelming inundation of information generated by electric media. It is difficult to study that which is difficult to notice by conscious technique. This difficulty has protected the subliminal realm of the preconscious mind from effective investigation.

From Recall to Recognition: The Preconscious and Subliminal.

When Wilson B. Key published *Subliminal Seduction*, he knew he would be hooted at by critics unaware of the embedding techniques used in some advertising to induce the seller to consume a particular product without actually knowing why. No one wants to admit that this is possible. Everyone manages to misunderstand what is meant by subliminal, a term which, for the purposes of this study, is coincident with the pre-conscious in its symplectic relationship with conscious awareness. The perceptual ambiguities of electric process mean that there is a sub-liminal dimension to everything, since everything is both itself and something else, especially when perceived by a different medium. The something else can be inserted below the level of consciousness to influence behaviour. Key outlined the following embedding technique.

> A photographer takes a photograph of a model and props. They
> are photographed at say at 1/150th of a second. A double exposure
> can be made at 1/1000th of a second in which only the word SEX
> is photographed as a faint impression across some portion of the
> original picture.[19]

The eye is drawn to the word "sex" as to nothing else. If you doubt this tendency of the eye, pick up a thick magazine and rifle through the pages quickly. Chances are that you will find in microseconds much of the salacious material it contains. Key baited his readers by pointing out about halfway through the book that his photograph on the dust cover was taken against a draped background on which he had embedded several SEXes. Humorously, Key mused that it would be interesting to know how many people purchased the book only because of such witty subliminal inducement. But seriously, it is important to know that such techniques work precisely because we don't notice them.

In *The Interpretation of Dreams*[20] (1900), Freud spoke of the mind's capacity for "repudiation." Establishing his firm belief that it is impos-sible for the individual to retrieve unconscious materials directly, he then asserted that psychoanalytic treatment actually takes place at the juncture of the conscious and preconscious areas of mind. This is an important observation, because it suggests that the preconscious is the pivot for mental health. Freud dogmatically regarded the contents of the preconscious as refined and liberated unconscious material, a volatile top of the unconscious, like steam rising from a mental stew. It seems more certain now that a great deal of the material affecting mental health collects just below the limen, or threshold, in the precon-scious, or subliminal, area of the mind. It appears that the preconscious is the entry point for all human experience. These rejected fragments of overloaded and undifferentiated experience are admitted to the preconscious directly from the environment and contribute to the shift in cognitive bias from *recall* to *recognition*.

To put it succinctly, conscious memory recalls, and preconscious memory recognizes. Television trains us to be recognizers; our recall faculty diminishes if we don't attend to it with rational, literate activity. Recall is developed through redundancy, through some repetitive practice like school, learning to play the piano, or training to be proficient at a sport. Recognition allows only critical awareness and does nothing to train the body to give it embodied memory. Our uniquely individual embodied memories may be all we have left to counter the systematized sameness of information technologies.

A heavy diet of mediated information, untempered by actual experience, will create in the user a deep burden of unreality. We can see this in the sense of unreality experienced by film and television actors on their psychological rollercoasters of rejection and adulation.

> Media effects occur at the boundary of the conscious and preconscious states. This is the domain of "unreality" associated with the mythic, archetypal, parapsychological, dream-like, hypnogogic, cinematic, and subliminal. It is the edge of awareness.

Heavy media use tends to make us feel mentally and spiritually diminished; we become highly susceptible to the vague negativity of the contents of our preconscious minds. The key symptom of internalizing massive amounts of unreal perception is depersonalization. Depersonalized individuals often feel themselves to be unreal, mired in a conflicted state between feelings of closeness and alienation with respect to their surroundings. The unreality of a life lived before a video display terminal is likely to produce some fairly bizarre attempts to compensate for the profound deprivations of direct experience.

Television brings interesting twists to this psychological disorder. What happens when the ecological surround lacks the high-action excitement of a world that is increasingly interpreted by cinematic values? Theme parks?

Inadvertent murders can, and have, resulted from such lack of clarity regarding what is real and what is mediated. Mankiewicz and Swerdlow have recorded many surreal events involving children raised on television and film who find it difficult to distinguish accurately between

> Television presents fantasy in the guise of reality, but if TV is perceived as "real," it can produce strong depersonalization.

reality and its mediated version because they have always assimilated fragments of media fantasy into their actual lives. One pre-teen murdered the only loving, nurturing, grandmotherly figure in his life because, he said, she caught him taking cookies and suddenly it was like a TV show and he knew he had to kill her. This neglected child skipped school almost every day and watched TV all day and night long.

A general tendency has developed for the most fantastic propositions to be entertained as possible reality by the gullible millions. Thus national lotteries succeed. *The National Enquirer*, *The Star*, and similar organs, which exploit the mindlessness of sensation-seeking gossip geeks, spring up and prosper. There is no limit to the moronic revelations of these types of papers, and their circulations are tied to increasingly preposterous headlines. Television programming is informed by a similarly grotesque underestimation of the audience's intellectual and emotional maturity.

> Viewing television lowers the threshold of awareness, lowers the energy level of voluntary attention, and reduces the intensity of the cognitive functions. TV shortens the attention span of viewers, especially of children.

Norman Dixon, one of the foremost mind scientists to have studied the preconscious, has put forth a startling argument for the existence of two cognitive systems.[21] Dixon's idea relies on the early work of Otto Poetzl and associates, who succeeded in demonstrating how subliminal visual stimulation registers and is retrieved. Poetzl, examining soldiers with damaged visual centres, discovered that there are two independent modes of visual perception: one *central* and the other *peripheral*. Poetzl discovered that the brain processes centred visual stimuli and peripheral stimuli in a fundamentally different way. This produces two kinds of mental organization in, for instance, the act of reading: one is normal, rational reading and the other is reading according to what Poetzl calls "dream process."[22] (Freud, who knew and admired Poetzl's work, likely drew from it the conception of "Primary Process" and "Secondary Process" thinking.) A major discovery ensued from his investigations, which indicated that "processes which arise in peripheral vision are normally excluded from consciousness."[23] Poetzl was then astounded to find that the parts of perception left out of central vision showed up later in dreams and hallucinations, and clearly had originated in the periphery of the central stimulus. In another type of experiment that involved showing pictures to his patients in fractions of a second, Poetzl found the picture parts that were not picked up consciously were retained as subliminal perception.[24]

The centred stimuli of the *action* mode are processed "normally," while the material peripheral to central vision remains in a *passive* mode, that is, a somewhat involuntary or subliminal mode. Dixon adds to this intriguing work, concluding that we possess "sufficient neurophysiological devices to account for the phenomenon of subliminal processing."[25]

W.W. Meissner, in reviewing Dixon's work, remarks on his theory of a "layered mental apparatus with two distinctly different cognitive systems," which can account for the peculiar faculty of subliminal cognition.[26] One system operates with lower levels of stimulation. This system tends generally to be more strongly affected by emotional states.

> Thus if two stimuli are presented, one at a supraliminal and the other at a subliminal level, the subliminal stimulus is more likely to have identifiable effects at a preconscious level of processing if it is more removed from the supraliminal stimuli in its strength and is different in its content.[27]

The tone of this constant state of subliminal cognition is consistent with EEG measurements of the state of mind produced by television viewing. "This state of relaxed, nonfocused receptivity is strongly linked to the presence of alpha waves in the EEG."[28]

With extended viewing, the preconscious, subliminal capacity fills up stressfully with rejected fragments of overloaded information. What we can't handle, we trash — but unlike computers,

> TV induces the dominance of alpha and theta waves in the brain-wave mix, and alters attention levels downward. Television produces a state of mind that maximizes subliminal cognition.

we never empty the trash. Similar findings are presented by the Emerys, whose work has been discussed earlier in this book.[29] One of the primary effects of this *subliminal cognitive system* is the enhancement of symbolic connections and relationships. The scope of artistic perception has been enlarged by the turbulent growth of the preconscious inventory. This system feeds our more holistic and more sensitive psychological needs. One's subjective response to a piece of art is almost certainly elicited from preconscious material. This study has barely been touched.

The second system operates with higher and more selective thresholds and is connected with consciousness. It tends to deal with stimulus material in a much more secondary-process, matter-of-fact, logical manner, as opposed to the primary system which operates to a greater extent through displacement and symbolism.[30]

The higher cognitive functions are linked to meaning and structure, and pursue logical, rational goals. We do seem to be dual-minded. There is a classical, analytical, formal side to the mind, and an intuitive, romantic, synthetic sense as well.

Freud, as early as *The Project for a Scientific Psychology* (1895), had noticed what he called "a primary thought defence" by which consciousness withdraws its attention from disturbing preconscious contents. Most of the rejected perceptual junk from TV viewing coagulates as preconscious inventory. Because of its overstimulation by television, the preconscious has become engorged by informational overload. Television, however, diminishes voluntary attention, making us less able to suppress these fragments from rising into general awareness.

Students who can't read, who spend an inordinate amount of time in video arcades, who skip classes and go home to catch a favourite soap, who have sound-bite attention spans from their *Sesame Street* training, who live conversationally in a desultory fog of chatter and dim recognitions — often about the previous night's TV offerings — this is an electric generation tuned to its preconscious.

Complete involvement in any attentive projection obliterates self-consciousness. Writing in *The Psychoanalytic Quarterly*, Owen Renik, an unusually perceptive commentator on the operations of the preconscious, observed that "depersonalization represents a defensive manoeuvre invoked to deal with threatening Preconscious thoughts. These are prevented from becoming conscious by the restriction of attention."[31] He notes that "[i]n states of depersonalization, attention is not permitted to range freely over incoming perceptual information,"[32] which suggests that a depersonalized individual is also severely inhibited.

Citing Arlow, Renik believes that "the internal danger of depersonalization may be treated as congruent with the perceptions of the external world."[33] This can mean that internally the preconscious grows at a same rate as the external overload of information. This is a revolutionary change in the way we look at the structure of consciousness.

It indicates that much of the real pressure on our lives comes from the preconscious. And advertising, being the principal technique for activating preconscious response, becomes a dominant form of communication — not a light and frivolous gloss on consumer desires, but an index to the emergence of a new, complex psychic condition derived from the structure of electric process.

Television powerfully restricts attention, altering the state of the brain to create diminished activity in the areas of higher cognitive function, ideas and beliefs that create physical well-being and spiritual growth. Inveterate television viewing renders people completely malleable to consumer inducements. More importantly, it renders them highly susceptible to an assault from preconscious contents on conscious stability.

> Even when repression is relatively adequate, particular *external*
> *circumstances* corresponding too closely to an unconscious fantasy
> can lead to the existence of intolerable preconscious thoughts.[34]
> (Emphasis added)

Electric media represent just such "external circumstances" for fantastic or fearful recognitions. This is a crucial insight into the relationship between external triggers and threatening preconscious contents. Films, reality, personal fantasies, and preconscious debris can fuse into a neurotic, cross-feeding system of great mental complexity. We do not yet have a psychotherapeutic way to sort this out.

Depersonalization appears to intervene in order to make the psyche proof against being overwhelmed by fantasy contacts in the environment. In television, the rhythm of commercials with news and "drama" helps in this balancing.

In the TV-viewing situation, the depersonalization of the user is useful in order to avoid intrusions by consciousness while the medium does its preconscious selling job. *Alternation is the key characteristic of depersonalization.* The subject's sense of reality fluctuates between real and unreal because the sense of unreality belongs properly to the threshold, or boundary, between the con-

As Renik observes, "Episodes of depersonalization function to keep disturbing Preconscious thoughts from becoming conscious."[35] Again we survive by becoming slightly less human.

scious and preconscious, the border of consciousness where psychotherapy and television effects occur.

The fragmentary, discontinuous structure of advertising and the symbolic dynamics of the preconscious are parallel forms. This is the realm of "subception," to use Poetzl's term; it is the level of perceptual training, a sort of pre-meaning recognition, to which we now return as we lose our grip on memory as recall. We protect ourselves from the uncontrolled entry of negative preconscious materials into consciousness by investing attention in a preconscious fragment, which we admit safely into consciousness as a thought.

Television, however, presents a situation in which preconscious materials can be set loose by the technical action of the medium on brain function. In a lowered state of awareness, one dominated by low-speed brain waves, normal defences are down and the alert, attentive function is significantly diminished. TV is unsurpassed in its ability to pile up, below the limen, a "heap of broken images," which do their subliminal job while evading the transformative powers of conscious attention.

Renik draws attention to another important aspect of the preconscious that suggests it has a role in giving communicative potential to the needs arising from instinct.

> An instinctual urge gaining association with a perceptual residue
> — generally the memory of an auditory perception, that is, a word —
> becomes capable of being attended to, or preconscious.[36]

A fragmentary lover's voice, husky with passion, saying the lover's name, can be remembered forever at certain critical moments.

> Advertising, particularly television advertising, links up instinctual urgency with perceptual fragments from the endless flow of preconscious subception.

By enhancing our ability to recognize and call up preconscious image fragments, and by suppressing conscious recall of verbal meanings, advertising is continually developing its power to subliminally divert our attention to product consumption. In order to maintain some control over our conscious lives, we must practice achieving a high level of attention, continually. This is impossible while watching television. For too many people, time away from the tube is limbo.

These observations are not meant to be taken as a moralizing rant. This is a study of electric process and its radical reshaping of the human condition. To say that one learns about reality from watching TV is a profound misunderstanding of the medium's psychological effects. People always strongly point out some high-quality programming available on some elite channel. They fail to recognize that *watching* is not enough *doing* to internalize such material in any useful way.

Lucubrations and Lacunae of the Mind

Kant saw a problem resulting from the setting up of "schemas" — what we would probably call mindsets — which guarantee that we reject experience that does not fit in with the tight organization of consciousness. Contemporary investigators in the area of neurochemistry try to find scientific answers to the metaphysical question of diminished sensation. But life transcends physics and chemistry.

> The preconscious is a buffer zone between the deep mind and its conscious top. Investigation of this relationship has been neglected — and no wonder.

In this Age of Angst, it is commonly felt that fending off disturbing perceptions and wilfully skewing attention is simply a useful mental tactic for avoiding anxiety. "Turn off" (civilized values), "Turn on" (drugs), and "Tune out" (stop receiving from the massive overload of information) — these ideas were slogans of the sixties. That was a generation still able to understand the deprivations of being the first full-fledged television society. They knew something was missing, however vaguely: their human grounding in a real environment. Today we have normalized the damage. We adapt to the artificial very well. We call it virtuality and admire its effects on psyche and soul.

Somewhere between Irving Goffman's "frames," the shared definitions of situations that draw people into conscious patterns of organization, and Pierre Janet's concern about the deleterious effects of narrowing the field of consciousness (by media or any other means), we may find a place to stand under the heavens, where there appear to be no black holes in human awareness.

The missing insight in these inquiries is recognition of the role played by electric process and media in shaping our inhibitive responses to life. To secede from the real world and live as consuming automatons in a culture of avarice is an endgame strategy with no chance for victory.

Mindless, progressive consumption dooms us to the fate of Erisicthon, who offended mortally against Nature and was cursed by the kiss of Hag Famine to succumb to an escalating hunger. Ovid describes this burgeoning hunger of the cursed king in the *Metamorphoses*. The more he ate, the more intense the pain of hunger became. Finally, there was nothing left to consume but himself, and thus he perished by devouring his own limbs — a nice parable for our times.

No one wants to believe that things will get this dramatic, but don't expect sweetness and light to prevail easily. We have a dark valley to cross before we find a new high ground that affords the moral panorama this fragile culture requires.

Media: In The Foyer of Consciousness

> In our exposure to mass media, a large amount of information is taken in that never reaches consciousness.

A music video, like any advertisement on television, feeds directly into the right hemisphere. Most of these videos have little or no narrative continuity or logical structure but instead make connections with the viewer symbolically. This is a completely subliminal communication modality. As Norman Dixon says, "All in all, when considered in conjunction with evidence that the right hemisphere is responsible for primary process thinking . . . susceptibility to subliminal stimuli is more pronounced in people showing right hemisphericity."[37] Put bluntly, as the Emerys' studies clearly indicate, the more one watches television, the more susceptible one is to subliminal inducements to consume and to respond predictably to social and political suggestions. The new kind of media-savvy governments understand this and pour hundreds of millions into the obvious, if scandalous, guarantee of power. Too many of us have inhibited this immoral manipulation. Instead of trying to engage in political life, many simply stop voting.

Through the operations of inhibition, much of one's direct experience of socio-political ideas is demoted from consciousness. Preconscious fragments of speech and image, filtered out of awareness, are retained in a subliminal limbo below the threshold of consciousness. There is a jumble of data in there: commercial jingles, catchy phrases from old songs, traces of threatening memories, bits of retained biases, commingled sensory and cognitive fragments — odours of fear or colours of hope — as well as shards of past joys.

The preconscious material is rejected outright: it is threatening or distracting stuff that is not assimilable into the unitary structure of consciousness. It appears to be stored as a growing reserve of psychic energy, which tends to undermine the integrated organization of thought and perception that characterizes the personality of the individual. Whatever one wants to call this shallow pan of random dissociative data, it is a source of variegated incoherence — a potential but suppressed source of radical change in consciousness.

Freud, curiously, neglected the phenomenon of threshold awareness. He resolved the question of the environmental influence on the psyche through the concept of repression. This concept, however, is incompatible with the vague but accessible out-of-awareness status of threshold materials. The preconscious antechamber to consciousness, which Freud did posit, had no significant function in his psychology except as a vestibule for certain unconscious materials that, having risen from the depths, were about to enter consciousness. Yet he believed that psychotherapy takes place at this juncture of the conscious and preconscious. Given what we know about the effects of electronic media on recognition and recall (see, for example, the Columbia School of Broadcast Journalism studies),[38] it is clear that the experience of the TV viewer is, like psychoanalysis itself, taking place at the junction of the conscious and preconscious.

The dynamic of Freudian analysis is significantly altered when it is understood that inhibited materials enter the preconscious directly and influence consciousness without having been an integral part of the deeper unconscious contents of the psyche.

> Individuals can recall, under their own power, considerable amounts of rejected materials from the preconscious, or subliminal, dimension of the mind.

Perceptions that never registered on consciousness can be brought into consciousness quite easily. Hypnosis is one technique for demonstrating this possibility. Another is depth advertising, which employs motivational research insights. The subliminal threshold is crossed as the preconscious ground contextualizes conscious perception without one's awareness that this is happening.

Materials from the inaccessible deep well of the unconscious, according to Freud,[39] can only be brought up into awareness through extraordinary efforts, usually directed by a trained therapist. It seems likely that the unconscious affects conscious behaviour in a fundamental, structural way, whereas the preconscious supplies the program content along these formative unconscious lines.

When we filter out information in the ordinary processes of perception, this rejected material doesn't sink into unconscious oblivion. It is only lightly restrained just below the limen of consciousness. We exercise this faculty every moment. It is possible to understand and control the subliminal action of the mind through the criticism of perception, which leads to expanded awareness. Running imaginative scenarios of possible but unlikely behaviour is an example of a critical approach to perception.

Because mysteries are written back to front, reading them forces us to develop the sharpness of our insights. We are aware that we are playing a game with perception, looking for clues to the whole pattern of events. In the case of preconscious materials, we use our imaginations in a similar fashion, digging up bits and pieces that our consciousness can deal with, even if this material is shocking or thrilling. Inhibition removes the most disturbing and challenging materials from conscious awareness and supplies us instead with a pattern of deep underlying structural meaning, which supplants the narrative line, or predictable story.

Electric process does the same sort of thing with the structure of meaning. Horror films and thrillers of the James Bond variety address themselves to this need. Their highly entertaining production values represent the entry of technical form into movie content.

Hemisphericity and the Subliminal

"In the course of being processed information may undergo transformation across four different orders of representation — physical, physiological, mental, and behavioural."[40]

Dixon calls for an effort to integrate complementary dimensions of psychology without resorting to metaphysical argument. His answer is the novel thesis of two centres of consciousness. He is looking for some "unifying biological frame of reference."[41] This frame is more than partly developed in the split-brain work of Sperry, Bogen, Tart, Gazzaniga, and others.

With S.H.A. Henley, Dixon had explored "the role of laterality in the effect of subliminal cues upon conscious perceptual experience."[42] Warning of the seductive speculations set loose by split-brain theory, Dixon nevertheless points out that besides the two parallel centres of consciousness (left and right) discovered by the pioneers in hemisphericity, there are other clear indications of two centres of consciousness. "In the intact brain, part of the unconscious exchange between the two hemispheres is presumably concerned with inhibition of the right by the left. As a result of this inhibitory influence . . . the right hemisphere remains silent."[43] Beyond the completely radical act of surgically severing the two hemispheres, Dixon points out other ways in which the right hemisphere shows itself to be the centre of another kind of consciousness.

> These other ways include hypnogogic states, sleep, hysterical dissociation, hypnosis and *the entry into awareness of the end products of subliminal stimulation* — end products which only emerge when arousal is low and the signal to noise ratio so reduced as to excite no attention by the left hemisphere.[44]
> (Emphasis added)

It is generally not appreciated that the simple act of watching television or attending to any cathode ray presentation, including those of video display terminals, produces moments of hypnogogic transfer of consciousness into and out of sleep — something the Emerys have shown with very strong evidence. People who know and can control this state often appreciate the epiphanies of clarity that are associated with it. These are moments between sleeping and waking when subliminal elements come into consciousness and increase the scope of conscious insight.

There is a telltale link between bimodal consciousness and whole vision, since the way in which information is generated and passes from side to side looking for balance greatly determines the quality of that information, its structure, and its meaning in conscious reality.

> As to the neuroanatomical bases of these two systems, there are grounds for the speculative hypothesis . . . that their manifestations are in part the products of the right and left

hemispheres respectively and that the switching over from one to the other is mediated by the arousal mechanisms of the brain.[45]

The word "mediated" is extremely apt. Electric media, in moving the focus of attention to the involuntary right hemisphere, are clearly operating in the domain of the subliminal. Early in his work, Dixon studied the investigations of Gazzaniga and Hillyard and agrees with their finding that subliminal stimuli are prevented from crossing the corpus callosum, that all-important neural connective layer between the two hemispheres through which information travels from one side to the other.

In the interests of achieving something of a synthesis of these ideas through his own work, Dixon establishes three concluding overviews:

> The first is that the brain may respond to external stimuli which,
> for one reason or another, are not consciously perceived. The effects
> of such stimuli may be almost as varied as those of sensory inflow
> which *does* enter consciousness . . .

> The second broad conclusion is that the characteristics of
> preconscious processing are indeed consistent with certain general
> principles of biological adaptation. According to this viewpoint,
> cognitive mechanisms evolved for the gratification of need. Hence
> organisms with the largest capacity for monitoring, analysing and
> storing inputs from both the external and internal environments
> would, perceptually, have had the greatest chance of survival. . . .

> Thirdly, since selection of appropriate responses may depend
> upon integrating the information from several sensory modalities,
> the foregoing speculations regarding the emergence of a conscious
> experience system are consistent with the ubiquity of subliminal
> effects.'[46]

Under normal waking conditions the second system is in control,

> but under states of reduced conscious domination, during fatigue,
> sleep, psychosis or when severely threatened from without or within
> the balance is upset and the secondary system becomes over-ridden
> by that other more primitive system which it normally holds in
> check.[47]

Thus the subliminal dimension of mind is set loose to dominate attention in such states, including that produced by electronic media — not so much because of a "threat" to mental balance, but because media are a pleasurable and entertaining substitute for real experience.

> The precise range of subliminal effects varies across the sensory array, but probably depends . . . upon such factors as the relative importance, from an informational and survival point of view, of the modality in question . . . By this reasoning, pain, taste and touch may be expected to have a small subliminal range while the proprioceptive and interoceptive senses remain almost entirely subliminal (as indeed we know they are). Because of the variety and importance of visual and auditory stimuli we would expect a relatively short subliminal range for these modalities and a much longer one for olfaction.[48]

Dixon illustrates his thesis simply in the following chart, which shows the escalating subliminal potentials of different sensory modalities. The chart tells us the hypothetical relations between preconscious/unconscious and conscious effects. No one should doubt these scientific findings, since they synch perfectly with what anyone might expect. Still, these findings are well worth setting down as an orderly observation in the context of subliminal effects.

······· Modality[49]	Sensory Effects ·······
Pain	
Tactile	
Auditory	
Visual	PHENOMENAL
Olfactory	SUBLIMINAL
Thermal	
Vestibular	
Kinesthetic	
Visceral interceptors	

The visceral, or proprioceptive, sense is always mostly subliminal. It's that peculiar feeling you might have when entering a room and sensing tension, perhaps because the room has fallen silent in such a way that you sense people have been talking unfavorably about you. This is not always a quasi-paranoid reaction; it can be a correct reading of subliminal cues, perhaps in the kinesic behaviour of the group. Pain floods consciousness with immediacy, leaving little room for the infiltration of subliminal additions to awareness. The areas in between, particularly the visual and auditory senses, are always ripe for subliminal inclusions.

The Tongue As Banana Peel

> The Freudian slip, a grammatical mistake caused by underlying emotional stress, can be extremely entertaining.

Man trying to collect a bill:
"All right then I'll see you on money . . . Monday."

"Yes, right away mum . . . err . . . ma'am" — a man's response to his female boss.

Some Freudian slips, or parapraxis, may truly connect with the unconscious, but it is most likely that the average slip touches mainly preconscious materials. You meet a gorgeous woman and say, "How nice to seize you." This may not touch down to the unconscious desire to rape. You may just not want the meeting to "cease." Since most slips tend to inspire humour in the perpetrator, there is a certain amount of immediate conscious awareness in the often tongue-fumbling recognition of the irony in the slip.

Taking syntax to mean "the right words in the right order," the type of slip that elides two words to make a nonsensical third is a slip that connects two thoughts, the one conscious and the other very near consciousness. Most people, in perpetrating this type of slip, stop and muse at the mistake's probable meaning on their own. They are aware that they have connected with something that is almost in their power to know. Since the unconscious is characterized by its intractability to individual attempts to discover its contents, it is most likely that the root of these slips, then, is embedded in the preconscious.

Even in some of Freud's more notorious anecdotes that record slips, a little simple association is all that is usually required to dredge up the interpretation. A frustrated swain might say to a reluctant partner, "I love your smiling mouth and your beautiful blue ice," thereby bringing out into the open her coolness to his advances. Such slips are of the moment and only preconscious.

In parapraxis, two things are being stated at once. It is a type of rudimentary poetry, a rune, an ideogram, an inadvertent metaphor. In *Finnegans Wake*, James Joyce quite deliberately exploits parapraxis in the creation of "portmanteau" multi-words: ". . . but one's only owned by naturel rejection. Charley, you're my darwing! So sing they sequent the assent of man."[50] This is simultaneously a reference to an old song lyric and an ironic treatment of Darwin's theory of natural selection and evolution in general.

While such slips may be accidental in life or poetic in prose, they are persuasive in advertising. Advertisers can effectively masquerade puns, or paranomasia, as parapraxis. Advertising works extremely well in embedding preconscious elements of persuasion in our minds that truly affect our purchase selections and political preferences, and that do not originate in the deep unconscious.

As the information overload of the environment increases, with the attendant increase in inhibition, the amount of rejected materials stored in the preconscious increases significantly, inflating far beyond what is normal the importance of this dimension of mind for understanding the dynamic of personality.

Parataxis: Syntax Tics

Parataxis, or "placing beside," is the arrangement of propositions one after the other without any direct reference to more holistic syntactic relations, for example: "He smiled; she blushed; they danced." The reader supplies the linkage. They are related forms. The opposite of parataxis is the hypotaxis of a "normal" sentence, which uses subordinate expressions to show the syntactic relation between the main elements of the sentence and its clausal qualifiers.

Parataxis is rarely used as a formal rhetorical device. But it is how people talk. Poet Charles Olson recognized the new-found relevance of parataxis in his famous "Essay on Projective Verse." Olson describes projective verse as "composition by field, as opposed to inherited line, stanza, over-all form, what is the old base of the non-projective."[51] Olson's poetry was, in contrast, a complex pattern of "conjunctional bits and pieces of sentences" that required the in-depth involvement of the reader to fill in the syntactical relations. His poetry, when recognized as the way we really speak, gave intense pleasure.

"Song 1," from *The Maximus Poems*, showcases Olson's technique of jamming together breathy clauses and shunning precise syntax:

```
colored pictures
of all things to eat: dirty
postcards
                And words, words, words
all over everything
        No eyes or ears left
to do their own doings [all
invaded, appropriated, outraged, all senses
including the mind, that worker on what is
                        And that other sense
made to give even the most wretched, or any of us, wretched,
that consolation [greased
        lulled
even the street-cars


song[52]
```

What Olson reveres is the unusual results one gets on paper by reproducing the patterns of breathing in actual speech, and the syntax that is thereby created. Olson believes that the percept of such speech far outweighs the repetitive literary assumptions of the concept of writing.

In the case of verbal slips, or parapraxis, the syntactic confusion demands the addition of a "subconscious" premise in order to make sense. If the individual can do this, then the added premise is not unconscious but preconscious. When inhibition rejects inadmissible ideas, downgrading them to mere negative "tendencies," they take a sub-syntactic, sub-ideational form in the preconscious. It is unlikely that the naturally deconstructed materials rejected by consciousness would have anything other than a broken, fragmentary existence as ideas —

the wholeness of ideas is by definition a characteristic of consciousness. At the same time, this tendency allows for the possibility of fragments gelling into ideas and entering consciousness. Parataxis works in a similar way; it is the conscious rhetorical exploitation of the fragmentary nature of the deep materials below consciousness that poetry — such as Olson's — tries to connect with. Readers, when triggering their deep responses to a poem, are doing this themselves. The words provoke deep awareness, *something not presently held in consciousness*.

Preconscious materials can be brought up in this way. Fully unconscious material can't be exhumed, except perhaps in very special cases, most likely musical.

Paratactic form in writing is the artful parody of the preconscious, subliminal stratum of mind, without which poetry cannot have strong effects. If it were to make its appeals to consciousness alone, poetry would remain forever light verse, with a dim, inhibited memory and penchant for sentimentality.

Parataxis involves the reader as co-producer, since the premises being implied in paratactic form create a large amount of room for interpretation. The mechanical forms of literature — the canzone, sonnet, sestina, and formal ode, for example — are forms that set limits to poetic utterance. These are closed systems to some real extent. Poets, like Houdini, have always tried to bind themselves in mathematical chains. The paratactic form, however, is open; all the physical bindings are left out, or appear to be, and the reader is left to bind himself to the truths of human perception.

Olson seems among the very first to notice the peculiar changes coming into speech from changes in the technological environment. Increasingly, perceptions are juxtaposed in multi-sensory patterns of extremely complex meanings. This is evidence that shows we have left the visual world and have re-entered acoustic space, a world where breathing matters.

> Electric Process is jamming perceptions together now.

In the world of advertising and show business, and in the technical denaturing of language with acronymic forms, half sentences, and the flipping of parts of speech — verbs for nouns, nouns for verbs — the fragmentary nature of the preconscious and the general effect of electric process come together to create profound changes in the role of language and print in communication.

The distortion of syntactic connections is one of several strategies that can be identified in advertising and other jargonized fields. Electric communication tends to truncate and implode language in ejaculatory bursts, acronyms, regional tribalisms, raw epithets, and the like:

> *Listen sucko*
> *Just do it!*
> *Go for it!*
> *Aw righhhht!*

We should also include the ubiquitous F-word, used everywhere in society, which is intended to cut off further communication. It's a verbal punch. Take this. Stop. In fact, the word likely means "die."

There seems little doubt that the central characteristic of modern electric culture is the inundation of the individual with fragments of visual and acoustic information not causally linked, but simply set loose to gel and dissolve in patterns of possible meaning.

From Subliminal to Sublime

Speaking in tongues, technically known to linguists as "glossolalia," is an interesting, if neglected, form of communication. Such "extemporaneous utterances of incomprehensible sounds,"[53] are not nonsense, studies have proven, or gibberish, and are probably not manifestations of divine connection. Glossolalia exhibits meaningful, internal communication, which can have outward forms like trancing speech, the fundamentalist euphoria of speaking in tongues, scat singing, the nonsense banter of children's baby talk, and the like.

There is an amusing anecdote on glossolalia recounted by Peter Farb, in his book *World Play*: "Samuel Taylor Coleridge, for example, told of an illiterate maid who, in a delirium, spoke in Latin, Greek and Hebrew. It was learned later that she had unconsciously assimilated these languages from a former employer who read aloud passages in them."[54]

The word "unconscious" here is unfortunate because it obscures the likelihood that the preconscious is the prime source of this conversation. Each of us has this ongoing talk with the little voice that monitors our behaviour and reacts to frustrations in the flow of events in the real world. It is also the voice we try to listen to when we read and that can play tricks on us when we tire.

The speaker in tongues is not just randomly pronouncing nonsense, but rather is following structured, somewhat decipherable patterns of speech, generally related to the speaker's first language. The fragments and bits likely emanate from the preconscious and not the unconscious. The point here is that a conversation between the conscious and preconscious provinces of the mind is at least capable of occurring, and, quite likely, is going on all the time across the psychic line that divides them. The important link between glossolalia and language with an underlying meaningful structure may be evidenced in the language play of Lewis Carroll in *Alice in Wonderland* and *Through the Looking Glass*, and the portmanteau language of *Finnegans Wake*.

Our recognition of a limen of consciousness, or threshold of awareness, is critical to understanding behaviour. But there must be a protective limen of awareness between the conscious and preconscious so that an emotional equilibrium can be maintained for psychological health. If the function of a limen is to stratify degrees of psychic awareness, then one also exists between the unconscious and preconscious, the limen of oblivion, the journey without return into the psychic depths.

Materials from below the unconscious limen tend to be extremely unpleasant when brought up by psychoanalysis, dreaming, or a hypnogogic accident between waking and sleeping. In contradistinction, the materials of the preconscious are sought after by the individual, to some degree, because they lend imaginative variety to established consciousness, and therefore give pleasure.

In respect to these thresholds or gates, Freud originally adopted the simple spatial metaphor of Maxwell's thermodynamic system. He even included the infamous "demon" at the gate, who allows only the slower, cooler molecules through, while ignoring the overly busy, rambunctious hot molecules.

The crudest conception of these systems is the one we will find most convenient, a spatial one. The unconscious system may therefore be compared to a large ante-room, in which the various mental excitations are crowding upon one another, like individual beings.[55]

Freud's insistence on a visually simple, spatial model for the strata of the mind can be explained by his unswerving devotion to the mechanistic metaphor of the nineteenth-century scientific paradigm. His obsession with attaining a concrete, empirical status for psychology allows him to risk trivializing his subject in the interests of scientific clarity. To us this seems an untenable obsession. Nevertheless, he goes on with his metaphor of the mind conceived as a Viennese apartment.

> Adjoining this is a second, smaller apartment, a sort of reception room, in which consciousness resides. But on the threshold between the two there stands a personage with the office of door-keeper who examines the various mental excitations, censors them, and denies them admittance to the reception room when he disapproves.[56]

Excitations rising from the turbulent unconscious throng the threshold of consciousness, but much of it is "incapable of becoming conscious" because this material is being "repressed," or held down, by forces only dimly understood, but which are in place to protect consciousness from the profound unpleasantness of facing the truth.

> But even those excitations which are allowed over the threshold do not necessarily become conscious; they can only become so if they succeed in attracting the eye of consciousness. This second chamber therefore may suitably be called the preconscious system.[57]

This is a very important distinction, even if Freud's mechanistic bias is producing a somewhat tenuous analogy. He himself, while recognizing that there is a certain crudeness to his conception, still feels that there is merit in this kind of distinction.

> Now I know very well that you will say that these conceptions are as crude as they are fantastic and not at all permissible in a scientific presentation. I know they are crude; further indeed, we even know that they are incorrect . . . At the moment they are useful aides to understanding . . . and, in so far as they assist comprehension, are not to be despised.[58]

It is very odd that Freud would insist on this model so strongly, all the while seemingly demeaning its significance. The only reason he could have had for persisting with this metaphor is that he believed it to be structurally correct. He says as much, though not quite clearly enough.

> Still, I should like to assure you that these crude hypotheses, the
> two chambers, the door-keeper in the threshold between the two,
> and consciousness as a spectator at the end of the second room,
> must indicate an extensive approximation of the actual reality.[59]

Freud is almost fixated with his static visual bias in describing these states of mind. He wants two chambers: the upper for housing latent or retrievable materials, and another, deeper one for the most repressed materials, which, purling in volcanic mental heat, threaten to erupt and destroy emotional stability.

Another aspect of Freud's view of the preconscious, and a feature of the preconscious that made it less interesting as a subject of investigation for Freud, is the belief that the latent unconscious, that is, the preconscious, is not "dynamic."

> We have two kinds of unconscious — that which is latent but
> capable of becoming conscious, and that which is repressed and
> not capable of becoming conscious in the ordinary way. This piece
> of insight into mental dynamics cannot fail to affect terminology
> and description. That which is latent, and only unconscious in the
> descriptive and not in the dynamic sense, we call preconscious;
> the term unconscious we reserve for the dynamically unconscious
> repressed.[60]

The important question implicit in Freud's analogy is whether or not the preconscious materials start off as truly unconscious, and then somehow rise to the unconscious top and leap across the limen into the "reception room," or parlour. It is most likely that preconscious materials never become deeply embedded in the unconscious in the first place.

It is certainly clear that Freud is saying here that preconsciousness is a state that is fundamentally different from either consciousness or unconsciousness. Though he offers no insights for denying a dynamic role to the preconscious, it is unlikely that he is correct in this supposition.

If Schelling and Fichte are right — and it seems to me that they may be — the preconscious appears to be the origin of fantasy formation, the general, illusive area of the imagination, and is the most probable source of individual artistic expression. How can the artist have power over the materials for his or her art if they are inaccessible to consciousness, by definition deeply repressed in unconsciousness? Freud's treatment of the preconscious avoids the most common questions about one's own power over deep mental functioning. Can he have it both ways?

Freud's genius divines the importance of the preconscious question. Freud believed that therapy takes place at the interface between the conscious and the preconscious. In the famous essay "The Ego and the Id" (1923), he asks, "How does a thing become conscious?" He suggests that the question be put differently: "How does a thing become preconscious?" He doesn't seem to know the answer, which may be that the preconscious simply admits materials directly from environmental sources.

Jung develops a nicer model. In discussing the ego's relation to the unconscious, he posits a triple-decked unconscious: (1) the subliminal, (2) unconscious material beyond voluntary call up, and (3) contents that are locked into the unconscious, never to see the light of conscious day.

> The somatic basis of the ego consists, then, of conscious and unconscious factors. The same is true of the psychic basis: on the one hand the ego rests on the total field of consciousness and on the other, on the sum total of unconscious contents.
>
> These fall into three groups: first temporarily subliminal contents that can be reproduced voluntarily (memory); second, unconscious contents that cannot be reproduced voluntarily; third, contents that are not capable of becoming conscious at all.[61]

The social and psychological effects of the "temporarily subliminal" are the most powerful transformative events we face. In electric culture, this force builds to an intolerable pitch. It is the preconscious that is overloaded by the information revolution, not the unconscious. Preconscious materials are easily invoked by advertising techniques.

Though the conscious has already rejected preconscious material, the sub-cognitive potentials in subliminal perception can resonate at critical moments with consciousness. Such reversals put pressure on our sense of reality. Advertising represents just such resonant patterning, whereby our conscious minds are induced subliminally to cooperate in connecting with preconscious materials. This "expansion" of consciousness has become a common daily occurrence in our lives. But the price we pay for this expansion is a decay in the unity of the conscious.

In respect to resonance — physical and psychological — each medium of communication has a distinctive frequency that allows for different sorts of material to be absorbed. A state of mind (a unit of dominant frequency) is a condition of altered ratios in the brain-wave mix. When one is alert and attentive, the rational, analytical processes keep out other perceptions. But a switch to the perceptual biases of another medium is a change to another state of mind. As discussed earlier, MRIs, and PET and CAT scans make it clear that the brain adapts the stimulus from each medium differently; each state of attunement thus created is a resonant psychological structure, appropriate to the structure of the technology of the transmitting medium itself. These psycho-technical states of mind could not exist without the media, which alters the rate of conscious absorption of materials from the preconscious that are of the same frequency. This process, which is so apparent in the rich fantasy associations that attend electric media, easily dominates the ways people behave in real life.

In using media, we entertain ourselves with varied physical states. At the low end, we are hardly attentive to contexts for perception. We can work our way up to strong, focused levels of whole attention through enhanced recognition of process patterns. This self-manipulation has a bias for innovation. But in the best sense of human achievements, innovation is always obsolescent. Language, in knitting together the best produced by mind and spirit, is still the primary satisfaction in life — though the titillations of interpretive technologies can be quite distracting entertainments.

Transliteration: Subliminal Reading

The powers of Miss X., as reported by James, are fairly normal these days, especially in an environment overloaded with information. The pervasive strategy of inhibition easily creates the appearance and impression of extra-sensory mysteries when, in fact, these are simply

> From illuminated manuscripts to advertising logos, the word can become an icon to be played with visually.

new perceptual strategies that have developed out of new media training. What is perceived by others as paranormal psychic power may actually be the result of an encounter with an ordinary perceptual event that occurs out of the range of conscious awareness. We habitually ignore these "strange" perceptions, which, when couched in a mystical context, appear to defy explanation. Yet almost everyone admits to having such odd experiences.

An interesting case of inhibition in transliterated language was disclosed in a test my colleagues and I conducted on a large class of freshman students. We mixed a series of words that transliterate into intelligible English with other, comparable words that are not the product of exact transliteration, as follows:

······· SALEM	LAGER	SPEAR	TRANCE ·······
1. Yacht	Grail	Hands	Enters
2. Meals*	Light	Throw	Canter*
3. Small	Glare*	Rapes*	Vanity
4. Males*	Regal*	Split	Cretan*
5. Measle	Coins	Spare*	Arcane

·······························

*Indicates an exactly transliterated word.

·······························

Without telling the students what was being tested, each unit of five words was exhibited for one minute to approximately one hundred freshmen. The signal word was then exposed for approximately one-half second. The students were asked to select one of the five words in the unit immediately, within five seconds. Scores were quickly recorded by a show of hands. The selection was made psychologically difficult by placing words that associate, but don't transliterate, in the mix — for example, salem and yacht, spear and throw. Also, certain incomplete matches were allowed as in the case of trance and arcane.

This was not a rigorous test, of course, but the impressive results can be trusted to at least strongly indicate that transliterations occur all the

······· SALEM	LAGER	SPEAR	TRANCE ·······	
1. Yacht: 23	Grail: 7	Hands: 2	Enters: 10	
2. Meals: 4	Light: 25	Throw: 23	Canter: 38	
3. Small: 16	Glare: 16	Rapes: 35	Vanity: 9	
4. Males: 44	Regal: 47	Split: 3	Cretan: 22	
5. Measle: 9	Coins: 5	Spare: 25	Arcane: 4	
	·······························			
Total number of				
respondents:*	96	100	88	83
Percent:**	50	63	68	72
	·······························			
Average percentage: 63				
	·······························			

*Scores were recorded very quickly. Some respondents were
too slow in responding to be included in the calculations.
**Percent of respondents choosing exactly transliterated words.

time without the slightest awareness on the part of any observer. This is a common and persistent habit in language perception that is the direct result of the inhibitors set up by formal language training. In addition, conscious play with this phenomenon is the basis of certain acrostic-style word puzzles, to say nothing of the obvious subliminal control factor available to any gatekeeper who wants better preconscious tools for managing public consciousness.

Doing the Cannes Con:
Where Do All the Commercials Go?

In another somewhat different investigation, the same students were shown ninety non-stop minutes of television commercials, the Cannes Film Festival award winners for that year. One hour later, a large majority of students could not recall more than two or three commercials and none wholly or competently. A startling number, about forty percent, could not recall any commercials coherently. They had to be helped to remember.

As the students' memories began to function under subtle prodding, fragments of specific commercials became confused with others in their minds. Witty and engaging commercials often obliterated their ability to remember the brand names of products. Associations between parts of commercials became mixed. Sometimes even the products were confused. It would appear that the information had been retained in a "pool" in which the various commercials were lodged as fragments of something more coherent — though no one could see what. The experience was one of simulated preconscious structure and content — much like the game Trivial Pursuit. As with games like Jeopardy, the preconscious fragments are loosely lodged like answers that need questions to compute them and let them out into consciousness.

As for the perceptual gimmicks employed in the creation of these very effective, prize-winning commercials, almost none of them were perceived consciously right away. With special emphasis in questioning, however, certain tricks could be made to surface like preconscious elements retrieved from that negative pool. To be fair, this is the "normal" state of affairs in the television viewing of commercials: they only work when out of conscious awareness and in subliminal form.

The Conundrum of Being Well Informed

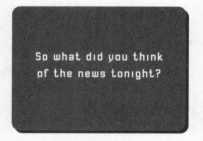

So what did you think of the news tonight?

Television is a negatively toned medium of communication. People have extreme difficulty in remembering anything that they have seen on television because, as the Emerys and others have shown, TV technology turns off the functions of the left brain — the verbal and analytical functions. It seems that nobody is paying attention to the news because we can't remember any of it, even only an hour after viewing it. How do we account for this?

The *Alfred I. DuPont–Columbia University Survey of Broadcast Journalism* reports:

> Andrew Stern of the University of California at Berkeley conducted an interesting experiment aimed at measuring news recall. 232 respondents who were asked, "What do you recall from tonight's

broadcast?" With an average of nineteen items to point to, 51%
could not recall a single story a few minutes after the newscast
was off the air. The remaining 49% who could remember something
from the news, remembered least well, almost not at all, the
sign-off item which often contained what little interpretation the
newscast offered.⁶²

Apparently this massive act of inhibition, whereby we filter out the
rational content of the news, is the predominant mode of news intake.
Low-level sensory involvement with the tube deflects attention from the
verbal and analytical properties of news itself. The ideas expressed
on the news, trivial as they may be in their television form, are nevertheless demoted to the preconscious. The material in the news that
threatens one's unity of mind becomes submerged below the limen of
consciousness as feelings with a strong negative tendency. If these tendencies were stored in a linguistically coherent form, they could not be
prevented from ascending to consciousness. Clearly, the preconscious
materials must be sub-syntactic, bits and fragments of barely verbal
materials, along with T.S. Eliot's "heap of broken images."

In the average news broadcast, where much of what the news presents is unexpected, only a few ideas can win conscious status and easy
recall. The news is coming to the viewer in a form that is relatively inadmissible to immediate consciousness and active memory. All the rest
must be demoted to the condition of preconscious tone and tendency.
To assume that nobody is paying attention is to seriously misunderstand
the real effects of television viewing in
shaping the preconscious psyches of North
Americans.

The perceptual modality of television
is opposed to the literate, analytical processing of information. It is natural that the
news should have become pure entertainment, completely incapable of in-depth

> Television technology
> alters the brain-wave mix.
> TV as a medium is inimical to
> rational, verbal, analytical
> involvement of any sort.
> TV news is a random game
> of emotional roulette.

treatment of any event. CNN rules the world. Wars are conducted
through its agency. Unexpected elements of the news — and the news
is, by definition, the unexpected — are least likely to gain conscious
status as ideas in the viewer's mind. The powerful unitary system of
mind will reject news that is merely discrete units of unexpected events.

Much of the news is just that — irresistibly forgettable. News to be assimilated into memory must be linked to ongoing processes. Increasingly, however, "news" is being packaged for easy assimilation, and lacks the qualities that create critical awareness. In short, some of the news is not really news, but rather trash to be immediately carted out to the preconscious garbage heap.

Terrorism is the perfect news story: the networks can feed for several days on the event's dramatic tensions, fraught with the immanence of real death — a low-budget show guaranteed to capture millions of viewers. Some dabbling with the hidden preconscious grounds that contextualize events is necessary if viewer involvement and memory retention are the objectives of the network news people. If their objective is, instead, to quickly gloss over the disturbing elements of the news so that viewers do not lose their focus on the commercials, then the news should continue to deal with items as discrete units.

The complex news coverage of investigative reporting is a redundant and exhaustive, but ultimately rewarding, process of making people care to even learn a little of what is really going on around them. Unfortunately, investigative reporting is barely possible anymore. The process of stressing detailed information and the building of larger and larger patterns of insight is inimical to the technology itself. The viewer, instead, is normally treated to a wash of cartoon reports in serial regress from anchorman to correspondents "on the scene" who at best can point a finger at something that seems important for the moment.

> Investigative reporting persistently brings ground awareness into consciousness, revealing perception as process.

Complexity of information destroys entertainment value. Redundant treatment of the news bores the audience. Successful news must be simple, quick, and trivial if it is to survive ratings pressure, and every major TV newscaster has warned us that this is the case. Still, almost eighty percent of the population gets its news mainly from television. What they get is simplicity, extreme condensation, and pseudo-objectivity — one-dimensional units that are figures without grounds — and most of this news is trashed into the preconscious mind.

News reporting is a method that uses pointing, runic gestures, which fade as fast as dance. The selection and interplay of items on the front page of a newspaper creates a juxtaposed pattern that never emerges into the consciousness of the reader. The mosaic structure of newspapers increasingly competes with the associative, non-linear aspects of television. At best, news supplies the bones for a do-it-yourself assembly of a skeletal reality.

The news rarely taxes the human capacity to adapt to new meaning. A discrete unit of news is not enough of a stimulus to dis-inhibit the system of organized consciousness. The "picture" of reality that the total news offering presents has a truly strong grip on awareness. People think they have independent opinions, whether they are weak or strong, and everyone says, "Nobody can tell me what to think!" But it is unnecessary to tell people what to think if you have the power to tell them what to think about. In many respects, it is laughably easy to manage public consciousness.

The ideas that are inhibited and demoted to tendency in preconsciousness amass as an overall negative tendency in the substrate of general awareness. This

> Ideas whose meanings run counter to the established mental order are shoved out of the way. They exist in a de-conceptualized, subliminal form below the threshold of consciousness.

dynamic of personality can go awry, and self-directed violence can break out. Kids symbolically maim themselves with tattoos, while adults cut and tuck their flesh in cosmetic operations. Wanting to look better may be a preconscious admission of a strong negative feeling of one's actual bodily condition. In fact, these negative adjustments are always happening in small ways as one tries to order one's existence.

As the environment becomes increasingly rich with information, the inhibition index for each person goes up, and the flip potential of each of us also increases. This self-violating inner force has to be tapped off into some sort of cultural activity that has the power to absorb great amounts of psychic energy. Electric media fit the need perfectly; like a powerful drug, they both fill and tap off the energy of preconscious build up, keeping us in an addictive circle.

As previously described, any system pressed to the limit of its capability to function reaches a sort of critical mass and flips into its opposite, or at least into something radically different. Since everything is rooted in its opposite, our psychic and material cataclysms can be spectacular improvements in the human condition. They can also trigger terrifying annihilations.

This tendency toward precipitous flipping into new and higher states of being is an important component of the post-atomic mindset, which is now assembling itself out of the rubble of the sloughed-off industrial world that has fallen to ruins at our feet. Whether the earth's magnetic polarity will flip again as it appears to have done before, whether the speed of light will remain forever a barrier we can't cross, and whether we shall have easy retrieval of the legion of lost minds who have flipped out, only time will telecast.

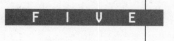

The Edge of Meaning

NATURAL DECAY IS ESSENTIAL FOR RENEWAL; so, too, is cultural decay. The first sign of decadence in a culture is a decay in meaning. This makes new meaning both possible and necessary. Decay of meaning, however, is extremely troublesome culture-wise. Our leaders believe that we cannot live without meaning, and tend to cling to old meanings, often violently, in order to consolidate their power. For example, the concept of war generated during the Second World War, which drew heavily upon national patriotism and a clear idea of right and wrong, was inoperative during the Vietnam War; the propagation of this obsolescent, divisive, and confusing concept of war produced in the American populace a response of massive civil disobedience that almost brought the government of the day to a halt.

We are presently experiencing a fundamental deterioration in the quality of experience as a result of the electrification of the globe. This is at once the worst thing and the best thing that could happen to us. The numbness we are experiencing, generated by the continuous hits of information assaulting our battered senses, results in a diminished appreciation of all our perceptions, especially our most cherished, inherited beliefs. On the other hand, getting away from the shibboleths of religion and party politics, an ineffective justice system, and a very inequitable redistribution of the commonwealth is a necessary separation from old experience. We are given a chance to reconfigure these formerly sacrosanct areas of thought and feeling.

What do our most important values mean in a society that has been trained to seek to satisfy its need for visual validation of everything it believes? Almost everything of true value in our electric times transcends mere visualization. This is a fundamental paradox. For example, in a court of law we say that a defendant must be found guilty "beyond a reasonable doubt." The rational, logical exercise involved in such legal determinations is highly abstract, especially for visually biased jurors.

In *Remote Control*,[1] there is a report on a case study pertinent to the prejudices of the television generation. A defence attorney sums up for the jury as follows:

> I have something important to tell you now. I have employed
> a private detective — a very good private detective — to find the
> person who committed this crime. The private detective is going
> to bring that person here and walk through that door in just a
> few minutes.[2]

Yes, the trick worked. As the attorney sat down to wait for his private detective's entry, of course all of the jury's eyes went to the door. The defence then rose and said to the jury:

> I just noticed that every one of you is glancing toward the door. You
> expected to see something. What does that tell you about whether
> you're convinced that my client is guilty beyond a reasonable doubt?[3]

The kinesic behaviour of the jury belies our perceptual training: through the close-up medium of television, we have become dependent on kinesic behaviour for understanding. TV greatly enhances the power of non-verbal communication, making it more important than language itself for establishing meaning.

Few investigators have wrestled more with the problems of meaning than Alfred Korzybski, the originator of general semantics. His lifelong concern was with the ways in which language does or does not represent reality. He sharpened awareness by pointing out language's deficiencies. "Language is supposed to communicate experience," he argued, "yet by its very nature it is incapable of doing so."[4] Korzybski is simply contrasting the essential difference between the concept expressed in language of a percept apprehended in the sensory order of things.

Still, if the language loses its ability to function for critical distinction, then our ability to survive is also seriously diminished. Meaning will return to magic: a belief in wacky sects, and a virtualized reality.

Meaning, in short, is deeply contextual and culturally determined. Especially in a multicultural society, it is difficult to ascertain solid meanings that cut across all groups. White middle-class meaning is certainly not always the same as black inner-city meaning. Political meaning is not the same as religious meaning, and meanings vary even between religions. Without consensus on meaning, how can we know what is moral, ethical, or even legal? Media treatments of the problem make matters exponentially worse.

The impoverishment of meaning is implicit in electric forms, where thought is based solely on images and cinematic structure. We must consider carefully what it will be like to live in a world in which meaning has become primarily graphic. In such a virtual world — as this one is quickly becoming — we are faced with the broadcast of morally confusing entertainments. Will our entertainments cure us of our need for meaning? Or kill us for lack of a clear understanding of socially healthy action?

In the early days of cold-war propaganda, the nuclear energy lobby advertized "Atoms for Peace." Such oxymorons didn't seem to rattle the public, but instead have effectively convinced most North Americans that they are getting cheap, clean, and safe energy from their atomic plants. On the contrary, this energy is not cheap, not clean, and certainly leaves a lot to be desired as a safe source of electricity. Our nuclear power plants are already decaying and threatening millions of lives. Faulty power plants deliver over-priced energy to users overwhelmed with guilt about pollution. The employees, themselves disgruntled and bored with their work, have been found to be high on hashish.[5] More insidiously, we suffer an inexorable erosion of the human spirit, impoverished by an addictive and escalating dependency on mass consumption. Increasingly, the only meaningful measure of cultural health is money, which is becoming monstrously misaligned in its distribution, as celebrity economics show.

The formula for celebrity economics is fairly straightforward. National brand goods achieve that status through television advertising. The mass consumer audience develops around the figure of an individual whose acting or playing becomes linked with the program's sponsorship. Star ads sell. Think of Nike. The goods associated with the celebrity have an inflated price because money is paid to the star for an endorsement; popularity also drives up prices. In the supermarket or department store, these more recognizable goods sell best. Great sales produce greater payment to the stars. How great? Multiple millions per year is normal when the selling power of the celebrity image is there. All that money comes out of the pockets of ordinary consumers — pennies at a time flowing into a river of celebrity wealth.

We still believe ourselves to be living in a democracy, having lost all sense of the real meaning of that political condition. Slaves and fools in supermarkets, we subsidize our own moral and spiritual downfall. Few people appear capable of even noticing what's wrong, let alone exhibiting the socio-political heroism of resistance to consumption. The standard that dominates our culture is greed for the realization of a fantasy of unlimited wealth.

Life in the West demands devotion to this form of selective ignorance, which suppresses anything that deflects us from our material benefit. In the long run, the job of getting on with business prevails over life values. Most of us have now become aware that we are not meant to notice the way electric media manage our conscious lives in support of this complex economic agenda. Like neurotics, we learn to love our disease. It would seem that we want to be deceived.

We don't know any longer if technology has any meaningful human purpose. We grow human ears on the backs of mice and put firefly genes into marker corn. We have grown sedentary and obese sitting and watching massive sports displays in the TV arena while athletes grow grotesquely rich from inflated television price structures. The electric technologies that aid our economic progress also create economies of scale that result in massive rationalizations of corporate personnel. The best we have are susceptible to ignorant neglect. Qualitatively, the fiscalization of reality drives everything in human affairs to social and political extremes. The media become the agencies of extremism.

Electric media create complex, chaotic relations between thought and feeling by severing one from the other. A reasonably simple view of any event can be gained through any one medium. But each medium is biased and presents a view of reality consonant with its technological structure, thus making all overview extremely complicated. While print can deal with complex inner realities, electric media can only intimate depth, at best creating strong feelings about events that are understood only superficially. We cannot overestimate the influence of a medium's form on perception and thought. Each medium has its own internal logic of meaning that depends on its perceptual bias. The attempt to recreate whole perception is implicitly complex.

The form of a new medium produces complete psychic and social change, and gives us a new way of looking at the world — providing another fragment of a whole reality. It changes our position in perceptual space. The intense visual effects of photography, for example, pre-empt abstract thought by overemphasizing feelings. Low-order visuality, as in print, emphasizes thought, thereby creating more complex, though less accessible, feelings than those associated with visual media. The true content of any medium is its unique sensory effects and how they alter the meaning of the story.

> A true content is now an amalgamation of old and new contents created by multiple media.

Without an understanding of the effects of the hidden structural ground of any medium of communication, the user is left with a disconcerting array of random accesses to reality, many of which are in conflict with each other.

Meaning and the Variance of Languages

When a fairly clear meaning crosses a language border, that supposed clarity becomes absorbed in the differences between the two tongues. Translating any meaning across a dozen languages completely garbles the hope for precision in meaning. Meaning is culture-bound, of course. Yet we depend on the possibility of coming to mutual understandings in our dealings with other peoples. Commercial and economic well-being rely on the sharing of clear meaning; the world's stock markets, for instance, must be linked by meaningful trade data. At least our communications should attempt to avoid a state of permanent war in the world. And besides, I would like this page to communicate something useful to you, the reader.

The conceptual patterns of languages, which have evolved over aeons of time, make it difficult to effectively translate across linguistic barriers while retaining the nuance of local difference.

> The untranslatable core of any language, what the French call the "ethnie" is a deep unconscious perceptual commitment to seeing reality in a certain way. This perceptual bias is definitively the source of tribal pride and identity. For example: a *nitpicker* in English is a person with hyper-fastidious concern for details. A nit is a body louse egg . . . In Italian, a nitpicker is one who will "cercare il capello nell'uovo" (search for a hair in an egg). The French regard such a fellow as one who would "encouler les mouches," (that is, bugger flies). Each language retains a unique perceptual facet of most metaphoric understandings.[6]

We see in this subtle set of differences in the perception of reality an English concern for cleanliness, an Italian focus on food, and a French — somewhat predictably so — expression of this matter sexually.

The serious side of this problem is nowhere better exemplified than in Bible translation. There is an inner resistance to most languages that makes clean, balanced translation impossible, especially with regard to the Bible.

> Portions of the Bible have been translated into some two thousand languages around the world and in every case the process of translation involved the loss of information originally in the Bible, the addition of new information, or the distortion of information.[7]

Eugene Nida, an expert in Bible translation, puts the matter succinctly: "The basic principles of translation mean that no translation in a receptor language can be the exact equivalent of the model in the source language."[8]

It is no wonder that more books have been written on the subject of language and its difficulties and challenges than on any other theme. But this leaves us still to wonder why we are addicted to the quest for perfect meaning. Even scientific principles vary in their interpretation and application from place to place. The Chinese invented gunpowder, but would not use it to make war. Darwinism has had a rough go in the schools of the southern United States. There is now an impressive slate of "creationist scientists" who deal with evolutionary data in ways that allow the literalist Bible zealots to ignore real science in the interests of narrow religious views. Scientific attitudes, applied to language and meaning, have had various results from Saussure (structuralism and semiology) to Chomsky (transformational-generative grammars). And although computer "languages" have a perfect logic to them, they simply do not encompass all that which is language. Stuttering, nasalizing, and the paralanguage of pitch, stress, and juncture — among many other aspects of true languages — are missing. Still the problem of meaning remains.

The answer may lie in the unlikeliest place: an understanding of comedy and its freedom from the tyranny of meaning. William Irwin Thompson put this together nicely in a paper for the *Tulane Drama Review* while he was still a graduate student at Cornell. He pointed out that if there is no meaning on which to base belief, then the world is simply, and in the last resort, absurd. I would add that while we may believe that we have been — and gone — through that old phase of absolutist, existential doubt and angst that leads to the view of the world as meaningless, we have missed the fact that electric process enfranchises and promulgates that view technologically. As Thompson says, long before Derrida, Foucault, and the rest, "All of this means that man is a comic being when he believes that he can act with support for his beliefs."[9]

Citing Pirandello's comedy *So It Is*, Thompson makes the point that "nothing is more hysterical than man's affectation to knowledge."[10] Facing such a ridiculous outcome to his intellectual activities, Thompson asks, "What can a man do in such a circumstance?" then answers, "He can think, and talk, and laugh; he can engage in no activity at all. Man waits for Godot, if there is a Godot, and in the meantime he fidgets in the void."[11] Drawing on an adage from Nietzsche — "Man would sooner have the void for a purpose than be void of purpose"[12] — Thompson finishes the insight by observing that "[t]hose who cannot laugh at theories and systems are not free."[13]

The person who brings us the knowledge that meaning has let us down is the absurd hero who makes no demands on our credulity, except that we see that "the universe is beyond mere belief and society is incorrigibly a hoax."[14] This is the comic world we inhabit, but our humour is based on grievances that can have deep meaning.

All this means is that comedy is the simple way out of recognizing the immense complexity of life. Railing about the inadequacies of language is futile and pointless. No one expects language to duplicate the experience of reality, but only to recall a draft version of it that allows for the creation of an emotional and intellectual analogy of the real. In fact, in electric culture, dominated by media formats, we derive meaning from symplexity, a recognition of both the simple and complex aspects of real events that operate simultaneously. Making the social register is not just about making friends, but that's where it starts if you follow the principles of money and class.

The fundamental symplectic action in all communication is the complex, self-preserving action of language itself under constant and escalating pressure from the simple assault on reality from the new media. The opening few minutes of Kubrick's *2001: A Space Odyssey* are a case in point, as is the wordless introduction to *Paris, Texas*. When the novel finds that its job of graphic descriptions has been co-opted by cinema, then language has to find ways to redevelop genres for its own survival. When e-mail destroys the epistolary art, then language has to address that loss. When the computer puts the electric vise of jargon on human expression, again language must find ways of remaining flexible and sensitive to a more nuanced mode of recording perceptions.

> Contents evolve as the survival strategies of language develop.

This evolution of content makes all ensuing contents more complex in view of the number of changes that language has gone through. A case in point is James Joyce's *Finnegans Wake*. Joyce's work purports to be the entire history of the world jammed into the portmanteau puzzles of a multiplexed, inventive language.

What Joyce forces language to do in this book serves as a parable of how language must behave in an electric environment. He has revivified language itself for us. And he has done this by playing with the very idea of meaning in a technique he calls the "abnihilization of the etym," or simply the recreation of meaning out of nothing. Joyce wanted the book to be a universal myth, so he incorporated dozens of the world's languages in his portmanteau, or overcoat, style; its punning words ensured some breadth of appeal. He got the idea from Lewis Carroll, who was first to combine several word fragments into entertaining neologisms, as in the poem "Jabberwocky." Still, few people have actually read *Finnegans Wake*. And has anyone exhausted its meaning? I think not. The multi-linguistic puns allowed Joyce to tell several stories at once, another complexifying aspect of the book. The words are several words sandwiched together — "No martyr where the preature is there's no plagues like rome."[15] — thereby creating symbolic resonances of extreme complexity.

As for content, *Ulysses*, Joyce's other masterwork, has a very simple plot that occurs in one day. The hero is banal and his movements trivial, but the language is extremely complex. Its content is really the story of language and the adjustment of language to the realities of the new technological and scientific environment. The "Wandering Rocks" episode of Ulysses has a structure based on the "observer orientation" of Einstein's Theory of Relativity. This famous central section of Joyce's novel was added to the Homeric model, and demonstrates quite clearly Edmund Wilson's original observation of Joyce as an "exploiter of the concepts of relativity."[16]

Many of the other great writers of our time follow similar paths. Their extremely long and complex novels give the reader a sense of the adamant obstinacy of literary forms of language in the face of an electronic environment that stands to destroy literature as we know it.

> Auditory perception leaves the user's imagination relatively free to image internally.

Created for the consumption of millions, a movie — by virtue of this fact — must impose its interpretation of events and leave little room for different views by its users. But the human imagination feeds on differences. Intense visual representation eliminates this source of imaginative power. Obviously, the elimination of difference establishes sameness. Eventually sameness arrives at the state of no change — the chaos of entropy. Films get substantially worse and technically better.

Ours is close to becoming a blue-box culture. Electric media trivialize and tend to eliminate serious interest in the past. They end history by their ubiquitous presence in recording it, an ironic state for the History Channel. With the past and the present impoverished, meaning fails. Is there a deeper order in the chaos created by electric media? Yes, new order is being computed all around us.

The hidden, deeper order of the overloaded environment is in the action of deep contents and the hope that such virtuality can be used to benefit humankind, as with virtual surgery and space travel. This deep order takes a positive form in selection, a technique for reducing and mitigating the schizophrenic intake of information.

Today, evolution is at war with information that produces an overall anti-evolutionary result. Cloning, and genetic research in general, ends the thrust of nature's program for preserving the species. From now on we're on our own, God help us. We no longer have to inhibit aspects of events that are not immediate to attention or survival. Our carefully balanced natural system has been thrown into critical disequilibrium by electric process. Work supports life through the creation and control of the technical means to subdue nature — a paradoxical ambition, made possible only by our power to inhibit the wholeness of nature with systems.

> Virtuality produces that which is true in effect, not in fact.

The Content Symplex

Advertising is a vast laboratory for testing meaning. This happens in a somewhat negative way. The doctor who wrote the following mad hat letter to *Harper's* magazine caught the spirit of this adverse advertising effect.

> When advertisers divorce words from their meaning and hijack
> concepts normally used to describe human behaviors or attributes in
> the name of selling automobiles or footwear, they trivialize language,
> consumerize our worldview, and cheapen important ideas.[17]

Advertising stands on the symplectic edge of our culture; neither art nor science, advertising nevertheless exploits those two fundamental dimensions of meaning.

The one fundamental effect of electronic technology on culture is to splice together the functions of simplification and complexification so that there can be no simple meaning anywhere on any subject; everything is made complex by technology, which has made the world symplectic — simultaneously simple and complex. Philosophy has become so inexpressibly complex that it can no longer be systematized for general use. Sociology has collapsed from the dead weight of the complexity associated with administering to the commonwealth on any simple basis. Economics has become so complex in its speed-of-light computerized forms that there is no way physically to control economic activity anymore.

A new paradigm always, at first, suggests a simpler way of viewing something that has become unmanageably complex. In the earth-centred view of the universe, the Ptolemaic diagrams of celestial motion required to keep the idea of circular orbits alive became a menagerie of Ferris wheels in the sky of such complexity that the system was constantly breaking down — it was no longer a mechanism for accurate interpretation of heavenly motion. A simpler way was found by Copernicus. This simplicity, however, has grown increasingly more complex. The simplifying activities of science always lead to increased complexity. We simplify in order to achieve new complexities.

Overall, as we pass through one paradigm after another, the complexity of our understanding becomes a layered complexity with receding but still significant grounds underlying everything we do. In other words, our perception of our position in the universe is evolving. The evolution of awareness is the true evolution. Physical evolution is so slow that it is of no real meaning to the development of human culture. Awareness of the world includes an understanding of ourselves, and thus must have both art and science motifs. These bimodal motifs, however, also bifurcate, and while it is clear that science adds complexity to life, we should also notice that the material expression of science — technology — creates an apparently more simple and convenient world for us. It promises simplicity, but by very complex means.

While the arts still attempt to make myth and give us coherence in our attempt to decipher the ineffable aspects of reality, we have arrived at a point in time when cultural coherence has become extremely muddled. Simple plays and stories, simple pictures representing real views of nature, simple sculptures, rugs, furniture, costumes — all have become collector's items, *objets d'art*. The boredom of acquisitive life is almost tragic. Young people, under complex social pressures to achieve, particularly economically, have invented raves, which bring a little simple danger or risk-taking back into their boring, regimented, affluent lives. The opposite of boring is ecstasy — the drug of choice at these virtual riots, which began in farmers' fields and have now moved to major venues in all the large cities.

When we look at literature, cross-culturally the effect of electric media becomes extremely apparent. The primary fact of all literary activity is the absolute attempt by language to survive changes militating against it. Literature evolves as it adjusts to major assaults on its cultural centrality.

With the invention of the phonetic alphabet, stories changed radically. Epic poetry, the Bible, and the Koran were transferred onto the manuscript page and priestcraft grew up around the new permanent records the new language of this technology afforded. This second dimension of literary reality drowned out the sound of the human voice as the exclusive modality of social communication.

In the early fifteenth century in Italy, glass technology and lens making changed the way the world sees objective space. Lens precision confirmed that we see space *totally* as a mathematical organization. This shift from iconic and symbolic uses of pictorial space to 3-D space, or the illusion of perspective, became the ground for the invention of print and its point-of-view enfranchisement of individual opinions.

Novels are born, newspapers work their subtle magic on language, and people begin to leave the ear for the eye *en masse*. A great graphic revolution occurs that makes language much more responsive to the imagistic needs of the user of literature. Great, fat *romans à clef*, which go on for multiple volumes, take to describing everything and everybody. While this new, third dimension of linguistic change is developing new contents, the old forms do not altogether disappear; they become embedded in the new forms and, with some writers, there is interplay between the various levels, or dimensions, of content. Dante is a particular case of a great writer who consciously set about to write his *Commedia* on four distinct levels, all of which interpenetrate, thus creating a very complex pattern of meaning.

In our time, with the introduction of electric media, a fourth dimensionality of content was created that coincided with the relativity theory of Einstein, which Joyce borrowed for the "Wandering Rocks" episode in *Ulysses*. The psychic depths had been reached by Freud, Adler, Jung — sex, power, and the hermetic tradition. This fourth dimension of meaning is the *anagogical*, or psycho-spiritual. The possibilities held out by some Eastern religions for the transformation of human consciousness to

higher states of existence gives language an additional power, something like prayer, but more a matter of deep reading and understanding,
as in the Tibetan *Book of the Dead*.

This fourth, anagogical dimension of content evolution has produced
writers who are environmentally sensitive to the technical changes that
electricity has brought into being. Along with Joyce, writers like T.S.
Eliot, Ezra Pound, and William Burroughs have been pushed back onto
deeper mythical grounds in order to preserve the ability of poetry to
communicate. Several of these writers, especially Joyce in *Finnegans
Wake* and Burroughs in *Naked Lunch*, have crossed over into the final
content paradigm, the quintessential fifth dimension. Language continues to find strategies for survival that preserve the possibility of deep
and novel meanings. The task of literature is now to survive the considerable threat from the Internet; it must avoid becoming jargonized by
computer geeks and yet retain the ability to reflect that reality.

The veiled meanings in books of this sort are now becoming spliced
with the fantastic meanings coming out of electronic culture. Literature
becomes fantastic, primarily because it takes up the cause of virtual
immanence. Is everything imaginable now possible, as writers like
William Gibson seem to believe? What is not possible? You can create
any effects you want with electricity, everything from condensing the
entire holdings of ancient Greek literature onto a single disk to performing nanotechnological surgery with microscopic robots as medical
slaves who travel to difficult sites to cut and sew, ream and plug.
Telepathic infusion of information is promised. Gibson shows us a
world in which our very flesh has been taken over into a new hyper-
tech reality as "simstim" — a near-future simulated stimulation medium
that apparently offers something a little better than virtual sex.

> Cowboys didn't get into simstim . . . because it was basically a
> meat toy. He knew that the trodes he used and the little plastic tiara
> dangling from a simstim deck were basically the same, and that the
> cyberspace matrix was actually a drastic simplification of the human
> sensorium, at least in terms of presentation, but simstim itself struck
> him as a gratuitous multiplication of flesh input.[18]

In this not-too-distant future world depicted by Gibson, normal sex is
as old fashioned or obsolescent as joy or happiness. The malaise of

informational mega-stress hangs over this world in all its bizarre extrapolations. As we actually depersonalize ourselves and really create a discarnate world of bodiless, virtualized information, flesh becomes merely something to play with.

The very senses are systematized technologically. Of course, everything that astounds the reader in this prescient and fundamental text of the future is just a fictionalization of what we have already set loose in our media-dominated lives. So what happens to all the knowledge that we have accumulated over aeons of time on the subject of the body?

The quintessential fifth dimension of content evolution puts the complex and the simple back together in remarkable ways. A great deal has happened in literature as fallout from Joyce's *Finnegans Wake*. Look at Beckett's *How It Is* and observe the almost maddeningly meaningless simplicity of the novel's structure, yet complex demands this work makes on the reader's wilful suspension of disbelief. Many books, in various literary styles, follow along this thin line between meaning and oblivion. All these styles are symplectic, in that they carry on the work of the arts in attempting to simplify experience, while also moving forward into ever more complex strategies for the survival of language itself.

Is there a solution to this question of meaning? Must we go on forever in this metaphysical muddle saving language by making it increasingly unreadable? I offer the following way to renew our understanding of the premises of meaning.

Meaning, like a strange attractor, describes a limiting spiral action around a point of perfect order that it can never achieve. One can be very accurate in one's meaning and get very close to the limit point of truth without arriving absolutely at that point. Still, this approximation is close enough to truth that it's worth basing one's actions on.

The strange attractor of cooking is seasoning. That perfect asparagus and porcini risotto you had ten years ago in Venice — what else was in it, you think, as you get closer and closer to that taste, though never quite put the whole context of the original together. Sex is all about the expectancies of touch: in good sex, a master learns what secondary spots to touch adjacent to the obvious erotogenic zones in order to set up cross-vibratory resonance in the partner. Find your own limit points.

If we take meaning to function like a strange attractor, the circuits of slightly variant and evolving meanings point to a truth upon which we can build our sensitivity. We can act on very dependable information, without having to worry about the lack of absolute truth and meaning.

A strange attractor creates its meanings through iteration — repetition with feedback. All this happens at electric speeds, which gives one the ability to project massive amounts of collected data into almost infinitely extensible configurations. We can see now this infinite extensibility. It is the image of the strange attractor.

We gravitate towards truth. But some truths are too powerful to be faced baldly. Certain truths are too elusive for us — just the fear of their possibility can overturn reason. Take Freud's clinical observations about family life, for instance: "Mothers and fathers love sons and daughters in physical ways." Well, who says that either Sophocles or Freud was right about this problem in family arrangements? Civilized modification of such drives replaces the deep truth. We know these things, of course; they have been the substance of psychological dialogue and much therapy from the inception of these fields. What has changed is that values such as these, when projected forward in media forms, produce different answers, ones that are probably less and less taboo.

As for the question of love within families, as Rod Gorney has suggested, one can see now that in the near future it is possible that incest laws will become increasingly violated until, perhaps, they are eliminated, as unthinkable as that might now seem.[19] Human sexuality has many forms, and as more and more variation is allowed, condoned — even legislated — it becomes increasingly likely that any form of sexual activity will become permissible, including incest.

Meaning has the role of focusing consequences. In other words, what follows an activity usually always follows that activity. Fluttering your eyes and smiling seductively usually brings sexual attention. All meaning intends to draw an appropriate response from the user. The law of appropriateness says that if you do this, such and such will follow. Depend on such meaning and guide yourself by it. It seems meaning is always moving and changing, but it is also always homing in on its truth, getting closer and closer until they almost, but don't quite, touch.

Electric process does not eliminate this possibility of establishing useful meanings. Rather, it sets up a new pattern for understanding that which we have left after eliminating the absolutist agenda, which has governed our philosophical speculation about meaning for far too long.

That the Deconstructionists' trivial insight into the limitations of

> It would be hilarious — if it weren't also maddening — that contemporary Deconstructionists are stuck on the idea that it is impossible to say definitely what anything means.

communication should be reason enough to trash tradition and all other forms of cultural continuity, with or without the aid of electric media, is simply silly.

Long before Deconstructionism, the great communications pioneer Colin Cherry believed in the *appropriateness* of selected meanings. Meaning for Cherry can be statistically precise in message and response while lacking perfection. For example, one might yell, "Fire" if there is an actual fire or to signal the need for help when being physically attacked. In communication, it is always the appropriateness of a message for eliciting a correct response that is the measure of its effectiveness, not the metaphysical imperfection of the message's ground or context. Communication is a practical art, even when dealing with epistemological questions.

The desire to interpret one's experience for others demands that meaning exist. To create a convergence and intensification of human intellectual energy in order to bring new things to life also requires meaning. Some think that meaning is a meaningless (sic) metaphysical category, like truth or honour, and that every concept exists in various forms that conflict in meaning. For example, some would say that heroism is simply a special way of channelling fear. Love is intense self-regard strongly reflected in a partner. These meanings do not elude us, nor does their ambiguity signal the end of useful communication.

As Robert Ian Scott has said simply in the December 1990 issue of *New American Review* about the currency of Deconstructionist views of meaning:

> Deconstructionists seem to think this variety of meanings "deconstructs" meaningful structures, shows they have no meaning, but structures are meaning. Deconstructionists suggest that we cannot know what anything means until we know everything else that might have been said or done, and all the possible meanings, as if we must learn everything all at once or not learn anything.[20]

The demand that we know everything about a thing or event before being able to say anything meaningful about it is Deconstructionism's "omniscience fallacy." Where else is the demand for wholeness pressed so tyrannically? Just stop using the verb "to be" in any form and the problem of identity between statement and experience is solved.

Electric technology has heightened the meaning stakes considerably. Many researchers now believe in futures dominated by thinking machines. Certainly, the addition of virtuality to our sense of reality greatly complexifies the question of meaning. Artificial intelligence has a grip on some minds, although this potentiality always gets pushed to impossible limits, like the suggestion that it will soon be possible to download the contents of one's mind, conscious and unconscious, into a computer.

Just before we all disappear bodily into information systems in a discarnate techno-based surreality, Humberto Maturana and Francisco Varela introduce the quasi-Jungian idea of *autopoesis*, or self-making.[21] Theirs is an idea closely linked to "embodiment,"* which turns the theory of cybernetic controls through feedback completely around.

> Autopoesis turns the cybernetic paradigm inside out. Its central premise — that systems are informationally closed — radically alters the idea of the informational feedback loop for the loop no longer functions to connect a system to its environment. In the autopoesis view, no information crosses the boundary separating the system from its environment. We do not see a world "out there" that exists apart from us. Rather we see only what our systemic organization allows us see.[23]

The problem with this formulization may be that all systems are, at least to some miniscule degree, open systems, suffering minute photonic adulterations. More interestingly, after Bell's theory, this formulation may be missing the distinct possibility that everything is actually linked to everything else. The idea of a closed system is not an absolute in either physics or philosophy.

Questions of the new paradigm of chaos and complexity hang over all our attempts to defend traditional values and cultural continuity. The embodiment thesis of autopoesis does away with the facile presumption that we are not open systems, bodily and mentally, and that we can

---

*Embodiment "is akin to articulation in that it is inherently performative, subject of individual enactments . . . always to some extent improvisational . . . for it is tied to circumstances of the occasion and the person."[22]

do away with the body through virtualization techniques. As Katherine Hayles puts it, and as Marshall McLuhan would have, "In the face of such a powerful dream, it can be a shock to remember that for information to exist, it must always be instantiated in a medium."[24]

Embodiment is a corrective to the Pollyanna views of cybernauts who want to believe that technological life is real life, who apparently can't tell the difference between a transistor and a thrombosis. This difference of opinion goes back at least to the debate that was raging at MIT when I was teaching there in the sixties, between Hubert Dreyfus and Marvin Minsky, MIT's famous cybernautic Nostradamus. Dreyfus, who seemed to be an isolated voice of dissent at MIT at a time when the computer was being treated as a panacea, was one of the first to publish the argument, in *What Computers Can't Do*, that human behaviour is embodied in such a way as to transcend being perfectly mimicked by computer systems.*

The hubris of the Minskyites led them to suppose that they could exactly duplicate all human characteristics and behaviours in cybernetic form. They were wrong, of course, and still are, though business still likes to support their economically useful, if philosophically failed, efforts.

In the end, the problem comes down to this: even if a completely functioning electronic surrogate of a mind is built whose artificiality can't be detected by a human mind, the virtual mind remains dependent on the imaginative, innovative discoveries of the human mind. Some may deny this, but consider what amount and quality of information would be required to duplicate the intellectual and emotional interactions of a high-powered think-tank. The human mind always stays ahead of its electronic offspring — a great deal ahead, at least in the area of innovation, the domain in which the species must do its best in order to survive.

As Lewis Thomas put it, "No one has yet programmed a computer to be of two minds about a hard problem or to burst out laughing."[25] These are unprogrammable, embodied functions. We meet utter failure when challenged to produce a program for playing hockey like Wayne Gretzky or for pitching a baseball like Pedro Martinez.

This hotly debated subject concerning humankind's individuation under technological conditions — virtualization versus embodiment —

---

*From Hubert L. Dreyfus's *What Computers Can't Do: The Limits of Artificial Intelligence*, rev. ed. (New York: Harper and Row, 1979).

seems to have missed the brilliant point made a long time ago by Teilhard de Chardin regarding the importance of "personality." Sir Julian Huxley discusses the importance of this Chardinian insight on "the supreme importance of personality" in the evolution of awareness:

> A developed human being . . . is not merely a more highly
> individualized individual. He has crossed the threshold of
> self-consciousness to a new mode of thought, and as a result
> has achieved some degree of conscious integration — integration
> of the self with the outer world of men and nature, integration of
> the separate elements of the self with each other. He is a person,
> an organism which has transcended individuality in personality.[26]

This question of transcendence is anathema to the demands of computer programming. The qualitative distinction is being made between one sort of individual, whom the computer can duplicate after a fashion, and the "person" who emerges from the higher state of consciousness. Any attempt to calculate the true condition of individuals who have "merged" with their environments runs into some version of the many-body problem, in which the unimaginable complexity of complete calculation outstrips any useful applications of computer duplication.

> [De Chardin] realized that the appearance of human personality
> was the culmination of two major evolutionary trends — the
> trend towards more extreme individuation, and that towards more
> extensive interrelation and co-operation: persons are individuals
> who transcend their merely organic individuality in conscious
> participation.[27]

Teilhard says that his work may be "summed up as an attempt to see and to make others see what happens to man" that results in his increasingly conscious awareness.

> To try to see more and better is not a matter of whim or curiosity
> or self-indulgence. To see or to perish is the very condition laid upon
> everything that makes up the universe by reason of this mysterious
> gift of existence.[28]

"To try to see more and better" is a matter of acquiring meaning, but meaning always turns out to be paradoxical. Paradox, however, does not destroy meaning; it creates it. No one-dimensional vehicle can hold truth. Truth is a way of seeing, one that recognizes that the results produced by split vision are results that lead to new paradigms of meaning. Before the atom was split, the world seemed indestructible. The obverse vision now dominates our view.

> Bodily knowledge individuates but does not necessarily create transcendent awareness.

The result of living under electric conditions is to deconstruct ourselves socially, politically, and spiritually. Everyone knows that all meaning is a form of deception. (Yet hastily I want to add: not this meaning!) Experience can encounter truth, but that truth then becomes a story interpreted. Interpretation introduces meaning and meaning is a metaphor — something that stands for something else but is not identical to it.

Katherine Hayles notes the destructive action of Descartes' causal thinking on context "by abstracting experience into generalized patterns."[29] On the other hand, she continues,

> [e]mbodiment creates context by forging connections between instantiated action and environmental conditions. Marking a turn from foundation to flux, embodiment emphasizes the importance of context to human cognition.[30]

All this talk about embodiment and virtuality and complexity and discarnate, or bodiless, information conditions needs some simple examples. Hayles borrows one from Paul Connerton (*How Societies Remember*). It's one I like and understand: liturgy, like the pattern of response at a Mass. "A liturgy, for example, 'is an ordering of speech acts which occurs when, and only when, these utterances are performed; if there is no performance there is no ritual.'"[31] In this instance, you are what you hear coming out of your mouth. It is the difference between dancing and attending the ballet.

Hayles and others in the embodiment clan are trying to make the most of the habitual behaviour that settles in under consciousness and is beyond the pale of conscious understanding, thus making this knowledge non-virtualizable, that is, out of the grasp of technology and its attempt to simulate consciousness. This involves many other aspects of human mental functioning: our sense of quality, novelty, and intuition, along with all the inexplicable semi-senses of proprioception, second sight, nirvana, and so on.

The subtleties of the new bodily awareness produce an electronic alchemy that strives not to find the secret of making gold, but of life itself. The truths that emerge from the Genome Project about human structures will all be strange attractors, not absolute mechanisms. We now know that schizophrenia plants its roots in a specific gene. Our genes are now the known seed plot of the gardens of ourselves.

The true transformation of consciousness that lifts us above ordinary individuation is beautifully articulated by de Chardin: "There is no more decisive moment for a thinking being than when the scales fall from his eyes and he discovers . . . that a universal will to live converges and is hominized in him."[32] The theory of self-reflexivity does not go far enough for those who know that the greater human action lies outside their individuated selves. It is the hope of this study to merge the two metaphysical notions of individuation and self-reflexivity with the principle of embodiment. In fact, this synthesis precisely defines the symplex.

The Edge of Meaning and Inhibition

To the extent that society allows itself to adopt the strategy of inhibition for its survival, general social and psychological entropy rises and meaning fails. Data supplant thought, systems replace nature, and simulacra replace reality. Meaningful interpretations fall behind the onslaught of undigested information. This effect is the opposite of communication.

> Carl Jung insists that "meaninglessness inhibits fullness of life and is therefore equivalent to illness."[33] Consider the corollary of this proposition: it is the function of meaning to counter inhibition in the interests of mental health.

Interpretation can only be as sound as the quality of perception on which it is based. Perception, if habitually reduced in acuity by inhibition, is unlikely to generate meaning of a quality that truly enriches life. The artificial environment of technology inhibits wholeness of perception by eliminating certain operations of sensory interplay. Try conversing or reading a book with the TV on, or watching a film and talking at the

> Knowledge comes only through thought and discussion, not by watching a flow of disconnected images. TV is TV is TV, regardless of content.

same time. Technology inhibits socialization. Individuals who spend an increasing amount of time with their media have little time for other people.

It appears more and more likely that television is a medium that trains viewers, children foremost, in an in-depth inattention to reality. One of television's main functions is to virtualize consumerism, so that as one goes through the day purchases are validated "as seen on TV." Real things matter somewhat less than the surreal things that magically get from the TV to your shop. You don't recall the announcement but you do recognize it. The recognition can easily be plucked from your preconscious with a little twitching by image. Significantly, television, a medium that defies memory, can nevertheless treat us as archives of commercial fragments, eliciting split-second recognitions at the point of purchase. Under electric conditions, we begin to be aware of something subliminal that has been done to influence us without knowing quite what. We mistakenly call this sensitivity paranoia.

There are powerful reasons why TV fails to add to our useful conscious knowledge. Nothing can be learned the first time through. Practice makes perfect. Redundant exposure to all aspects of an event is required for learning. Since viewers cannot readily recall what they have seen on television, nothing from the preconscious is actually "learned," that is, submitted to conscious scrutiny and judgment. The preconscious, as we know, is only a storehouse of apparently meaningless fragments, a pool of odds and ends — a chaotic archive. This subliminal dynamic fades long-term memory and emphasizes short-term memory. Overloaded with information, few can expend the energy that memory requires. Who needs memory, anyway? Everything is on tape, film, disk, or even the head of a pin.

The Mass Art of Meaninglessness

David Letterman deals in meaninglessness. He puts on everything. He almost never strikes a serious note. Disorganization, confusion, and downright anti-social nastiness predominate his shows. Running like an undertone through his shows is a powerful negative tendency to turn everything on its head. He expects nothing but foolishness of people and is seldom disappointed. Very often, he is so inexplicably rude and boorish that he seems out of emotional control.

> David Letterman puts on literacy: shirt, tie, and jacket. He looks like the antithesis of his audience, a bookish, disgruntled figure out of the past. His speech is punctiliously grammatical and he intimates conservative Midwestern values.

Letterman's guests are there simply as foils for his nasty barbs and embarrassing put-ons. He reduces everyone to nothing. He eliminates all pretension to meaningful values. Once he was called an "asshole" on the air and he left the incident on the broadcast tape. In such an environment of arch-meaninglessness, nothing has the power of true thought or feeling. It is the perfect content for a medium that mainly has no content, just smart personalities saying smart lines in banal situations. Any aspect of real life is made to seem trivial against the nothingness of the overall backdrop.

To the uninitiated, his show seems a stupendous waste of time, during which he presents idiotic silliness as entertainment. This entertainment — the barely satirical diddling with things and people of absolutely no consequence — is always the same, lent support by an important media network and a highly paid star. Nothing is learned, nothing need be remembered; in fact, the sooner forgotten, the better for his show. It makes the reruns easier to take.

Something Happened, the name of a book by Joseph Heller, would be an apt title for this show. Letterman is at his best pretending to be exasperated when things go wrong, when some planned business turns out to be futile and meaningless. He poses as the reasonable man in an unreasonable world; the audience loves it. It must remind them of their lives.

Whole experience is a state, not a statement. But conscious understanding comes only through the statements we make about our whole experience. In the beginning was the word and this conundrum: Without *Homo sapiens*, there is no

> All media present interpretative reconstructions of direct experience. They distort and limit perceptions and meanings.

language; without language there can be no *Homo sapiens*. Buckminster Fuller has described himself as a verb. Everything we possess culturally exists fundamentally as language — words out of which we create our endlessly varied reconstructions of experience. This is an almost infinite process of refining, a process of perpetual re-evaluation of culture and all statements about it.

Every reconstruction or interpretation of events is biased toward the technical capabilities and limitations of the interpretative medium. Each interpretation by another medium adds to the linguistic growth and wholeness of an event. In terms of whole perception, therefore, we need to know what is lost and what is gained in the interpretations of each medium through time. Events have passed; we want to hold on to them as accurately as possible. This tenacity of cultural purpose may invoke science or mathematics or art, but always, at base, the reconstructions are linguistic.

French psychiatrist Jacques Lacan believed that in the unconscious mind, what is found at base is the word. It seems that we *are* verbs. Even the operations of the four basic constituents of the DNA molecule are described by George Beadle as fundamentally linguistic. The word, too, has its limitations, but the crucial difference between language and all other forms of communication is that the verbal process includes and encompasses all the contributions to understanding of all the other media.

Only language retains that power of primacy and control. All other media usurp the established functions of language in order to give free play to their innovative technology and their stimulation of the senses in new entertaining and informative relationships.

Language always moves toward greater understanding by refining the story of experience, whereas other media present reality just at, or below, the limen of idea and coherent syntax. If one wants to "know" the world, language is indispensable. You have to tell yourself what you've experienced in order to make any sense of it and to retain a useful memory of it. A pan shot or an instant replay can only recreate the feeling of an experience.

Words in artful order, as in great poetry, are resonant with meaning. Words in a novel of genius pile up strata of meanings, a geology of etyms like tectonic plates giving rise to original thought. Print is capable of being delicately plied. Ezra Pound once defined poetry as "language charged to the utmost possible degree with meaning." There is an over-whelming wholeness to the total verbal record of human existence; it is an evolving cross-cultural awareness of our position in time and space.

Other media can intensify feelings, but they are not able to use words in a way that exploits their power to aid understanding. Words work against strong visual bias by preserving the ambiguities of acoustic space. Higher-level abstract thought is only possible when freed from visual tyranny. Electric process is invisible and retrieves acoustic space, where things are connected by the operations of the resonant intervals of electromagnetic forces, which retrieve a more balanced ratio between the other parts of the sensorium. The ear comes back, as does touch.

The fundamental property of any medium of communication is its effect on the word. Electric media inhibit the power of the word, though each medium does this differently. The telephone elicits paralanguage and verbal shorthand. Radio, as described earlier, has become an adjunct to music and the telephone. TV will soon be all talk and much smut. All of these effects show up in the way we use language. Precisely at a time when competency in language is being undermined through the exclusive use of one medium — television — language becomes more important than ever.

Meaning at the Edge of Awareness:
A Look at Apperception and Projection

Leibniz introduced the term "apperception"[34] to mark the two-phased phenomenon of experiencing ourselves experiencing. We can be surprised, for example, by a noise that we have inhibited from reaching our conscious awareness until it stops. A ringing in the ears, the after-effect of the noise, draws our attention to the act of hearing. We may even become bemused by the dim apprehension of our powers of inhibition. But we seldom take it further than that. The meaning of the event is in its ceasing to exist.

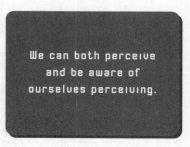

We can both perceive and be aware of ourselves perceiving.

Apperception, as a psychological term, refers to the process whereby new experience is assimilated to the established unity of the conscious mind. The new input is transformed by the residuum of past experience to create a new organization of the conscious whole. The residuum of past experience is the so-called apperceptive mass.[35]

A shock of awareness or of recognition, the flash of an epiphany or insight, Augustine's ontological illumination, and the spiritual enlightening in the conversion of Paul on the road to Damascus are extreme examples of a transformation of the conscious whole into a radically new form once one perceives oneself perceiving. This action brings the preconscious together in radical juxtaposition with the conscious order. Sometimes a completely opposite or flipped pattern of conscious organization follows; other times, the changes, though less dramatic, still result in a reversal of the accepted/rejected polarity that governs consciousness.

The process of getting in touch with preconscious meaning and defusing it of its negative potentials is a basic transformative process, much like dialectic discourse. Two people, engaged in discourse with the objective of rising by mutual effort to a higher level of understanding than either has consciously achieved, must sift through preconscious materials to add to the conscious. If unconscious materials can be thus exposed, made conscious, and a higher synthesis obtained, dialectic discourse becomes a form of psychotherapy.

Synthesis is a powerful faculty of mind localized in the right hemisphere, and is the obverse of left-brained semantic analysis. Meaning, therefore, is poised at the edge of these two mental modes of understanding. This position is precisely where apperception takes place, with one hemisphere able to monitor the other. Music is produced in a similar way: the mathematics of it on one side monitors the flow of feeling on the other.

The pattern of one's inhibitions is revealed in the way one projects. Robin Williams, for example, seems almost entirely connected to his preconscious; he plays it with virtuosity and to great comic effect. The unique character of one's walk, talk, and thought patterns is a clear message about the inhibited aspects of individual personality. Handwriting can also be revealing of inner states. Mimes thrive on this aspect of human behaviour and give pleasure simply by bringing into awareness certain rejected facts about personality and gestural behaviour.

> The synthesis hoped for in traditional dialectic exchange is a basic function of electrically trained perception. Electric process enhances the individual's power of synthesis.

The media of communication are technical forms of projected inner states. We have learned to experience in the way required by each medium, each a different way of perceiving. But we are seldom aware of how this perceptual learning is also a set of instructions on how to inhibit perceptions not relevant to the use of the individual medium.

> The media of communication force us to become masters of inhibitive meaning.
> The proposition put to the user by each medium: ignore perceptions not part of that particular technical mode of translating experience.

It is possible to make a positive value out of the perceptual limitations of any medium. The verbal force of print produces the great pleasure of interior imaging. The research that goes into a period film can seduce the viewer through the technical accuracy of its visual effects. Even a humble telephone call allows one to put the best image possible to the voice at the other end of the line.

We are not supposed to notice these translations — otherwise, the trick of making each medium credible as part of reality would be lost. Within the perceptual frame of each medium, our wilful suspension of disbelief must be maintained. We are not supposed to study the inner workings of our watches, our cars, our refrigerators, or our perceptual lives. The media, especially, require an inhibition in viewer awareness, which hides important aspects of perception but lets the specific medium have its best effects.

A one-medium user is the new illiterate. High users of all media, but especially those well grounded in language, are probably best off in the media-overloaded environment. The benefits are somewhat the same as the advantages enjoyed by the fluent speaker of several languages. It takes strong mental effort, however, to become perceptually expert in both print and electric forms of communication. Some deliberate study is involved in acquiring such expertise. If people are not rigorously educated to such virtuosity, it is unlikely to happen by accident.

Schools presently have no pedagogy capable of doing this job. Although "media literacy" programs do exist in most school districts, they tend to be advertising biased and fairly superficial. They still focus on content to the general exclusion of technology's virtual additions to that content. An in-depth sensibility training in media forms would be a much more useful way to educate today's children. Programs in media literacy must be grounded in a strong understanding of media effects on the whole being of the user if they are to work. Generally, however, teacher education leads in the opposite direction, urging just social commentary on content.

The superficial addition of "visual aids" to the child's day simply creates confusion in the child's mind about the nature of informational structure. A little light discussion of film meaning through character behaviour is not enough to inculcate the sensibility required for survival in our overloaded environment. Teacher training must result in first-rate film and video criticism.

The education children do receive introduces them to a limbo-like world in which they are attracted naturally to environmental forms like media, video games, and computers that are at odds with the watered-down literate game being played in the classroom. They fall between two stools; not literate enough to achieve useful levels of critical judgment, they are also uncritical consumers of general environmental communications. Such an education should produce citizens unable or unwilling to act in any politically or socially demanding capacity.

The Explicit Limits of Meaning

> To the extent that it aspires to be whole, the process of thought is always failing. Even in the most adamant quest for the truth, it is impossible to avoid contradiction.

At base, even the most rigorous philosophical system is autobiographical. No mind can construct a vision of life and the world that is large enough to contain all that is in the author's mind. The selection by an author of what he deems most important in his thought is, in fact, the expression of an enormous bias.

A history written by a misanthrope, as in the case of H.G. Wells, is history terribly skewed. A psychology produced by a man obsessed by machine metaphor, as Freud was, is likely to become obsolete when the dominance of that metaphor fades from culture. Autobiographical biases underlie all so-called objective treatises.

The scientific thread that strings together Ptolemy, Copernicus, Galileo, Newton, and Einstein falsely emphasizes the continuity of thought in their work. In fact, each was an idiosyncratic individual, steeped in his own experiential knowledge, and bent on overturning his scientific forebears and rivals. We stand on the shoulders of giants in order to be in a better position to kick their teeth out.

Even an illustrious philosopher functions historically more like carrion for those who come to carry away only the fragments that serve their more specious appetites. The largest picture possible of all philosophy is just a mosaic of interplaying parts that is constantly changing. What was thought of Newton in 1750 and what we think of him now is a difference marked by our increased familiarity with him as an idiosyncratic man and the disintegration of his world view.

> The history of human knowledge is mainly the history of complex personalities.

Every thinker, systematic, traditional, or desultory, is one of a kind. The illusory simplicities offered by the myth of objectivity belie the complexities of deep personal motivations. Bias creeps easily into any system of thought. The best we can hope for is that deeply rooted personal experience will accurately reflect the spirit of the age in which the writer lives. All systems of thought become falsifiable as whole systems, but nodes of permanent wisdom live forever in some, in isolation, as percepts. Thus universal thought forms in personal contexts.

Science strains to ignore, as far as possible, the metaphoric relations between all things, yet everything, even in science, is both itself and something else. Poetic genius (after the fashion of Vico's argument)[36] is the substrate of all direct experience. Prose, the explicit mode of communication, flattens language out into fewer layers of meaning. Poetry no longer has an honoured place in our society. The schools do their best to stamp it out. The best we can hope for

> Each person's work is an extended and complex metaphor of self, expressed in corporate terms.

in literature is that more of an author's experience can be brought into utterance. Great poetry comes closest to achieving this goal, but poetic form has been usurped to some extent by the lens and splice of film.

Such a reappraisal of the grounds of communication becomes increasingly necessary if we expect to clarify bases of action in an impossibly overloaded informational environment. Our perception of reality must increasingly be based on an understanding of the structure of information. We must understand as well what a medium *can't* do.

Given the intense current interest in the bimodal model of consciousness, it should not be surprising that we are double-minded about the nature of knowledge in general. Michael Polanyi underscores his perception of a split: "We always know tacitly that we are holding our explicit knowledge to be true."[37] We may know it, but we don't admit to such awareness in our explicit thought patterns — the mask of professionalism, or seriousness, guards against mixing the two modes of thought. This in spite of the fact that "tacit knowing is . . . the dominant principle of all knowledge."[38] The tacit experience of every human makes her or him unique.

Tacit knowledge is not absolutely whole, but is much wider in scope than the narrow specializing focus of explicit knowing. An analogy exists here, for example, between the true, wide, 240-degree vision that we actually experience and the narrow, vanishing-point perspective of 3-D space, framed like a photograph.

Tacit knowing is suppressed in the interests of getting things done. Simplifications are necessary in order to make life comfortable and profitable. We have given up a lot of freedom to build up our institutions. Now, through electric media, however, we have been turned inward to encounter more holistic experience and the serious limitations of institutional values to give our lives sufficient meaning.

> Electric process tacitly exposes and overturns explicit cultural conventions and reshapes the meaning of morals.

The essential difference between the two kinds of knowledge, tacit and explicit, is that we can critically reflect on something explicitly stated, but we cannot easily reflect on our tacit awareness of experience. Ironically, the explicit leads to a reflective posture and the tacit to an active, rather than passive, relation to thought. The understanding that flows from tacit knowledge leads inevitably to the recognition of the essential incompleteness of all reflective thought. So every time we acquire tacit knowledge consciously, we enlarge the world, the world of humanity, by something that is not yet incorporated into the objects of our explicit knowledge, and in this sense a comprehensive knowledge of man must appear impossible.

Polanyi tries to show that the relations between the tacit and the explicit are almost mathematically precise, at least an elegantly balanced set of forces rooted in language and linguistic utterance. In order to describe experience more fully, language must be less precise. But greater imprecision brings more effectively into play the powers of inarticulate judgment required to resolve the ensuing indeterminacy of speech. So it is our personal participation that governs the richness of the concrete experience to which our speech can refer. Only by the aid of this tacit coefficient could we ever say anything at all about anything.

The cultivation of the tacit and its transformation into the explicit is the real business of language. When the job of language is complicated by electric media, however, we see a reversal of this process. Film and television start with simple descriptive language (a script) and then create surrogate forms of tacit experience. This is a reversal of civilized, literate procedures, and a process that trivializes experience itself. We have become more aware of the limits of formal thought.

Media destroy metaphysics; we run scenarios full of shallow gestures in place of careful thought. Media lead us to prefer the tacit over the explicit. Truly, our sense of the world has become a kaleidoscopic flux of impressions, many of which we must inhibit in order to get by without serious thought.

The idea of a "sixth sense" is trying to be born. Starting with the scientific inquiry into proprioception, or body knowledge, we must also consider topographic knowledge — the nuanced feel in a great athlete's movements, for example, that result from exquisitely fine training on an exquisitely fine nervous system. The important meanings generated by this dimension of human sensitivity are part of a general and healthy destabilization of meaning brought into

> The depersonalized and discarnate effects of computer technology are being challenged by the ineffably humane knowledge being developed in the "embodiment" movement for mind/body uniqueness.

play by the various forms of the theory of embodiment. Science cannot describe absolutes because of the unique autobiographical bias of the investigator. The quest for new systems of knowledge re-establishes a role in serious inquiry for those aspects of our humanity that science has rejected as mystagogic obfuscations of the real. Serious attention is now accorded parapsychological phenomena, orthomolecular medicine, acupuncture, therapeutic imaging, radical nutrition, psychochemistry, electrotherapy, and more.

Echoing William James' concern for the complexity of "attention" in human perception, Polanyi attempts to reconstruct the actual conditions of consciousness attendant to the apparently simple act of reading a letter.

> When I receive information by reading a letter and when I
> ponder the message of the letter I am subsidiarily aware not only
> of its text, but also of all the past occasions by which I have come
> to understand the words of the text, and the whole range of this
> subsidiary awareness is presented focally in terms of the message.[39]

Even this simple form of communication presents us with a complex mosaic of interplaying perceptions, which focus on parts of the letter as well as the medium as a whole. *It is a distinction between form and content that is at the root of the creation of meaning.* The message comes in layers of awareness, interplaying and influencing the meaning of one another.

> This message or meaning, on which attention is now focused, is
> not something tangible: it is the conception evoked by the text.
> The conception in question is the focus of our attention, in terms
> of which we attend subsidiarily both to the text and to the objects
> indicated by the text. Thus the meaning of a text resides in a focal
> comprehension of all the relevant instrumentally known particulars,
> just as the purpose of an action resides in the co-ordinated
> innervation of its instrumentally used particulars.[40]

Not to put it too crudely after such a fine set of distinctions, this "focal awareness" refers to the figure/ground relationship between the figures presented to perception and the ground of the operations of tacit subsidiary awareness. The intrusion of hidden grounds into a controlled situation, such as a particular medium of communication, can destroy the special effects of that medium. A bad film cut or a phony rear projection can kill a movie's effect; an inept rhetorical figure can draw attention to the hidden agenda in printed communication. In Polanyi's words: "While focal awareness is necessarily conscious, subsidiary awareness may vary over all degrees of consciousness." And can it be partly preconscious? It seems unavoidably so.

This figure/ground problem, in one form or another, has bedevilled philosophers who have recognized it for the conundrum it is. Polanyi cites A.N. Whitehead: "There is not a sentence which adequately states its own meaning. There is always a background of presupposition which defies analysis by reason of its infinitude."[41] The permeation of

Heisenberg's Uncertainty Principle into philosophical thought is reflected in Polanyi's early use of the notion for illuminating the limits of meaning.

> The irreducible indeterminacy inherent in the meaning of all
> descriptions and the origin and function of this indeterminacy in
> relating meaning to reality was affirmed and elaborated in . . .
> Science, Faith and Society.[42]

As soon as direct experience is lined up on the grid of semantic interpretation, it acquires a clarity and coherence that the original experience lacked. This perceptual habit is linked to our being able to select from an array of environmental actions the one action that most puts our safety in jeopardy.

There are even higher uses for this faculty. Nietzsche, I believe, first suggested that metaphysics is based on forgetting; metaphysics can't cover everything that is the experience of the metaphysician, especially the Dionysian or irrational side. Incompleteness again! We survive by forgetting all that our senses pick up but do not focus attention on.

Things are further complicated, Polanyi insists, by our tendency to take what we learn from others as having the same standing as direct experience. "Remember that the overwhelming part of our factual beliefs are held at second hand through trusting others." Much of the training of children is devoted to cutting them off from direct experience and imposing the second-hand knowledge of culture on them.

Life, if lived thoughtfully, becomes less false, and perhaps decreasingly unhappy. Polanyi works his system of thought in just such a context.

> The principle purpose of this book [*Personal Knowledge*] is to
> achieve a frame of mind in which I may hold firmly to what I believe
> to be true, even though I know that it might conceivably be false.
> The cultivation of thought in general is only examined as the context
> in which truth may be upheld.[43]

To further underline the isolation of the thinker, Polanyi makes an appeal similar to that of Carlyle or Marcuse for heroes: "Men are valued as men according to their moral forces."[44] In a world seething with almost instantaneous change, moral bedrock is vital; reaching a moral consensus, however, appears impossible. Perhaps the call has never been clearer: like Robert Frost, we must learn that the only revolution possible is the revolution of one human. The enemy is the social science mentality, divorced from human sources by specious adherence to statistical methods and the mass values of consensus morality, the mass that Ortega defines as "all that which places no value upon itself."[45] The agenda of the mass is always explicit; tacit knowledge is individual knowledge.

If the world is descending by the agency of electric process into cultural entropy, is our only hope the irreducible primacy of tacit knowledge as a corrective to the aberrations of science and technology? The breadth of personal experience in an over-rich informational environment stimulates more comprehensive patterns of awareness when one transcends the protections of inhibition. A new age of individualism may be upon us.

Socrates had more knowledge than anyone in Athens, yet he died, he said, knowing nothing. His meaning in saying this was highly paradoxical, but paradox is a very powerful form of meaning. It took him an entire lifetime of intense introspection and active dialogue to divest himself of his opinions, and to learn that all opinions are mental mechanisms for shutting out an awareness unencumbered by cultural shibboleths. Such a free mind can establish tolerance, peace, and understanding of differences.

> Simple opinions always create complex responses. A man who wants to avoid the trouble of thinking (or who lacks the capacity) will despise paradox and ambiguity.

Knowing nothing, as well as understanding why he knew nothing, Socrates became most wise. Knowing nothing, his teaching became most instructive. Knowing nothing, he became most sensitive to the true nature of human inquiry. Knowing nothing, he learned that it is futile to take any action against a man save exposing the ignorance of his opinions. Only by ignorance does culture grow.

For anyone interested in taking action on some solid basis, this is an insupportable solipsism. Life is messy. Thought is imperfect. A man must eat. Never mind that "all is vanity" — one has to make a showing in life. This desire for simple meaning, unfortunately, develops into a stance that militates against any exploration of the hidden grounds essential for useful interpretations of events. Life becomes a welter of surface confusion in which nothing means very much at all. Narrowness does not save us the pain of not knowing.

Propaganda, a theoretically complex process, requires a public that wants to be simply informed. It is the business of successful propaganda to remove from awareness any contexts that do not serve the interests of those who would manage meaning for public consciousness. The necessity to investigate hidden grounds is obviated by ideology. Ideologies are massive institutional systems of inhibition. The powerful, regressive force of nationalist ideology — in Ireland, Scotland, Belgium, Quebec, Iran, and elsewhere — underlines the extent to which an inhibited perception of the real forces of globalization can go.

We live within an enveloping global information network that obliterates local differences with global meaning, at least to the extent that our present state demands a global scale of interchange for the purposes of economic and political survival. The true collectivist values of our times are the planetary values of information technology. Every square foot of the globe is technically under broadcast control, though not quite politically.

This network reality presents us with serious problems. The less diversity there is between things and events in the world, the more the world runs down into cultural entropy. The eventual state of no change, in which all differences have been eliminated, is the ultimate cultural nothingness. Money abhors cultural difference, which is why global fiscal activity opposes cultural diversity.

The random chaos of an environment overloaded with information is the dangerous stage of a system showing advancing cultural entropy. It is not likely that such a tendency to sameness in the world will go undisputed by the forces, Eastern and Western, now accumulating beneath the apparent calm of global business as usual.

We seem to have become a perfectly propagandized zombie constituency. A great irony seems to have been let loose upon the world. At the very time when the new spirit of a higher humanity based on the etherialization of knowledge through information economies is trying to be born in the world, anti-human forces are being created by those who see electric process as a complex weapon for breaking down resistance to consumer values.

We may become angels or trolls, depending on how addicted to inhibition we remain. A nation crying out to be spared understanding is a nation easily dictated to. The wisdom produced by awareness is the only authority we have. One wise individual is a polity unto him- or herself.

Of Form, the Content of Content, and Pure Ignorance

Interpretations of the relation between form and content appear to be inexhaustible. In fact, every philosopher has a way of approaching this thorny problem — though each, in the end, becomes only a revelation of the biases implicit in that particular philosophical view. The view that form proceeds from content, for example, or is an "extension of content" (see Olson and others, for instance) is naive; it presupposes that the problem is dualistic enough to allow for such a simple manipulation of the terms.

To have a useful knowledge of forms, one must at least consider both *the form of the medium* as well as the *form of the content*, since every medium has as its content another medium. Every filmgoer, while familiar with the demands of film form, often lacks knowledge of the literary forms on which film content is based. The problem of form and content is one of multiple regress, as in a system of self-reflecting mirrors. The medium, even without a content, is the meaning.

This ignorance of the out-of-awareness aspects of any medium of communication is where action and change occur, particularly as one moves from one medium to another. We want to know whether there is a form/content relationship that holds true for all media of communication. An affirmative answer to this question is possible: *content consumes form*. How could *The Wizard of Oz*, *Gone With the Wind*, or *La Dolce Vita* be imagined apart from their medium's form, which has entered and become fused with content? No matter how spectacular the production values of a film, the contents of that film consume it.

> All strict philosophical discussion of form ends up rooted in our incomplete knowledge of human perception.

Forms tend to formalize, of course, though at some point they came from pure invention: someone wrote the first sestina or the first ode. But who was the first person to use alphabetized language? (It probably wasn't the mythic Cadmus, who likely was illiterate.)

Clearly, the form of the medium is of primary importance to meaning; the form of the content, which is part medium and part literary genre, proceeds from it secondarily. Other parts of the form of the content are style, structure, voice, and the self-conscious part that assimilates aspects of the medium's form.

New aesthetic forms are created in response to a new medium. After many novels have been absorbed by a reading populace, life itself becomes novelistic. All other, secondary forms are variations on the new kinds of sensory interplay that the medium has made possible — and that's the meaning of the new medium. The strictly literary notion of form and content is too narrow to be applied to other media. New forms are a function of new technologies for projecting inner states of mind. All art is nothing if not first the quest for new forms. And that means discovering new techniques for altering perception and new ways to construct contents to make that possible.

Contents tend to lose their novelty through assimilation. Anyone working in a genre will subscribe to some extent to its formally entrenched rules, which, by habit, have become requirements of the form, in order not to frustrate audience expectations. A novel, however experimental, has to look novelistic to a recognizable degree. Human nature appears incapable of handling very much novelty in a short period of time. Novelty of form tends to be rejected outright or assimilated very slowly. Novelty threatens established conscious standards of expectation. When we say we seek the new,

> Art always forces meaning to the edge of awareness.

what we often want are variations of the old, something still recognizable. Most of us don't want *Finnegans Wake*, we want Saul Bellow or A.S. Byatt. Contents tend to redundantly confirm a fixed view of reality, the "eternal verities."

It is likely that novel meaning comes from a part of the mind that is below the conscious threshold. We use the word "imagination" to describe this contact with the substrate of consciousness. Sometimes we admire this faculty, other times we resent its intrusion into the drudging business of everyday existence. We tend to resist the imaginative inputs of novelty, thinking they conflict with reality. We like ritual repetition in the arts. Only after some effort to assimilate the new does its content overcome the alienating features of the new form.

> The content of the content is the medium.

As in all communication, content is a

mixture of what is expected and what is unexpected. Novel elements in any medium are part of both the form and the content. The most ordinary story done as a film, in which all the latest production techniques are employed to overwhelm the senses, has a novelty that is not part of conscious awareness. A story that has no narrative line, but which exploits psychological relations, runs the risk of having too much new information in its content for the common user.

The old wisdom suggests that nothing that expects to succeed should ever be more than five percent new. People generally can't handle more than that without help and a long period of time for processing. Imaginative, unexpected, "newsy" material is severely restricted in its ability to communicate by the primary demand for redundancy — the expected elements of a message. Content, therefore, normally mixes the richness of novel elements with recognizable and pleasurable variations on the expected. It's one thing to get exactly what one expects and quite another to get an ingeniously subtle variation of it. When the medium enters into content, the virtual relationship between the medium and the content pulls the two together.

Artists and media producers dredge up preconscious elements as part of the novel aspect of any media program. This gives the appearance of real imagination, since the result has little to do with the expectations of consciousness. It may be instead that real imagination, as Coleridge suggested, is linked to unconscious sources, whereas fancy, which we easily mistake for deep imagination, is only linked to the fairly accessible preconscious elements in the psyche.

The preconscious, sub-syntactical elements in communication (a poetic image, a metaphor, a violent scene) can be employed more richly in electric media forms where the strict linear demands of literacy are much less in force. Here, new literary forms are emphasized: lists, stream of consciousness writing, hypertextual anti-stories, and the like.

Only the most difficult works of literary genius, like *Finnegans Wake*, dare to have the novel, multiplexed form of a music video. Music videos tend, on the whole, to traffic in accessible preconscious materials. Their lack of traditional content form severely restricts their capacity to communicate semantic meaning, but they are very powerful in conveying the *psychological tendency* implicit in the medium. In a medium like television that is dominated by audile values, the visual dimension is appropriately organized by symbolic resonance.

Form is a mixture of both the technical aspects of a particular medium and the uniqueness of such technology in dealing with particular states of mind. A dream rendered in film, in print, or in a painting is not the dream itself, obviously, but an interpretation of the dream experience. These interpretations give us insight into the unique way media translate states of mind into forms appropriate to those media.

Each new medium is in reality a parable of the limitations of that technology, which is new knowledge about primary experience. A babbling brook, a description of a brook in Wordsworth, a Wyeth stream plunging headlong, a postcard dimly recalling brooks, a filmed brook dashing over rocks, and videotape of a brook visited — experience grows and complexifies as an aggregate of interplaying simple views. The experience expands awareness synergistically, the whole becoming greater than the parts.

The technology of any medium must be ignored in order for the effects of its contents to attend to the appeals of reality. The illusion thereby created takes on the characteristics of a higher reality; these technical simulations then create a strong desire for the hyper-real. As Edmund Carpenter has shown in *They Became What They Beheld* and *Oh, What a Blow That Phantom Gave Me*, primitives see through our media instantly, and are the first to correctly determine that they have deleterious effects on psychic health. It is we who do not perceive the effects of the media we use on mental and spiritual conditions. The more we use various media, however, the more we become inured to the novelty of their perceptual effects and conditioned to their bias toward meaning.

> It is obvious that media alienate us from direct experience. But media also immeasurably enlarge the scope of our ignorance about experience.

The illusion of the superiority of the hyper-real is so powerful because we recognize instinctively the greater pleasure to be gained in probing the preconscious. Media are instruments of psychic interplay. Add to this the thrill of toying with the powerful and lively materials that we have rejected in the interests of orderly, and somewhat deadly, institutional values, and it is easy to see why we have an inescapable attraction to media. The fact that media offer an entirely new way to structure meaning, especially economic meaning — consider the salaries of celebrities and televised athletes — is not lost on us either.

The profound unreality of electric economics unexpectedly introduces whole new realms of ignorance into our daily lives, confusing us morally and ethically.

> Content is the style of perception demanded by the technology of any medium. The form of any medium is its grammar.

A style of perception has to do with the sensory ratios established by the medium and that ratio's spin on the whole experience. The grammar of any medium is the formal set of technical requirements that account for the illusion-making power of the medium. One ought never to "see" the grammar taking precedence over the "story."

Just as there are figures of speech in language, so, too, do electric media have figures of perception that bind the way we perceive reality in their interpretations. Film, for example, has a precise and elaborate grammar: establishing shots, pans, zooms, the reversal rule of 180-degree line of motion, the relations between moving camera and/or moving subject, the symbolic transformation of body parts when isolated by the lens, standard relations between close-ups, medium close-ups, full shots, long shots, and so forth.

Television's long-standing inability to communicate subtle detail makes it subscribe to a grammar of extreme visual simplicity — close-up shots, tight-to-frame performance, an avoidance of pans, and an adherence to simple shot composition. Besides trivializing the perceptual habits of the inveterate viewer, this characteristic of television permeates every formal aspect of the medium. Nothing can be treated in its true complexity due to the low-definition of the small screen; everything on television is a perceptual and conceptual cartoon. Even digital technology has not converted TV into a "hot" medium because the video display terminal is a right-brained stimulus.

Telegnosis:

The Deep Meaning
of Electric Process

*"Well, I think that we live in post-history
in the sense that all pasts that ever were
are now present to our consciousness and that
all the futures that will be are here now."*
— MCLUHAN[1]

WE ARE ENTERING INTO THE FIFTH DIMENSION of cultural evolution, a living myth of the increasing etherealization of the human condition. Our unavoidable obsession with information in all its forms turns our once-simple life of physical contexts into one of discarnate relations in which our bodies mean less and less in our work and play. The characteristics of the present condition of the human spirit represent a new gnosticism, a retrieval of the archaic outlook of searching for wisdom, this time in the new dimension of language coded by electric conditions. Gnosticism is an esoteric attempt to redeem the lost spiritual element in man. Gnosticism promises a way of achieving deep understanding that reveals the hidden truth of reality. Instead of rational thought, gnosticism relies on epiphanies of insight, grand happenings in a flash, which are hopefully more potent than the news bulletin that interrupts regular television programming.

We have begun living a Telegnostic reality of virtual transformations in which our media simulate otherworldly connections, if not with heaven, at least with cyberspace. We are fed intolerably large amounts of insistent information by media from an emergent bolus of barely suppressed preconscious materials. This rejected psychic stuff coming up into consciousness can feel mysterious, at times like true epiphanies.

Learning the secrets of such new and powerful electric forces amounts to the creation of a new gnostic depth to the human condition. Gnosticism is a system of symbolic and linguistic transformations that enable the practitioner to retrieve hidden knowledge and deep truths from the shadowy world of marginal or subliminal awareness. Just as electricity has retribalized society, deepening local realities against global sameness, so there is an electric dualism to contemporary experience that underlies information technology. It is an electric form of gnosticism that generates new secret knowledge.

Seekers after secret information flood the Internet looking for everything from pornography to cures for cancer and plans for building an atomic bomb. Deep shifts in economics are studied and arranged by power brokers before they overwhelm ordinary citizens. The shift now from markets and the holding of goods to the sale of *access* to the short-run experience of ownership presently marks our most basic deep thought about business.

Above all, observe that this new gnosis is technologically driven and is thus ultimately real and practical in determining important new aspects of the human condition. All things thinkable are now technically possible, though in terms of time, energy, and money often somewhat implausible.

Everyone always wants to know, individually and collectively, "Where are we going?" It is the question of life — silly, yet profound. The answer, in all great systems of speculative thought, is "to find the way": the soul's safe way out of the world. Taoism follows the *tao*, or the right way; Christ called himself "The Way"; and Buddhism's way, with its steps of spiritual growth, is the "True Path." But the realm of the supernatural seems always just out of reach of the strongest minds, and a matter of unconvincing faith in the weakest, though the truly humble sometimes give us pause in what they achieve spiritually. Nevertheless, ours is a world in which earthly realities prevail. This earth and its technological articulations ought to be mysterious enough for anyone. And as Alexander Pope insisted, "The proper study of mankind is man."[2] Telegnosis promises a new way to discover one's soul.

The Gnosis* of Marshall McLuhan

McLuhan was fully aware of the deep hermetic, or gnostic, base to communications theory. Language is connected to the deepest roots of the human psyche. Through the proper study of language, deep truths can be released into consciousness, not unlike psychiatric operations on the unconscious. Consider the flash of deep insight, epiphany, or ontological illumination, if you like, that can occur while studying a poem or prayer. Such things happen, if only rarely.

McLuhan studied the tradition of hermetic grammarians and their gnostic knowledge for his dissertation at Cambridge. This work examined the crucial changes, occurring in the late medieval period, that gave way to the "modern" mindset embodied by Peter Ramus. Ramus' new way of thinking challenged Aristotelian controls that had been officially in place for centuries. Ramus' primary effect was on language, though his work also focused on logic and new ways of thinking about the material world.

As McLuhan brilliantly described in his Cambridge dissertation, this new way of the "moderns" left behind the "ancients," the grammarians who used language in its full paradoxical richness, not scientifically.

> The great alchemists, the Paracelsans from Raymond Lully to
> Cornelius Agrippa, were grammarians. From the time of the
> neo-Platonists and Augustine to Bonaventura and to Francis Bacon,
> the world is viewed as a book, the lost language of which was
> analogous to human speech. Thus the art of grammar provided
> not only the 16th century approach to the book of Life in
> scriptural exegesis but to the book of Nature as well.[3]

This approach to the "book of Nature," or science, prior to Bacon's experimental thrust was arrested by obsolete Aristotelian views.

*The terms gnostic, hermetic, alchemical, or esoteric are forms used interchangeably here, although subtle differences divide them in other contexts. In part, the belief in gnostic knowledge is centred on the lost preternatural condition of man before the Fall. The hope of reconnecting to this higher state is what motivates the quest for superhuman status through the acquisition of secret knowledge. The original gnosticism offered devotees "knowledge of the otherwise hidden truth of total reality as the indispensable key to man's salvation."[4] The system was developed as a sidebar to the main hermetic tradition that taught the importance of converting material know-how into spiritual gain. ("By their works you shall know them.")

One very large question hovers over McLuhan's deep and extensive knowledge of the gnosticism of the grammarian tradition: as a grammarian himself, could he be steeped in such knowledge and still be a Catholic in good standing? What kind of Catholic was he? McLuhan gave away his true feelings to his old student Walter Ong when he complained movingly in a letter that "I find few I can talk to among Catholics. Fewer and fewer too."[5] Obviously, as a Catholic, the man was lonely. I am convinced that the unconventional implications of McLuhan's scholarly views and his deep understanding of the philosophical tradition were always at odds with the dutiful, orthodox practice of his new religion, but he managed both to the end.

McLuhan writes to Ong that he has been reading Aquinas and the Pseudo-Dionysus, two theologians central to the Church. After a garbled reference to a discovery in Aquinas, McLuhan exclaims, "My eyes bugged out! And Thomas is not quite one-third right on this point I think."[6] Correcting Aquinas is heady business in Catholicism; it shows that McLuhan still maintains a rebellious streak that does not docilely accept all Catholic orthodoxy.

McLuhan's mention of Giordano Bruno, who comes into modern literary awareness through his important role in the work of James Joyce, is also telling. Joyce saw in Bruno a symbol of his own battle with the Church, a tussle that resulted in the Church burning Bruno at the stake for a heresy that basically amounted to his premature espousal of the Copernican system. McLuhan, the arch-modern in spite of protesting otherwise, has his Catholic psyche split between Joyce the actual apostate and Joyce the artist with whom McLuhan most closely identifies literarily. He reserves the highest praise for Joyce, an artist who makes art of his actual apostasy. If McLuhan has no Catholics to talk to, he can always turn to Joyce and a little heretical reading in *Finnegans Wake*.

The extensive knowledge that McLuhan had gathered of the various gnostic grammarians, along with his general apprehension at the power and pervasiveness of secret societies, stayed with him throughout his life — because these things do exist and they touched him actually in his real life. McLuhan the grammarian could not have missed the irony that in siding with the ancients in his dissertation, he appeared to be in the same position as the Masons. In looking, as he did, at the Masonic code, he could see that the Masonic view of the ancients was that they were like the preternatural Adam before his Fall.

> [They] were once in conscious conversation with the unseen world
> and were shepherded, taught and guided by the "gods" or discarnate
> superintendents of the infant race, who imparted to them the sure
> and indefeasible principles [Wisdom, Strength and Beauty] upon
> which their spiritual welfare and evolution depended.[7]

Masonry says that it is the living continuum of the once-powerful gnostic tradition of the grammarians, a tradition that contains all of the esoteric knowledge in man's possession. McLuhan could not help but see that it was a failure in the Church that saw it relinquish its primary role as gnostic receptacle and continuance. He may have felt that the loss was retrievable. One could more easily say of the mysteries of the Catholic Church, as of Masonry, "Our teaching is purposely veiled in allegory and symbol and its deeper import does not appear upon the surface of the ritual itself . . . The deeper secrets of Masonry, like the deeper secrets of life, are heavily veiled; are closely hidden."[8] And that behind each symbol is a "realistic fact."[9]

The Masonic objective is to build men morally and bring them to power over all aspects of life.

> This — the evolution of man into superman — was always the
> purpose of the ancient Mysteries, and the real purpose of modern
> Masonry is, not the social and charitable purposes to which so much
> attention is paid, but the expediting of the spiritual evolution of
> those who aspire to perfect their own nature and transform it into
> a more god-like quality. And this is a definite science, a royal art,
> which it is possible for each of us to put into practice.[10]

Wonderment plays over this entire question of esoteric knowledge and coincidence in McLuhan's life. It is certainly merely coincidence, but everyone knows now that *Annie Hall* (which is Diane Keaton's real name), Woody Allen's film, has a cameo appearance by McLuhan whose grandmother's name was Hall and whose close colleague was Edward T. Hall. But more brow-knitting is the strange significance of the name Lewis in his life. Wyndham Lewis, a great, difficult, and curmudgeonly friend and mentor to McLuhan, had a deeply arcane mind. And the maiden name of McLuhan's wife Corinne was Lewis, apparently no relation to the English novelist.

Still, McLuhan could not have missed the esoteric meaning of the name Lewis in Masonic code. "'Lewis' is a modern corruption of Eleusis,"[11] a reference to the ancient rites of the pre-Christian religion that lasted at least a thousand years before Christ right up until his time. McLuhan was steeped in the supposition and the actuality of systems of secrecy, so it is little wonder that he remained focused on powers emanating from this region of human activity.

Long after the esoteric research for his Cambridge University Ph.D., we find McLuhan still focused on secret rituals and codes in the very important and revealing letter to Walter Ong dated May 31, 1953:

> For the past year I have been exploring the relations between the Secret Societies and the Arts. A grisly business. I don't know what you know, but I know there isn't a living artist or critic of repute who isn't playing their game. I mean their rituals and doctrines as basis of artistic organization.[12]

Such revelations have often been taken as proof of McLuhan's alleged paranoid streak — typically shoved aside by the faithful and deemed a serious fault by his denigrators. But one should not be so quick about what McLuhan is wrestling with here: his deep understanding of the functions of secrecy in power relations anywhere and everywhere.

The reference in the Ong letter probably reflects McLuhan's attempt to understand the interest of Pope and Swift in Rosicrucianism and Masonry, and the continuance of such interests through the academic world. He was certain that the highest senior officials and colleagues at the University of Toronto were top-ranking Masons conspiring to hold power secretly. The arch-exponent of this condition was Northrop Frye, whom McLuhan believed to be a thirty-third degree Mason. Why did he concern himself about these things?

For one thing, when McLuhan converted to Catholicism, his knowledge of the foundation philosopher of the Catholic Church, St. Thomas Aquinas, was associated with Aquinas' teacher, St. Albertus Magnus, *Doctor Universalis*. Albertus was a thoroughgoing occultist, having written a book on alchemy (he was also said to have developed some of the early Masonic symbols),[13] and had shown legendary interest in magic. (The story circulated widely that when one visited Magnus, the door was answered by a robot who took your hat and cloak and announced you within.) Aquinas himself is thought to be the author of the *Aurora Consurgens*,[14] a treatise that attempts to marry the esoteric tradition with Christianity. Almost all of the major grammarians were given to esoteric biases. McLuhan understood this.

Now, McLuhan's problem was, again, that he wanted passionately to remain a Catholic in good standing — no easy role for someone as gifted and intellectually dynamic as McLuhan. Again the Ong letter holds clues. "Odd how Dominicans seem to have [a] yen for gnostic techniques of *gnosis* via passions. Bruno, Savonarola, Campanella."[15] The dangers to one's faith and health in holding such esoteric views, as in the cases of Bruno and Savonarola, is quite clear. But Campanella is a different story.

Thomas Campanella (1568–1639), author of *City of the Sun*, dealt in the fantastic; rejected Aristotle, and thus, by implication, Thomas; promoted intuition (passion) over reason; championed doubt in the face of Church certainty; and, antedating Descartes by twenty-eight years, established a highly individualistic protestation in the first proposition of his theory of cognition and doubt. As he writes: "I myself think," that is, "the certainty of self-consciousness is the primary truth."[16] Does he seem like a Protestant and a Catholic melded together? It is enough to say that it's extremely likely that McLuhan had too much knowledge to be an ordinary Catholic, and that he never gave up his attachment to this arena of deep theological controversy. He may have seen himself as a Catholic of the future: faithful, yet esoteric in the knowledge of the true Church.

The Cambridge dissertation was the perfect place to work these communications issues out. McLuhan was studying the revolutionary changes brought into education as epitomized in the watershed debate between the "ancients" and the "moderns," two movements headed by Thomas Nashe and Gabriel Harvey, respectively.

What is at stake in this formative debate, which now seems somewhat arcane, is the passing of the old system of education, the trivium of grammar, rhetoric, and logic, and the emergence of a new approach based on Ramus' revolutionary shift away from Aristotelianism and Thomism, which was paving the way for the new experimental science championed by Francis Bacon, and for Protestantism and capitalism.

The old system of education, steeped in the traditional study of grammar, used etymologies and rhetoric to create a way of communicating that preserved and emphasized the dual nature of speech, oral and written. In the new system, print culture allowed for, even demanded, precise definitions and standardized syntax, which tended to eliminate ambiguities in grammatical meaning. The deep understanding of language and the paradox in meaning was lost on ensuing generations. The aural tradition died. The ancients lost, only to return recently in electric guise. Belief in the power of language to connect deeply with the collective unconscious has made a return in psychiatry, modern literature and art, and the mass media.

The archetypes of the collective unconscious, and the gnostic meanings of those symbols, have returned in the psychology of Carl Jung. Both McLuhan and Frye studied the archetype as a connection to the ancient mind. But McLuhan's book *From Cliché to Archetype* is a highly simplified interpretation of the Jungian view. According to McLuhan, media mark the difference in the meaning of archetypes, which are simply old clichés retrieved from unconscious suppression.

> It might be argued that a main cause of the merging of the archaic attitude to cliché with the modern notion of archetype as a more intense reality resulted from our great variety of new techniques for retrieval. Both past cultures and primal individual experiences are now subject to ready and speedy access.[17]

Pursuing the notion that electric process lifts us out of historical time and retribalizes our own modern awareness, McLuhan sees a new role for both cliché and archetype. After quoting Mircea Eliade on archaic man — that "[h]is life is the ceaseless repetition of gestures initiated by others"[18] — McLuhan, disregarding the function of the totem, for example, adds the following:

> For archaic or tribal man there was no past, no history. Always present. Today we experience a return to that outlook when technological breakthroughs have become so massive as to create one environment upon another, from telegraph to radio to TV to satellite."[19]

The deep psychic experience of archetypal awareness is made possible for archaic man only through language. "To archaic man language is an immediate evoker of reality, a magical form."[20]

All our new technologies, especially electric process as embodied in mass media, have had the effect of recreating post-literate conditions that are similar to the experience of early humankind.

> The idea of words as merely corresponding to reality, the [modern]
> idea of matching [as opposed to early man's making] is characteristic
> only of highly literate cultures in which the visual sense is dominant.
> Today in the age of quantum mechanics, for which the "chemical
> bond" is, according to Heisenberg . . . and others, a "resonance," it
> is perfectly natural to resume a "magical" attitude to language.[21]

The mysterious operations of the mind in its play with language, in its holographic internal relations — point to point, region to region, hemisphere to hemisphere; the new roles for language in the context of the computer; the post-modern tendency of texts to subscribe critically only to their own authority — all this panoplied, anarchistic activity around our cultural institutions suggests that something deeper and more mysterious is happening.

Since McLuhan always regarded Joyce's work as the fundamental communications archive, it is in Joyce that we find its deep roots. In his essay "Joyce: Trivial and Quadrivial"[22] (which comes directly out of his Ph.D. dissertation), McLuhan, explains Joyce's belief that "[e]very letter is a Godsend," as follows: "[E]very word is the result of a complex mental act with a complete learning process involved in it."[23] Thus regarding words "not as signs but as existent things,"[24] their deeper psychic power is affirmed.

> [Joyce] is concentrating on the submerged metaphysical drama
> which these meanings tend to overlay. His puns in the Wake are
> a technique for revealling this submerged drama of language, and
> Joyce relied on the quirks, "slips," and freaks of ordinary discourse
> to evoke the fullness of existence in speech.[25]

McLuhan's views are virtually coincident with Joyce's. The two operate like Sherlock Holmes looking for deep hidden patterns of meaning where one might least expect them. "All his life [Joyce] played the sleuth with words, shadowing them and waiting confidently for some unexpected situation to reveal their hidden signatures and powers."[26]

One of the disconcerting powers of electronic information systems is the elimination of personal privacy. Special interest groups and business agencies mine uncontrolled amounts of personal data all the time.

> There is power in secret knowledge, as the Electric Age knows only too well.

We live completely out in the informational open. There is nowhere to hide. The owners of the controlling knowledge secretly use data about each of us to make us more susceptible to their management of our lives.

Politics and economics have always operated in secrecy. In information circles, media gatekeepers are the functionaries of the new gnostics. Cyberspace bandits, information high priests, chaos investors, hacker terrorists, bank presidents and IMF globalists, drug and biotech researchers, communications moguls, and sundry other infocrats cross the data desert of the Internet in one-person caravans.

There is something fundamentally mysterious about the operations of electric process. Every square centimetre of earth has become a holographic point containing all of the transmissions over the face of the globe. The elimination of time and space in human interchange is a big enough revolution to completely change all social values — virtualized, bodiless people can make no real society. The discarnate realities of electric process and their great economic power may be the problem, not the solution to our futures.

········ The Way of Telegnosis

Because of electric technology we have come to a rare millennial shift upward to a fifth dimension of awareness that has all the characteristics of gnosticism.

The search for underlying structure is the only way to make sense of the electric world.

Gnosis is hidden knowledge, that is, knowledge of the hidden ground.

Today we see not so much an unfolding of Darwinian reality as an acceleration of de Chardin's evolution of awareness — progressive extensions of mind and soul through improvements in the transmission of knowledge.

The global mindset is the materialization of the collective unconscious through technology.

The subliminal, out-of-awareness part of thought is burgeoning into reality through media use.

We will teach our children how to ask the most useful and involving questions, and give up the attempt to restrict their intelligence by imposing obsolescent answers on them.

Tradition and traditional values will be perceived as that which is eternally new. The oldest things are the newest things. Discovery of origins shall dominate all attempts to educate. ········

Coda

THE SOCIO-PSYCHIC LANDSCAPE is full of hidden forces. Who in the fifties saw the sixties coming? Can anyone remember life before the computer? What about life after the computer? What shift in reality will follow the assimilation of this technological love affair? How soon before we get beyond the speed of light? Will all reality finally be virtualized, including love and birth? What anti-environments await us there? Are we at the end of something?

Cultural hysteria flares quietly around the edges of our reality like a setting sun. The news of our present reality is as garbled and manic as the tapes in a crashed jetliner's black box. Psychotherapy and feel-good drugs are sought by millions who cannot access their inner selves in a world where they have access to almost everything else.

Building a sense of reality requires a lot of careful leaving out. But ignoring engenders ignorance. Still, culture is based on selective ignorance. Unprotected by a strong inhibitive shield, the psyche seems completely vulnerable to the schizophrenic anxieties and disorders of the electric world. Not only are we saturated with negativity through the operation of our preconscious, but we have learned to thrive on our dire condition, possessed as we seem to be of a lust for lostness. We resist change as though addicted to a drug. If anyone tries to take our sickness away, we panic.

An anti-environment in the form of an immanent, new technology is always there, somewhat invisible, but ready to take over at a moment's notice whenever a new age demands. No matter how adept we become at our inhibiting tactics, we remain completely vulnerable to technological change. As long as we have artists, however, we should have some awareness of a changeable reality. Art is still a fairly dependable early warning system of cultural change.

Difficult art reconnects people to the powerful stuff stored below the threshold of consciousness. Few of us want to face this. It seems dangerous to mental stability.

Our contemporary art is more symptomatic than vatic. The great artists of classical times seemed to have prophetic vision; they appeared possessed of the knowledge of what is eternally true. Today, that vatic posture is gone. Our artists seem more egocentric and speculative. Between good art and bad art lies the domain of advertising. These worlds interpenetrate. Consumerism confuses the real world with advertising, and advertising with art.

We can see only the giant, undeflectable motion of global culture toward the fiscal embrace of electric process. It didn't happen all at once. The deep pull on our sense of reality is the effect of an underlying drift in the tidal suctions of our ebbing and flowing awareness of global conditions.

In the end, the enemy is always oneself. But considering how media reshape us, it is difficult to know how to be true to thine own discarnate self. Computerization denigrates the body, which can disappear into information like an oyster sucked down with scarcely a murmur of protest. We must seek to individuate ourselves, perhaps through "embodiment," perhaps by a reversal of consumption. We must learn to respect, once again, those creations of character that speak of a soul beyond the virtualized reality of the computer. We must move beyond the solipsistic Deconstructionists — Derrida, Foucault, de Man, et al. — those who believe that nothing much meaningful can be said about anything.

This grand cultural struggle to find a new home for the head and heart is a quest for an evanescent simplicity in the face of the inescapable complexity of electric culture. We are, I'm sure, trapped between these two forces. The awareness of the dilemma is a state of mind I call symplexity.

It is well known that there is not much information in simple systems, so why would we want them? Well, there is also not much entropy in simple systems, and that means that the essence of simplicity, if it isn't obvious, is stability. Stability of mind and heart generates happiness and peace — good conditions for social welfare. But the problem runs deep. In modern particle physics, we have discovered that "simplicity is not the most natural state of matter. At the quantum level, of course, matter is extremely complex, and grows more so the deeper scientists probe into its secret depths."[1]

Things in the classical world were always made to balance — the proper behaviour of mechanical systems. With electricity, however, systems lost their equilibrium and became open, dynamic, and complex. The isolated laboratory specimen gave way to the environmental system. As science became increasingly immaterial, the emphasis shifted from force and object action to knowledge of information theory.

> The new departure made by modern information theory was that it broke away from classical ideas about communication. It abandoned determinism, and with it simplicity. Information theory did not regard a message as a separate, independent object, but as part of an organized system."[2]

Jeremy Campbell, in *Grammatical Man*, makes a symplectic observation about the nature of information: "The lesson of information theory is that choice and constraint can coexist as partners, enabling a system, be it living organism, a language, or a society, to follow the arrow not of entropy but of history."[3]

And so we wrestle with the forces that assault consciousness and manage our lives from below our general awareness. But consciousness is not so easily co-opted. "Consciousness," as Merleau-Ponty insists, "is in the first place not a matter of 'I think that' but of 'I can.'"[4] We can, and must, educate ourselves to reinvent the simplicity of "I can" and find new grounds for the complex meanings in the age of computerized chaos.

NOTES

Introduction: The Bias of McLuhan

1 Harold Adams Innis, *The Bias of Communication*, Canadian University Paperbooks, 26 (Toronto: University Press, 1964).

2 H. J. Chaytor, *From Script to Print: An Introduction to Medieval Vernacular Literature* (Cambridge: W. Heffer, 1950).

3 C. K. Ogden and I. A. Richards, *The Meaning of Meaning: A Study of the Influence of Language upon Thought and of the Science of Symbolism*, Harvest Book, HB 29 (New York: Harcourt, Brace & Co., 1962).

4 Marshall McLuhan, *Understanding Media: The Extensions of Man* (New York: McGraw-Hill, 1964), 7.

5 Marshall McLuhan et al., *Letters of Marshall McLuhan* (Toronto: Oxford University Press, 1987), 492.

6 T. S. Eliot, *The Waste Land: And Other Poems* (New York: Harcourt, Brace & World, 1962).

7 C. G. Jung, *Aion: Researches into the Phenomenology of the Self*, 2d ed., Collected Works of C. G. Jung, vol. 9, pt. 2, Bollingen Series, 20 (Princeton, N. J.: Princeton University Press, 1968), 267.

8 James Joyce, *Finnegans Wake* (London: Penguin Books, 1992).

9 T. S. Eliot, *Four Quartets*, rev. ed. (London: Faber & Faber, 1979).

10 Leo Tolstoy, *The Death of Ivan Ilych: And Other Stories*, Signet Classic, CT354 (New York: New American Library, 1960).

11 Marshall McLuhan, *New Media & the Arts: An Address by Marshall McLuhan*, audiotape, SUNY, Spring 1965.

One: The Media Symplex

1 I. Prigogine and Isabelle Stengers, *Order Out of Chaos: Man's New Dialogue With Nature* (New York: Bantam Books, 1984), 188.

2 Ibid., 189.

3 Ibid.

4 Marshall McLuhan, *The Mechanical Bride: Folklore of Industrial Man* (New York: Vanguard Press, 1951).

5 Gillian Dyer, *Advertising As Communication*, Studies in Communication (London: Methuen, 1982).

6 James Joyce, *Ulysses*, rev. ed., The Modern Library of the World's Best Books (New York: Modern Library, 1961).

7 William York Tindall, *James Joyce: His Way of Interpreting the Modern World* (New York, 1950), 96.

8 William Hazlitt, *The Round Table: A Collection of Essays on Literature, Men and Manners*, 3d ed.,ed. Harold Bloom (New York: Chelsea House, 1983), 146.

9 Prigogine, xvii.

10 Gustave Flaubert, *Madame Bovary*, Classiques Garnier (Paris: Garnier, 1971).

11 C. G. Jung, *Answer to Job*, 1st paperback ed., Routledge Paperbacks (London: Routledge & K. Paul, 1979).

12 Archibald MacLeish, *J.B.: A Play in Verse* (Boston: Houghton Mifflin, 1958).

13 Marshall McLuhan and Barrington Nevitt, *Take Today; The Executive As Dropout*. (New York: Harcourt Brace Jovanovich, 1972), 297.

14 Michael Polanyi, *Personal Knowledge: Towards a Post-Critical Philosophy* (New York: Harper & Row, 1964), 103.

15 Colin Cherry, *On Human Communication: A Review, a Survey, and a Criticism*, 3d ed., Studies in Communication (Cambridge, Mass.: MIT Press, 1978), 103ff, 182ff.

16 George Beadle, *The New Biology and the Nature of Man: An Address by George Beadle at the Fagerburg Memorial Lecture* (MIT, 1963).

17 Mary Wollstonecraft Shelley, *Frankenstein*, Everyman's Library (New York: Dutton, 1973), 56.

18 James Burke, *Connections* (London: Macmillan, 1980), 76.

19 Ibid., 76.

20 Frank Zingrone, "The Pentad and Technical Syncretism," in *McLuhan Studies*, vol.1, no. 1 (1991).

Two: The Myth of Electric

1 Alfred North Whitehead and Lucien Price, *Dialogues of Alfred North Whitehead* (Westport, Conn.: Greenwood Press, 1977), 24.

2 Laurence J. Peter, *Peter's Quotations: Ideas for Our Time* (New York: Morrow, 1977), 248.

3 Colin Murray Turbayne, *The Myth of Metaphor*, rev. ed. (Columbia: University of South Carolina Press, 1970), 21.

4 Ibid., vii.

5 Claude Levi-Strauss, *Réalités* (1968).

6 Chaytor, 8.

7 Joseph E. Bogen, "The Other Side of the Brain: On Appositional Mind," in *The Nature of Human Consciousness: A Book of Readings*, ed. Robert E. Ornstein (New York: Viking Press, 1974), 119.

8 Ibid., 120.

9 Arthur Deikman, "Bimodal Consciousness," in *The Nature of Human Consciousness: A Book of Readings*, ed. Robert E. Ornstein (New York: Viking Press, 1974), 67ff.

10 Georg von Békésy, *Sensory Inhibition*, Herbert Sidney Langfeld Memorial Lectures, 1965 (Princeton, N.J.: Princeton University Press, 1967).

11 Albert Einstein and Carl Seelig, *Ideas and Opinions*, Laurel Edition (New York: Dell, 1976), 35–36.

12 Alfred North Whitehead, "Mathematics and the Good," in *Essays in Science and Philosophy* (New York: Philosophical Library, 1948), 81.

13 Giorgio de Santillana and Hertha von Dechend, *Hamlet's Mill: An Essay on Myth and the Frame of Time* (Boston: Gambit, 1969), xi.

14 Ibid.

15 Ibid.

16 Ibid., 268.

17 James Thomson, "Autumn," in *The Seasons*, 2d ed. (London: Printed by N. Blandford for J. Millan, 1730).

18 Prigogine, 147ff.

19 Prigogine, 148.

20 Jeremy Rifkin and Nicanor Perlas, *Algeny* (New York: Penguin Books, 1984), 211.

21 Ibid., 212.

22 Ibid.

23 John Briggs and F. David Peat, *Turbulent Mirror: An Illustrated Guide to Chaos Theory and the Science of Wholeness*, 1st Perennial Library ed. (New York: Harper & Row, 1990), 53.

24 Wolfgang Köhler, *The Task of Gestalt Psychology* (Princeton, N.J.: Princeton University Press, 1972), 98.

25 Lewis Thomas, *The Lives of a Cell: Notes of a Biology Watcher* (Toronto: Bantam Books, 1975), 131.

26 George Bernard Shaw, *The Sanity of Art*. "Open Letter to Mr. Benjamin Tucker," regarding Nordan's book *Degeneration* (1898), (London: July 1907), 69.

27 Polanyi, 198.

28 Ibid., 199.

29 Ibid.

30 Gary Taubes, "An Electrifying Possibility," *Discover 7*, no. 4 (1986): 63ff.

31 Ibid., 66.

32 Merrelyn Emery, "The Social and Neurophysiological Effects of Television and Their Implications For Marketing Practice (Vol. 2) An Investigation of Adaptation to the Cathode Ray Tube" (Ph.D. diss., Australian National University, 1985), 700ff.

33 Ibid., 627.

34 Ibid., viii, 620.

35 Ibid., abstract.

36 Krugman, 3–9.

37 Alexander R. Luria, *Language and Cognition* (New York: Wiley and Sons, 1981), 315.

38 Taubes, 66.

39 Herbert E. Krugman, "Brain Wave Measures of Media Involvement," *Journal of Advertising Research* (1971): 3–9; F. E. Emery and Merrelyn Emery, *A Choice of Futures*, International Series on the Quality of Working Life, vol. 4 (Leiden: Martinus Nijhoff, 1976); A. R. Luria, *Human Brain and Psychological Processes* (New York: Harper & Row, 1966); Thomas Mulholland and Erik Peper, "Occipital Alpha and Accomodative Vergence, Pursuit Tracking and Fast Eye Movements," *Psychophysiology*, no. 5 (1971): 556–75.

40 James Gleick, *Chaos: Making a New Science* (New York: Penguin Books, 1988), 76.

41 Mircea Eliade, *The Forge and the Crucible*, 2d ed., a Phoenix Book (Chicago: University of Chicago Press, 1978), 34ff.

42 John N. Bleibtreu, *The Parable of the Beast* (New York: Collier Books, 1971), 61.

43 Ibid., 212.

44 W. Ross Adey, "ELF, Magnetic Fields and the Promotion of Cancer," in *Interaction Mechanisms of Low-Level Electromagnetic Fields in Living Systems*, ed. Claes Ramel and Bengt Nordén (Oxford: Oxford University Press, 1992), 22–46; W. Ross Adey, "Collective Properties of Cell Membranes," in *Interaction Mechanisms of Low-Level Electromagnetic Fields in Living Systems*, ed. Claes Ramel and Bengt Nordén (Oxford: Oxford University Press, 1992), 47–77; Carl F. Blackman, "Calcium Release From Neural Tissue," in *Interaction Mechanisms of Low-Level Electromagnetic Fields in Living Systems*, ed. Claes Ramel and Bengt Nordén (Oxford: Oxford University Press, 1992), 107–28.

45 Emerys.

46 Peter Tompkins and Christopher Bird, *The Secret Life of Plants* (New York: Harper & Row, 1973).

47 Edward Twitchell Hall, *The Silent Language* (Garden City, N. Y.: Anchor Press, 1973), 29.

48 Floyd W. Matson, *The Broken Image: Man, Science and Society*, Anchor Book (Garden City, N. Y.: Doubleday, 1966), 135.

49 Ibid., 134.

50 Ibid., 133.

51 Ibid., 137.

52 Niels Bohr, *Essays on Atomic Physics and Human Knowledge* (New York: Vintage, 1966), 4.

Three: Inhibition

1 Bleibtreu, 3.

2 Ibid.

3 Ibid.

4 Ibid.

5 Ibid.

6 Ibid.

7 Ibid., 4.

8 Cherry, 107.

9 McLuhan used this term conversationally, but in the introduction of *Understanding Media* he says "mythically and integrally".

10 Jacques Ellul, *Propaganda: The Formation of Men's Attitudes* (New York: Vintage Books, 1973), 22.

11 Polanyi, 200.

12 Barrington Nevitt, *The Communication Ecology: Re-Presentation Versus Replica* (Toronto: Butterworths, 1982), 31.

13 Ibid.

14 Von Békésy, 8.

15 Fritjof Capra, *The Turning Point: Science, Society, and the Rising Culture* (Toronto: Bantam Books, 1983), 148.

16 Jean Baudrillard, *Simulations*, Semiotext(e) Foreign Agents Series (New York: Semiotext(e), 1983), 2.

17 Norbert Wiener, *The Human Use of Human Beings: Cybernetics and Society*, Discus Books (New York: Avon Books, 1973), 44–49.

18 Von Békésy, 11–12.

19 Ibid., 9.

20 Ulric Neisser, "The Processes of Vision," in *The Nature of Human Consciousness: A Book of Readings*, ed. Robert E. Ornstein (New York: Viking Press, 1974), 201.

21 Ibid.

22 Ibid.

23 Ibid., 201–202.

24 Ibid., 17.

25 Ibid., 18.

26 Norman Oliver Brown, *Love's Body* (New York: Random House, 1966), 72.

27 George Burr Leonard, *The Transformation: A Guide to the Inevitable Changes in Humankind* (New York: Delacorte Press, 1972), 166.

28 Ibid.

29 Von Békésy, 19.

30 Roderic Gorney, *The Human Agenda: How to Be at Home in the Universe Without Magic* (Los Angeles: The Guild of Tutors Press, 1979), 257.

31 Von Békésy, 4–5.

32 Ibid., 220.

33 Ibid., 39.

34 Ibid.

35 Ibid., 225.

36 Ibid., 227.

37 Ibid., 215–16.

38 Karl H. Pribram, "Holographic Memory: Interview With Daniel Goleman," *Psychology Today* (1979).

39 Von Békésy, 217.

40 Ibid.

41 Neisser, 202.

42 Chaytor, 9.

43 Ibid.

44 Ibid., 6.

45 Ibid., 8.

46 Jane M. Healy, *Endangered Minds: Why Our Children Don't Think* (New York: Simon and Schuster, 1990).

47 Ibid.

48 Chaytor, 35.

49 John R. MacArthur, *Second Front: Censorship and Propaganda in the Gulf War* (New York: Hill & Wang, 1992).

50 Susanne Katherina Knauth Langer, *Mind: An Essay on Human Feeling*, vol. 1 (Baltimore: Johns Hopkins Press, 1982), 324.

51 Ibid.

52 Ibid., 326.

53 Matson, 115.

54 Ibid.

55 Ibid.

56 Ibid., 117.

57 Christopher Cerf and Victor S. Navasky, *The Experts Speak: The Definitive Compendium of Authoritative Misinformation*, rev. ed. (New York: Villard Books, 1998), 302.

58 Sigmund Freud, *Civilization and Its Discontents* (New York: W. W. Norton, 1967), 38.

59 "Reamalgamerge" from James Joyce, *Finnegans Wake* (New York: Viking), 49. The reference is to the "Identities of Indescernibles" of Leibnitz, a theory that states that no two things (monads) in the universe can be the same.

60 Cerf.

61 Nevitt, 126.

62 Ibid.

63 Ellul, 22.

64 Erik Barnouw, *The Sponsor: Notes on a Modern Potentate* (New York: Oxford University Press, 1978), 19–26.

65 Ivan Petrovich Pavlov, *Conditioned Reflexes: An Investigation of the Physiological Activity of the Cerebral Cortex* (New York: Dover Publications, 1960), 73.

66 Marshall McLuhan and Eric McLuhan, *Laws of Media: The New Science* (Toronto: University of Toronto Press, 1988).

67 Pierre Teilhard de Chardin, *The Future of Man* (New York: Harper & Row, 1969), 11–25.

68 Werner Heisenberg, *Physics and Beyond: Encounters and Conversations*, in *World Perspectives* no. 42, Ruth Nanda, ed. (New York: Harper and Row, 1971), 70–81.

Four: The Preconscious

1 Frederick Charles Copleston, *A History of Philosophy*, vol. 8 (London: 1963), 305.

2 Paul Edwards, *The Encyclopedia of Philosophy* (New York: Macmillan, 1967), 192–96.

3 Sigmund Freud, "A Note on the Unconscious in Psychoanalysis," in *Collected Papers*, 1st American ed. (New York: Basic Books, 1959), 25.

4 Ibid., 27.

5 Sigmund Freud, "The Unconscious," in *Collected Papers*, 1st American ed. (New York: Basic Books, 1959), 105–6.

6 See Wilhelm von Humboldt and Northrop Frye in Marshall McLuhan, *Essential McLuhan* (New York: Basic Books, 1995), 3.

7 William James, *The Will to Believe and Other Essays in Popular Philosophy* (New York: Longmans, 1910), 314.

8 Sigmund Freud, *A General Introduction to Psychoanalysis* (New York: Washington Square Press, 1960), 306.

9 James, 314–15.

10 Ibid., 315.

11 Ibid., 302.

12 C. G. Jung, C. G, *Memories, Dreams, Reflections*, rev. ed. (New York: Vintage Books, 1963), 117ff.

13 James, 317.

14 Ibid., 325.

15 Daniel J. Boorstin, *The Image, or, What Happened to the American Dream* (New York: Penguin, 1962), 216.

16 Ibid., 226.

17 Ibid.

18 James, 315.

19 Wilson Bryan Key, *Subliminal Seduction: Ad Media's Manipulation of a Not So Innocent America* (New York: New American Library, A Signet Book, 1974), 109–10.

20 Sigmund Freud, *The Interpretation of Dreams*, translated and edited by James Strachey (New York: Basic Books, 1959).

21 Norman F. Dixon, *Subliminal Perception: The Nature of a Controversy*, European Psychology Series (London: McGraw-Hill, 1971); Norman F. Dixon, *Preconscious Processing* (Chichester, N. Y.: John Wiley & Sons, 1981).

22 Charles Fisher, "Introduction to Poetzl's 'The Relationship Between Experimentally Induced Dream Images and Indirect Vision,'" *Psychological Issues* 2, no. 3, monograph 7 (1960). The distinction Poetzl is making is probably a reference to a much-neglected aspect of hemispheric specialization, the fact that there is some verbal capability in the right hemisphere: child-like, simple, dreamy. This right-side verbal activity is not actively part of the dominant verbalization on the left associated with Broca's and Wernicke's areas but still has a passive role in verbal activities.

23 Ibid.

24 Otto Poetzl, Rudolf Allers, and Jakob Teler, "Preconscious Stimulation in Dreams,

Associations and Images," in *Psychological Issues* 2, no. 3, monograph 7 (1960): 108ff. Originally published by Poetzl in Z. Neurol. Psychiat. 37 (1917): 278–349.

25 W. W. Meissner, "Review of Dixon's Preconscious Processing," *The Psychoanalytic Quarterly* 52 (1983): 109.

26 Ibid, 110.

27 Ibid.

28 Ibid.

29 The Emerys have produced an excellent study of the selling of educational television: and the *Sesame Street* case in particular. See Merrelyn Emery, "The Social and Neurophysiological Effects of Television and Their Implications For Marketing Practice (Vol. 2) An Investigation of Adaptation to the Cathode Ray Tube," (Ph.D. diss., Australian National University, 1985).

30 Meissner, 110.

31 Owen Renik, "The Role of Attention in Depersonalization," *The Psychoanalytic Quarterly* 57, no. 4 (1978): 588–605.

32 Ibid.

33 Ibid.

34 Ibid.

35 Ibid.

36 Ibid.

37 Dixon, *Preconscious Processing*, 73.

38 Martin Barrett, ed., *The Politics of Broadcasting: The Alfred I. Du Pont–Columbia University Survey of Broadcast Journalism* (New York: Grosset & Dunlap, 1970–1971), 5–38.

39 Freud, "A Note on the Unconscious in Psychoanalysis," 25.

40 Dixon, 261.

41 Ibid.

42 Ibid., 34.

43 Ibid., 215.

44 Ibid.

45 Ibid., 266.

46 Ibid., 262.

47 Ibid.

48 Ibid.

49 Ibid., 266.

50 Joyce, *Finnegans Wake*, 252.

51 Charles Olson, *Selected Writings*, ed. Robert Creeley (New York: New Directions, 1966), 16ff.

52 Charles Olson, *The Maximus Poems* (New York: Jargon/Corinth, 1960), 13.

53 Peter Farb, *Word Play: What Happens When People Talk* (New York: Bantam Books, 1981), 73.

54 Ibid., 74.

55 Freud, *A General Introduction to Psychoanalysis*, 305.

56 Ibid.

57 Ibid., 306.

58 Ibid.

59 Ibid.

60 Ibid.

61 C. G. Jung, *Psyche and Symbol: A Selection From the Writings of C.G. Jung* (Garden City, N.Y.: Doubleday, Anchor Books, 1958), 3.

62 Barrett, 7ff.

Five: The Edge of Meaning

1 Frank Mankiewicz and Joel L. Swerdlow, *Remote Control: Television and the Manipulation of American Life* (New York: Times Books, 1978).

2 Ibid., 352–53.

3 Ibid., 353.

4 Farb, 194.

5 *Toronto Star*, 20 August 1997.

6 Frank D. Zingrone, "Electric Reality, Retribilization, and the Global Village: Japan's Econo-War With the United States," *Canadian Review of American Studies* 27, no. 3 (1997): 146.

7 Farb, 227.

8 Ibid.

9 William Irwin Thompson, "Freedom & Comedy," *Tulane Drama Review* 9, no. 3 (1965): 225.

10 Ibid.

11 Ibid.

12 Ibid.

13 Ibid., 227.

14 Ibid., 230.

15 Joyce, *Finnegans Wake*, 465.

16 Marvin Magalaner and Richard Morgan Kain, eds., *Joyce: The Man, the Work, the Reputation* (New York: Collier Books, 1962), 203.

17 *Harper's*, June 1999.

18 William Gibson, *Neuromancer* (New York: Ace Books, 1984), 55.

19 Rod Gorney.

20 Robert Ian Scott, *New American Review*, December 1990.

21 Humberto R. Maturana and Francisco J. Varela, *Autopoiesis and Cognition: The Realization of the Living*, Boston Studies in the Philosophy of Science, vol. 42, 1st ed. in Spanish (Dordrecht, Holland and Boston: D. Reidel Pub. Co., 1980).

22 N. Katherine Hayles, *How We Became Posthuman: Virtual Bodies in Cybernetics, Literature, and Informatics* (Chicago: University of Chicago Press, 1999), 196–97.

23 Ibid., 10–11.

24 Ibid., 13.

25 Thomas, 131.

26 Pierre Teilhard de Chardin, *The Phenomenon of Man*, 2nd ed. (New York: Harper & Row, 1965), 19.

27 Ibid., 20.

28 Ibid., 22.

29 Hayles, 203.

30 Ibid.

31 Ibid., 203–4.

32 Teilhard de Chardin, 36.

33 C. G. Jung, C. G, *Memories, Dreams, Reflections*, rev. ed. (New York: Vintage Books, 1963), 340.

34 In epistemology, "the introspective or reflective apprehension by the mind of its own inner states." In psychology, "the process by which new experience is assimilated to and transformed by the residuum of past experience to form a new whole. The residuum of past experience is called the apperceptive mass." Dabobert D. Runes, ed., *Dictionary of Philosophy* (Paterson, N. J.: Littlefield, Adams, 1956), 15.

35 *Encyclopedia Of Philosophy*, 15.

36 Giambattista Vico, *The New Science of Giambattista Vico*, trans. Thomas Goddard Bergin and Max Harold Fisch (Ithaca, N.Y.: Cornell University Press, Cornell Paperbacks, 1970).

37 Polanyi, *Personal Knowledge* 92.

38 Ibid.

39 Ibid.

40 Ibid.

41 Ibid., 88.

42 Ibid., 95.

43 Ibid., 214.

44 Ibid., 215.

45 José Ortega y Gasset, *The Revolt of the Masses*, 25th anniversary ed. (New York: Norton, 1957), 14.

Telegnosis: The Deep Meaning of Electric Process

1 Marshall McLuhan, "Reply to Northrop Frye on Communications," *The Listener* 84, no. 2167 (1980): 475–76.

2 Alexander Pope, *An Essay on Man* (London: The Penguin Poets, 1950), 121.

3 Marshall McLuhan, "The Place of Thomas Nashe in the Learning of His Time" (Ph. D. diss., Cambridge University, 1943), ix.

4 *Encyclopedia of Philosophy*, III, 336.

5 McLuhan, *Letters of Marshall McLuhan*, 238.

6 Ibid.

7 W. L. Wilmhurst, *The Meaning of Masonry* (New York: Gramercy Books, 1980), 173.

8 Ibid., 50.

9 Ibid.

10 Ibid., 47.

11 Ibid., 186.

12 McLuhan, *Letters of Marshall McLuhan*, 237.

13 *The Encyclopedia Britannica*, 9th ed. (Akron, Ohio: Werner Company, 1906), 748.

14 Thomas von Franz and Marie-Luise von Franz, *Aurora Consurgens: A Document Attributed to Thomas Aquinas on the Problem of Opposites in Alchemy* (London: Routledge & K. Paul, 1966).

15 McLuhan, *Letters of Marshall McLuhan*, 238.

16 *Encyclopedia Britannica*, 9th ed., 757.

17 Marshall McLuhan and Wilfred Watson, *From Cliché to Archetype* (New York: Viking Press, 1970), 117.

18 Ibid., 119.

19 Ibid.

20 Ibid., 117.

21 Ibid.

22 Marshall McLuhan, "Joyce: Trivial and Quadrivial," in *The Interior Lamdscape: The Literary Criticism of Marshall McLuhan* (McGraw-Hill, New York, 1969), 23–47.

23 Ibid., 37.

24 Ibid.

25 Ibid., 37–38.

26 Ibid.

Coda

1 Jeremy Campbell, *Grammatical Man: Information, Entropy, Language, and Life* (New York: Simon & Schuster, 1982), 255.

2 Ibid., 255–56

3 Ibid.

4 Maurice Merleau-Ponty, *Phenomenology of Perception* (London: Routledge & K. Paul, 1962), 137.